The Complete Guide to

•••••••••••••• RTI

The Complete Guide to RTI

An Implementation
TOOLKIT

DOLORES BURTON   **JOHN KAPPENBERG**
with Invited Contributors

CORWIN
A SAGE Company

CORWIN
A SAGE Company

FOR INFORMATION:

Corwin
A SAGE Company
2455 Teller Road
Thousand Oaks, California 91320
(800) 233-9936
Fax: (800) 417-2466
www.corwin.com

SAGE Ltd.
1 Oliver's Yard
55 City Road
London EC1Y 1SP
United Kingdom

SAGE India Pvt. Ltd.
B 1/I 1 Mohan Cooperative Industrial Area
Mathura Road, New Delhi 110 044
India

SAGE Asia-Pacific Pte. Ltd.
33 Pekin Street #02-01
Far East Square
Singapore 048763

Acquisitions Editor: Jessica Allan
Associate Editor: Allison Scott
Editorial Assistant: Lisa Whitney
Production Editor: Amy Schroller
Copy Editor: Cate Huisman
Typesetter: C&M Digitals (P) Ltd.
Proofreader: Victoria Reed-Castro
Indexer: Michael Ferreira
Cover Designer: Karine Hovsepian
Permissions Editor: Karen Ehrmann

Copyright © 2012 by Corwin

Printed in the United States of America

Library of Congress Cataloging-in-Publication Data

A catalog record of this book is available from the Library of Congress.

ISBN 9781412997096

This book is printed on acid-free paper.

11 12 13 14 15 10 9 8 7 6 5 4 3 2 1

Contents

Acknowledgments

This book would not have been possible without the collective efforts of a battalion of individuals with a passion for improving educational opportunities for all children. Many individuals contributed to the knowledge base that is the foundation of the book. We are grateful to the New York State Higher Education Support Center for SystemsChange and Dr. Gerald Mager, Dr. Peter Kosik, Iris Maxon, and Steve Wirt, who developed and maintained a venue to keep us in the company of scholars and the resources to share expertise to improve teacher education and student outcomes.

For Chapter 2, many thanks to colleagues, past and present, who gave their time and expertise to develop the skills and techniques discussed, and to the S³TAIR Project staff and partners for sharing their experiences, which contributed to these best practices.

For Chapter 4, we honor the memory of Alice Koontz, fellow of the Orton-Gillingham Academy; she was a teacher, mentor, and friend.

For Chapter 5, we wish to acknowledge the editing assistance of Dr. Charlotte Rosenzweig.

For Chapter 8, we thank Joanne Cashman and Patrice Linehan of the IDEA Partnership for their mentoring and commitment to communities of practice and collaborative work. Dr. George Goldstein provided expertise and insights into the administrative aspects of parent involvement. Dick Maitland, of the Sesame Street Workshop, was a continual source of inspiration and technical expertise throughout this project. Misty Burch provided valuable research into the implementation aspects of the RTI process.

For Chapter 9, we acknowledge the contributions of Dr. Charlotte Rosenzweig and Dr. Karen Siris.

We heartily thank all of our contributors—Harold J. Dean, Arlene B. Crandall, Erin E. Ax, Lynn Burke, Sarah McPherson, C. Faith Kappenberg, Helene Fallon, Patricia Ann Marcellino, and Lydia Begley for sharing their expertise. We are thankful to all of our past teachers and professors, who assisted us to develop the understandings and habits of mind that resulted in this book, and we offer our regards to Jessica Allan, senior acquisitions editor, Amy Schroller, production editor, and Cate Huisman, copy editor, all at Corwin, who supported us during its completion.

This book would not have been possible without the generous support of President Guiliano and the New York Institute of Technology, which provided a sabbatical that gave Dolores Burton the time to pursue the scholarly core of this book.

Finally, words cannot express the thanks we owe to our spouses, Bernard Burton and Faith Kappenberg, for their patience, encouragement, and assistance throughout this extended labor of love.

Publisher's Acknowledgments

Corwin gratefully acknowledges the contributions of the following reviewers:

Elizabeth Alvarez
Math & Science Coach
Chicago, IL

Erin E. Barton
Faculty
University of Colorado Denver
Denver, CO

Sue A. DeLay
Teacher-Math Interventionist
Oak Creek-Franklin School
    District
Oak Creek, WI

Esther M. Eacho
Education Specialist
McLean, VA

Lisa Graham, NBCT
Program Specialist, Curriculum
    & Staff Development
Vallejo City Unified School
    District, Special Education
Walnut Avenue, Vallejo, CA

Lori L. Grossman
Academic Trainer
Houston ISD
Houston, TX

A. L. Hough-Everage
Associate Professor of
    Education
Brandman University,
    Chapman University
    System
Victorville, CA

West Keller
Kindergarten Teacher (SPED/
    Social Skills Blended
    Kindergarten)
McGilvra Elementary
Seattle, WA

Sara Lynne Murrell
Teacher, 5th Grade
Bethel Elementary
    School
Simpsonville, SC

Lyndon Oswald
Principal
Sandcreek Middle School
Ammon, ID

Lois Rebich
Instructional Support Teacher
Ross Elementary School
Pittsburgh, PA

Dr. Rose Cherie Reissman
Licensed Literacy and ELL
    Educator, Literacy/ELL
    Consultant
Chief Academic Officer, Mind
    Lab
New York, NY

Victor Simon III
Principal
John C. Dore Elementary
    School
Chicago, IL

Michelle (Drechsler)
    Strom
Teacher, Language Arts
Carson Middle School
Colorado Springs, CO

Deborah D. Therriault
Special Education Teacher
Clarkston Community
    Schools, Clarkston High
    School
Clarkston, MI

Karen L. Tichy
Associate Superintendent for
    Instruction and Special
    Education
Archdiocese of St. Louis,
    Catholic Education Office
St. Louis, MO

Russell Vaden
Assistant Professor of
    Educational Psychology
Coastal Carolina University
Conway, SC

Marian White-Hood
Director of Academics,
    Accountability, and
    Principal Support
Maya Angelou Public Charter
    Schools and SeeForever
    Foundation
Washington, DC

About the Authors

Dolores Burton, EdD, has spent 36 years in education as a teacher, administrator, professional developer, consultant, and author of instructional software and numerous publications. She has presented papers regionally, nationally, and internationally on response to intervention, universal design for learning, differentiated instruction, brain-based learning, mathematics instruction especially in inclusive settings, strategic planning, professional development, and the use of technology to enhance teaching and learning. She has served on the board of directors of the Northeastern Educational Research Association and has held offices in numerous educational organizations.

Dr. Burton believes all children can learn and have a right to be in an educational environment that facilitates their academic successes. Her writing, presentations, and teaching reflect this belief. She is included on the Fulbright Specialist roster and has consulted locally and internationally. She received her bachelor's and master's degrees from the State University of New York (SUNY) at Stony Brook and holds professional diplomas from both Long Island University and Hofstra University. Her doctorate was earned at Hofstra University. She taught courses at SUNY at Stony Brook and currently is a professor and chair of the Division of Teacher Education at New York Institute of Technology.

John Kappenberg, EdD, has spent 40 years in education as teacher, professor, district administrator, writer, speaker, and consultant to school districts and professional organizations. He has been director of research, planning, and quality at the Sewanhaka Central High School District in New York, where he led its long-term strategic planning program, and director of educational leadership and technology at

New York Institute of Technology. He has taught school finance and law, Total Quality Management, strategic planning, and educational technology at Hofstra University on Long Island and at Argosy University in Sarasota, Florida. Dr. Kappenberg served on the board of directors for the Governor's Excelsior Award program (Empire State Advantage) in New York, as regional liaison for the Higher Education Support Center for SystemsChange, and as vice president of the Long Island chapter of the New York State Council on Exceptional Children (CEC). He received his bachelor's degree in biology from Fairfield University (Connecticut), master's in the history of ideas from New York University, and doctoral degree in educational leadership and policy studies from Hofstra University. He has produced more than 40 instructional, motivational, and public information videotapes and DVDs for schools, universities, and professional and state organizations.

About the Contributors

Erin E. Ax, PhD, is a nationally certified school psychologist. Erin obtained her doctorate in school psychology from the University of South Florida, where she collaborated with Reading First schools, the Florida Center for Reading Research (FCRR), and community partners in a problem-solving/outcomes-driven approach to service delivery. She has consulted with schools across the country on implementing an RTI model focused on both academic and behavior support. Dr. Ax has served on the adjunct faculty in the master's of education degree programs at Hunter College and Pace University and in the doctoral program in school psychology at City University of New York.

Lydia Begley, EdD, is associate superintendent for educational services of the Board of Cooperative Educational Services, an organization that serves the 56 school districts of Nassau County, Long Island. She has been a public school teacher, a school administrator in public schools, a district superintendent, and an adjunct professor in an educational administration program working with graduate students who are preparing for careers as future administrators. Dr. Begley has presented at local, state, and national conferences on leadership, women in the superintendency, and instructional issues regarding integrated skills and curriculum mapping. Both a practitioner and researcher, her scholarly and research interests include gender issues and women in the superintendency.

Lynn Burke, MS, an educational consultant, works to improve instructional results for learners of written alphabetic languages. Her primary focus is helping teachers to integrate "the missing piece" (i.e., explicit, sequential, cumulative, phonetically based multisensory reading/writing/spelling instruction) into existing language arts curricula. Ms. Burke is currently serving as president of the International Dyslexia Association—Long Island Branch, and is a board member of the Learning Disabilities Association—Long Island Branch.

Arlene B. Crandall, MA, has worked in education for over 30 years as a teacher, school psychologist, special education administrator, and staff developer for the New York State Education Department. She is one of the authors of the 2009 New York State training resource for the Committee on Special Education/Committee on Preschool Special Education. Ms. Crandall has served as the president of the New York Association of School Psychologists (NYASP) as well as delegate and regional director for the National Association of School Psychologists. She is currently the president of ABCD Consulting, Inc., a company that provides professional development for school districts, and an adjunct instructor in the department of school counseling at New York Institute of Technology.

Harold J. Dean, EdD, is an administrator with the Eastern Suffolk Board of Cooperative Educational Services. A lifelong Long Island resident, he has taught special education in inclusive, self-contained, resource-room, and consultative settings. He has presented locally and nationally on topics including best practices in special education, student intervention, and instructional strategies.

Helene Fallon, MEd, has a background in social work and education with extensive training in advocacy for children and young adults with disabilities. She is the parent of two children with special needs. Working nationally as a professional development specialist, she conducts trainings on many topics, always focusing on collaboration and effective communication in education.

C. Faith Kappenberg, PhD, LCSW, has been a clinical social worker in the fields of autism, child development, special education, psychotherapy, and social work education for over 30 years. She has served on the faculties of Molloy College and Adelphi University teaching practicum supervision, organizational behavior, human development, and psychopathology. Dr. Kappenberg is a founder and clinical director of Westbrook Preparatory School, the first residential therapeutic school in New York serving high functioning adolescents on the autism spectrum.

Patricia Ann Marcellino, EdD, is an associate professor in the Educational Leadership and Technology Program at the Ruth S. Ammon School of Education at Adelphi University. She has cross-disciplinary expertise in the fields of both business and education; she possesses an MBA in management and an MA in education. Dr. Marcellino has experience in both fields as an administrator, instructor, and consultant. Her research agenda includes the development of teams, groups, and partnerships in the areas of distributed leadership, team learning, and professional relationship building. She is the author of numerous papers and presentations on these topics.

Sarah McPherson, EdD, holds a master's in reading and doctorate in special education from Johns Hopkins University. She is chair of the Department of Instructional Technology and Educational Leadership at New York Institute of Technology and current president of the International Society for Technology in Education Special Interest Group for Teacher Education. She is also on the board of directors for the New York Society for Computers and Technology in Education and the Long Island Council of Exceptional Children, and she serves on the Long Island Task Force on Quality Inclusive Schooling. She has written articles and book chapters and has presented at numerous national and international conferences on instructional technology for K–12 inclusive education, universal design for learning, RTI, virtual online education, web 2.0 tools for globalization, and e-portfolios.

This book is lovingly dedicated to Richie and Matt, who have been my inspiration and my joy.

Dolores Burton

. . . and to Geoff, Eric, and Kirsten, my dreams for the future.

John Kappenberg

Introduction

PURPOSE OF THE BOOK

The Complete Guide to RTI offers a toolkit of resources for introducing response to intervention (RTI) to professional educators in K–12 schools and to teacher candidates in colleges and universities. A growing library of monographs on the topic is available, which raises the question of why a new book on RTI is needed. The answer lies in recent political developments impacting American schools, in particular, the strong federal recommendation that all schools adopt RTI as part of their general and special education programs:

> Consensus reports and empirical syntheses indicate a need for major changes in the approach to identifying children with SLD. Models that incorporate RTI represent a shift in special education toward goals of better achievement and improved behavioral outcomes for children with SLD. (Assistance to States for the Education of Children With Disabilities, *71 Federal Register, 46647,* 2006, codified at 34 CFR 300)

Influences on the way curriculum is taught in American schools are escalating, coming from educational, political, scientific, business, and professional spheres, and driven by forces at national, state, and local levels. They impact teaching and learning in much the same way that health care legislation is changing the practice of medicine. In light of this, a reform as fundamental as RTI should not be introduced as solely a new, "scientifically based" teaching technique, to be learned, practiced, and applied in the classroom. It has been aptly described as a sea change and paradigm shift (Jimerson, Burns, & VanDerHeyden, 2007; Sansosti & Noltemeyer, 2008), and it is poised to usher in the most consequential alteration in American schooling since the shift from curriculum-centered to child-centered learning in the 1960s.

When a school adopts RTI, it changes its basis for making instructional decisions from reliance on past practice, training, experience, and professional expertise to reliance on a formal, scientifically based model of practice based on data gathering and systematic problem solving.

The way we introduce this new form of practice to professional educators needs to be configured accordingly: It needs to be presented not as a new educational program with content that needs to be learned, but as a different way of looking at the practice of education, a new *method* for using the vast array of educational techniques that are available to professionals. RTI does not provide the educational interventions that will help students learn; it provides a method for deciding when an intervention is working and when it needs to be changed. The difference between a school that uses RTI and one that does not is in the standard for deciding whether an intervention is successful. In traditional settings, the standard has been the judgment of professionals, based on their experience and expertise; within RTI, the standard is the evidence of data.

This is the same scientific method that guides practice in fields as diverse as medical research, psychotherapy, and clinical psychology (Clark & Alvarez, 2010). It seeks to standardize the basis for decision making in areas such as a child's success in specific areas of learning, causes of and responses to inappropriate behavior, and whether or not a child should be classified as in need of special education services. Under RTI, decisions of this type, which were previously made on the basis of past practice and policy, are made according to a systematic, scientifically based process similar to that used, for example, by the FDA to evaluate the safety and effectiveness of a new medication (Tilly, 2002). RTI needs to be presented to professionals as a *method* for educational decision making, not as a new body of content for educational practice.

DESIGN OF THE BOOK

This book is designed to be a hands-on resource for educators and others in the educational community who work within the day-to-day pressures of the current changes in American education leading toward scientific, data-based instruction.

Coping With a Paradigm Shift in Education

Depending on one's disposition, the pressures of change may be challenging or threatening, but they are never easy. Since the advent of the No Child Left Behind (NCLB) Act in 2001, developments in areas such as technology, accountability, and data gathering have been fast, scattered, confusing, and unpredictable. (Note: Congress passed NCLB in December of 2001, and President Bush signed it in January of 2002. Throughout this book, we will refer to its passage with the more commonly used date of 2001.) Many professionals, particularly the young, may see this as a rare opportunity. Others will see a decline from stability to uncertainty.

According to Robert Harvey, both views are correct; the differences lie in the individual's perception of change: "The new technology has been pulverizing big business. . . . Optimism and pessimism are code words for how we deal with change" (Harvey, 1995, p. 189). Max Planck, the iconic 20th-century physicist, gave a description of how these pressures operate in the field of science: "A new scientific truth does not triumph by convincing its opponents and making them see the light. Rather, it must grow until its opponents eventually die and a new generation grows up that is able to understand it" (1949, pp. 33–34).

We can't wait for a generation of educators to retire before RTI becomes fully accepted. But Planck's experience ought to lead us toward a practical starting point: The most effective introduction of RTI should be directed toward a new generation of teachers and educational leaders—whether they be novice or veteran—and it needs to be presented as a transformational, rather than incremental, change in educational practice.

An Approach to Meeting the Changes Ahead

In light of the changes that educators face, the book is based on four foundations:

1. *A focus on the technology.* The text is permeated with references to instructional technology that provide a basis for future instruction and professional development within RTI. Each chapter includes annotated online resources leading to further study in the topics presented.

2. *A broad collaborative base of contributor expertise, demonstrating the wide range of RTI applications.* Contributor expertise includes early childhood, childhood, and middle and secondary school research; college and university teacher education; educational policy development; clinical services; educational psychology; professional organizations; school leadership; and parent advocacy. Applications of RTI are organized into four areas: (a) *foundations,* including its educational and political history, as well as its scientific and data-driven approach in both general and special education, (b) *content area applications,* including reading, literacy, mathematics, positive behavior support, and school administration, (c) *the use of technology* in teaching RTI skills and in applying RTI in classroom settings, and (d) *collaboration among professional and nonprofessional stakeholders* in the introduction of RTI, including parents, students, and communities.

3. *A hands-on, results-oriented focus on teacher preparation for RTI in both general and special education.* With the accompanying technology resources, the book is designed as both an *introduction* to the historical, political, and educational foundations of RTI and a rich *resource* for teaching RTI as a required skill in the years ahead. In an October 22, 2009, speech, Education Secretary Arne Duncan described the need to reform the way we prepare future teachers:

> Teachers say two things about their training in teacher education schools. First, most of them say they did not get the hands-on practical teacher training about managing the classroom that they needed, especially for high-needs students. And second, they say they were not taught how to use data to differentiate and improve instruction and boost student learning. (Duncan, 2009)

The Complete Guide to RTI responds to both of these challenges. It takes into account recent state and federal department of education policies that mandate scientific justification of instruction and adherence to the peer review standards of research science. RTI is not presented dogmatically, as a fixed body of knowledge or as a skill for aspiring teachers to simply learn and put into practice. It has had scientifically proven success in a variety of local applications, but it will need to grow, adapt, and be enhanced as it is applied on a national scale. Case studies throughout the book provide context for the application of RTI principles to local school practice.

4. *Linkage of the book's content to foreseeable developments in state and national educational policy.* One of the most controversial aspects of the current paradigm shift toward RTI is the increasing role of state and federal agencies in enforcing standards for schools that have traditionally thought of themselves as locally controlled. In this process, RTI has come to embody policies that mandate scientific and data-driven educational standards in virtually every state. These requirements are emphasized in the area of teacher preparation. The secretary of education has announced a national agenda that some have found inspiring, and others deeply disturbing:

> America's university-based teacher preparation programs need revolutionary change—not evolutionary tinkering. But I am optimistic that, despite the obstacles to reform, the seeds of real change have been planted. . . . Real change, based upon the real outcomes of children—revolutionary, isn't it? (Duncan, 2009)

Whatever one's response to the changes underway, the data-driven and progress monitoring strategies presented throughout the chapters will help teachers to examine the outcome of their work in terms of student response. This book is designed to keep in-service teachers aware that what they are learning about RTI is not education as usual, but is instead the leading edge of changes that are, in the words of America's top educator, "revolutionary"—and to prepare preservice teachers for the educational environment they are entering.

Keynote

1

Reasons and Resources for Learning Response to Intervention

Dolores T. Burton and John Kappenberg

FOUNDATIONS OF RESPONSE TO INTERVENTION

Shifting Paradigms of American Education: Historical Perspective

A *paradigm shift* generally describes a fundamental change in the way large numbers of people think about and do things. If we understand response to intervention (RTI) as a form of scientific method applied to making decisions about the educational programs of individual children—applying scientific method in day-to-day educational practice (Clark & Alvarez, 2010)—then its widespread adoption would qualify as a paradigm shift by any normal use of the term. To see the importance of this, we need to briefly review the educational paradigms that have appeared and "shifted" during the past 50 years.

The Curriculum-Centered Paradigm: World War II Through the 1950s

During and after World War II, Americans tended to focus on their emergence as a superpower and cold war competition with the Soviet Union. The struggles during these years included the nuclear arms race, begun with the first Soviet atomic test in 1949, and the related space race, ushered in by Sputnik in 1957. Both of these shaped the way Americans viewed their educational system. The Eisenhower administration responded with a massive federal investment—more than a billion dollars through the National Defense Education Act of 1958—into American schools in hope of improving the competitiveness of their graduates (Ambrose, 1990). The effect was to introduce what we now call a paradigm of American education: School became a place where students were supposed to develop the learning and skills they would need to help their country survive the challenges of modern life. Curriculum was the center of the educational process, and the purpose of curriculum was to serve the society, not just the individual child.

Echoes of the curriculum-centered paradigm could be heard in President Kennedy's "Ask not what your country can do for you—ask what you can do for your country" (Clark, 2004, p. 4) and his call for "achieving the goal, before this decade is out, of landing a man on the Moon and returning him safely to the Earth" (Murray & Cox, 1989, pp. 16–17). Publishers took advantage of a wave of mass interest in learning, for example, selling millions of encyclopedias at supermarket checkout counters. Mortimer Adler's 60-volume *Great Books of the Western World* series sold more than 50,000 sets in 1961 (Mayer, 1993). Within this cultural background, schools of the 1950s and early 1960s placed a heavy emphasis on academics—particularly math and science, on moving more graduates into higher education, and on teaching children responsibility to society.

The Child-Centered Paradigm:
The Late 1960s Through the 1990s

By the early 1960s, the civil rights movement was taking shape and moving American values in a new direction: from responsibility of the individual to society, toward responsibility of society to guarantee the rights and fulfill the needs of each individual. Part of the fallout from the civil rights movement, the youth movement, and the anti–Vietnam War movement of the late 1960s was a dramatic shift of perception about the purpose of schooling in America, that is, a paradigm shift. During the same years that educators focused on what they and their students could do for their country, a new voice was building momentum, demanding equal protection of the laws for all citizens, and eventually, an educational system that valued the needs of the individual child as its overriding purpose.

The drive to "meet the needs of all students" became a mantra for districts throughout the nation. During the 1970s and 1980s, hardly a school calendar was published that did not carry some variation of that statement in its masthead. American schools and academic programs focused on the needs of children, not the demands of society.

Reaction to the Child-Centered Paradigm: From A Nation at Risk *to No Child Left Behind*

On June 16, 1980, *TIME Magazine* published a startling cover story: "Help! Teacher Can't Teach!" For the first time in living memory, Americans saw their public schools held up to ridicule in the national media: "Like some vast jury gradually and reluctantly arriving at a verdict, politicians, educators and especially millions of parents have come to believe that the U.S. public schools are in parlous trouble. . . . Ever since the mid-1960s, the average achievement of high school graduates has gone steadily downhill" ("Help! Teacher Can't Teach," 1980, screen 1, para. 4, and screen 4, para. 3).

Similar stories followed in *Newsweek, U.S. News & World Report,* and dozens of national and local publications and public service documentaries. The child-centered educational system of the past generation, with its focus on the affective, rather than cognitive, aspects of students' growth, was perceived as fallen into a state of crisis. As part of his initiative to disband the U.S. Department of Education, President Reagan convened a National Commission on Excellence in Education, which published its report entitled *A Nation at Risk* in April 1983 (Vinovskis, 2009). Rather than argue for a downgraded federal role in education, the study increased the level of national alarm over the state of America's schools:

> Our Nation is at risk. Our once unchallenged preeminence in commerce, industry, science, and technological innovation is being overtaken by competitors throughout the world. . . . The educational foundations of our society are presently being eroded by a rising tide of mediocrity that threatens our very future as a Nation and a people. . . . If an unfriendly foreign power had attempted to impose on America the mediocre educational performance that exists today, we might well have viewed it as an act of war. As it stands, we have allowed this to happen to ourselves. (National Commission on Excellence in Education, 1983, Opening section, paras. 1 & 2)

Among the causes for the decline, the commission recognized the child-centered approach to education, seen in "the multitude of often conflicting demands we have placed on our Nation's schools and colleges . . . [which] are routinely called on to provide solutions to personal, social, and political problems that the home and other institutions either will not or cannot resolve" (National Commission on Excellence in Education, 1983, Opening section, para. 3).

Through the late 1980s and 1990s, calls for reforming education according to a more rigorous and competitive paradigm came from a wide range of special interests, particularly the business community. Groups within public education—teachers, administrators, state education departments—tended to see change driven from outside their profession as a threat. They resisted most of these efforts as insensitive to the complex problems of working with children. From 1983 to the inauguration of the Bush administration, these two educational paradigms—child-centered versus society-centered—struggled to a draw, with little fundamental change in either the functioning of schools or the achievement levels of students (Vinovskis, 2009).

The No Child Left Behind (NCLB) Act of 2001 (Public Law 107–110) represented a breakthrough for those advocating the rigor of scientifically based practice to the struggling field of education. Professional organizations, particularly teacher unions, strongly resisted its insistence on testing, data, and accountability—including the new mandate that "schools and districts are encouraged or required to implement programs that are proven to be effective through scientifically based research" (U.S. Department of Education, 2002, p. 25).

As a directive, this represented a paradigm shift with an illusive play on the word "child." The popular name given to the 2001 reauthorization of the 1965 Elementary and Secondary Education Act (ESEA) (Public Law 89–10) became "No Child Left Behind." This provided reassurance that the child-centered paradigm of the past generation would be carried forward. However, it was clear that, under the new law, the *methods* that districts were required to use for educating individual children would radically change. In place of accumulated experience, past practice, expertise, professional judgment, and training as the basis for decision making, the standard for educational practice would be the scientific method:

> Systematic, empirical methods . . . rigorous data analysis . . . observational methods . . . experimental or quasi-experimental designs . . . [that] allow for replication . . . [and accepted] by a peer-reviewed journal or approved by a panel of independent experts through a comparably rigorous, objective and scientific review. (President's Commission on Excellence in Special Education, 2002, p. 47)

RTI A Paradigm for
Scientifically Based Educational Decision Making

Debate over the appropriateness of using the scientific method in educational practice carried on during the early 2000s and is beyond the scope of this book (Melnyk & Fineout-Overholt, 2005; Shavelson & Towne, 2002). But the outcome of the discussion, and the paradigm shift it is generating, are critical to any school intent on adopting RTI. From 2002 through 2010, policymakers and local educational leaders searched for a way of applying the methods of scientific research to the challenge of improving the way children learned. They needed a technique that was rigorous, data based, and peer reviewed (i.e., scientific); it also had to be focused on the growth of individual children rather than aggregate groups, nonintrusive to educational programs, within the capability of educators to implement (i.e., adaptable to a child-centered value system), and finally, cost effective and affordable (i.e., practicable). It was a formidable challenge.

While consensus on an effective approach for a majority of schools is not yet in sight, the technique that is the most widely known, supported, and practiced is RTI. Perhaps most important, the principles underlying RTI were strongly endorsed by the NCLB legislation in 2001 (Neuman, 2002), and in the reauthorization of the Individuals with Disabilities Educational Improvement Act (IDEIA) in 2004 (Public Law 108–446, §614 (b)(6)(B)).

ROOTS OF RTI

RTI originally developed in the wake of the Education for All Handicapped Children Act (EAHCA) of 1975 (Public Law 94–142, reauthorized in 1990 as the Individuals with Disabilities Education Act [IDEA]). Beyond its effects in the schools, the law produced a wave of research into the instruction and evaluation of children with special needs. In terms of classification and eligibility for mandated services, the law introduced what became known as the *discrepancy model* for identification of learning disabilities. It set the standard for classification as a demonstrated gap in performance between a student's tested IQ (on an instrument such as the WISC-IV) and the level of performance that would be expected for a child of his or her age in class and on achievement tests (such as the Woodcock Johnson Achievement Test).

Some researchers were disturbed by this idea and soon dubbed it the "wait to fail" approach to evaluation. In their eyes, it required the child to demonstrate the need for special services by allowing a gap in performance to develop over a period of time, which could run from one to two years or longer. Their response was to search for scientific methods of identifying learning disabilities with a diagnostic, rather than a reactive, approach. They were also interested in finding ways of maximizing the effectiveness of evaluation and instruction for special needs children.

The first movement in this direction arose in the late 1970s, when it was known as data-based program modification (DBPM), or progress monitoring (Deno & Mirkin, 1977). When Stanley Deno and Phyllis Mirkin published the first research on DBPM in 1977, it was one of the earliest peer reviewed approaches to what we today call *data-driven* instruction. The goal of their research was to identify a method to give teachers data in the kind and quantity they would need to literally "drive" their approach to instruction.

In spite of these and hundreds of other efforts from research, the actual practice of both general and special education changed little during the 1980s and 1990s. Evidence for scientific, data-based education ran counter to the child-centered paradigm that had guided education since the 1970s. (If national media attention from publications like *TIME*, *Newsweek*, and *A Nation at Risk* could not produce reform, it should not be surprising that educational research would be largely ignored.) Change came only with the passage of the NCLB legislation in 2001 and the reauthorization of the IDEIA in 2004. Combined, these two pieces of legislation came close to mandating that scientifically based programs be at the foundation of American educational practice. Specifically, the diagnostic practice that had evolved and expanded from progress monitoring (now known as RTI) was strongly recommended by the Department of Education. Since 2004, this federal endorsement has transformed RTI into one of the most highly studied developments in the past half-century of American education.

REVIEW OF RTI

RTI is a multitiered approach to identifying and supporting students with learning and behavior needs. Its focus is to provide high-quality, scientifically based instruction in the general education classroom. The RTI process includes ongoing student assessment and monitoring of individual student progress (progress monitoring) that tracks the results of targeted and "tiered" interventions. These interventions are introduced first to all learners (beginning at the elementary school level), and then increased for those who show a need for additional support. This additional support comes from a multitiered approach that provides differentiated instruction to develop their skills.

While no single RTI model is universally practiced among all grade levels, generally, the three (sometimes four or five) separate tiers of specific learning strategies offer increasing levels of intensity of instruction to accelerate students' rates of learning, based on their individual needs.

Most RTI models include a three-tier, or three-step, process of increasing levels of support for students that includes high-quality classroom instruction and screening interventions (Tier 1), targeted small-group interventions (Tier 2), and intensive interventions *in addition* to core instruction and comprehensive evaluations (Tier 3) (Buffum, Mattos, & Weber, 2010). Figure 1.1 presents the organization of RTI used throughout this book.

Figure 1.1   Response to Intervention: Tiers and Spheres

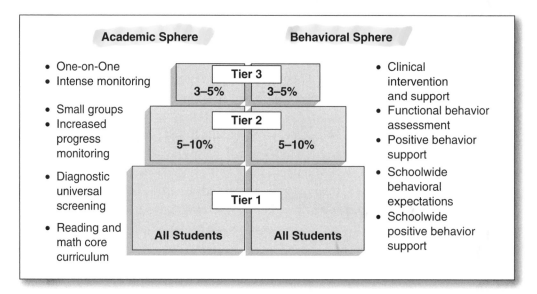

The illustration shows the RTI process as a three-tier composite of academic and behavioral spheres and suggests that these reflect and reinforce one another. This model is based on the clinical understanding that academic performance is a form of student behavior (see Chapter 7). The two spheres are interdependent and inseparable, and so, an effective RTI program needs to evaluate the full range of each student's performance in school: curriculum work (academics, which is a form of behavior) and social interactions (behavior, which strongly affects academics).

Within each tier, general education teachers, special education teachers, and specialists (including support staff) monitor student progress with increasing intensity, adjust instructional and behavioral intervention according to the level of response, and work collaboratively within instructional support teams (ISTs) to routinely review each student's progress. Data are collected and analyzed and become the basis for decision making. Ultimately, members of the IST share these data with the student's parents in an effort to make educational decisions collaboratively on behalf of the student.

The chapters of this book attempt to provide an overview of the components of an effective RTI implementation. They take the reader through the foundation and history behind RTI to its implementation in the specific content areas of mathematics, literacy, and reading and on to engaging members of the educational community, including parents and administrators. The book is not written as a comprehensive text but rather as a user-friendly introduction to using RTI to improve outcomes for all students.

Chapters of the Book

Chapter 2. Progressing With Progress Monitoring
(Harold J. Dean and John Kappenberg)

Chapter 2 presents progress monitoring as the source, growing since the 1970s, from which RTI would develop in the 1990s. It discusses the current relationship between RTI as a diagnostic program focused on improving instruction, and progress monitoring as a data-driven approach to making educational decisions that support individual students.

The authors include a history of curriculum-based measurement, the research supporting progress monitoring, and a hands-on description of how teachers should administer these techniques. This includes six basic steps: (1) Define a behavior to be monitored; (2) select a measurement strategy; (3) establish a baseline; (4) create a goal to be achieved; (5) develop a chart to monitor progress toward the goal; (6) create a plan for making decisions based on the data from progress monitoring.

The chapter concludes with a review of the benefits of progress monitoring over other forms of assessment within RTI (such as outcome assessment, screening assessment, and diagnostic assessment) and includes a reference to progress monitoring tools and Internet resources.

Chapter 3. The Instructional Support Team: A Foundation of the
RTI Process (Arlene B. Crandall, Erin E. Ax, and Dolores T. Burton)

This chapter focuses on the IST as an essential component of an RTI program. After defining the key kinds of ISTs (teacher assistance team, prereferral intervention team, mainstreaming assistance team, school-based consultation team) and the problem-solving model, the authors reinforce the concept that RTI represents a paradigm shift in our educational process, changing the focus from testing as a summative assessment to testing as an instructional and diagnostic tool. An essential part of this is the benefit of instructional and diagnostic decisions made not by individual professionals but by an IST.

The authors present research supporting the effectiveness of ISTs followed by a detailed and hands-on analysis of the IST meeting process, including the steps needed before the meeting, during the meeting, and after the meeting. The section discussing the meeting includes six key elements needed for success. The chapter includes a case study of the IST meeting process, which illustrates in detail each of the elements included in the chapter.

Chapter 4. Literacy Instruction: Tier 1 (Lynn Burke and John Kappenberg)

Chapter 4 introduces the role of RTI in diagnosing and supporting individual students who struggle with reading. It focuses on understanding the background knowledge in literacy needed to properly apply RTI in a Tier 1 setting. The chapter presents the process through the eyes of a teacher who is learning how to introduce RTI into her instruction, and her own struggle to make sense of the transition from traditional methods to a data-based model. The chapter includes an update on recent developments in our knowledge of the neurological foundation of reading as a complex skill and as the foundation for almost every other academic discipline. This information is described as essential to selecting effective interventions within RTI. It concludes with a prospective on future developments of RTI in the area of reading.

Chapter 5. Literacy Intervention: Tiers 2 and 3 (Sarah McPherson and Dolores T. Burton)

This chapter continues the application of RTI to reading and presents material needed to understand its use in Tiers 2 and 3. It begins with a discussion of several common myths about literacy, along with the most recent findings from research, particularly those that have a direct bearing on the way reading is taught and evaluated in an RTI setting.

The chapter presents a hands-on account of some of the most effective techniques currently known for the introduction of RTI into school reading programs. Topics include the following:

- definitions of learning disabilities
- early childhood assessment and intervention

- interventions used in Tier 1, Tier 2, and Tier 3
- discussion of NCLB and IDEA mandates for assessment of learning disabilities, alphabetics, and other specific reading issues
- the Zabala four-step SETT framework
- quality indicators for literacy in childhood, middle level, and high school level literacy programs
- universal screening
- progress monitoring in reading
- curriculum-based measurement reporting
- instructional tools for RTI
- resources for the introduction of RTI into reading programs (National Research Center on Learning Disabilities; RTI Action Network; Reading Rockets)

This chapter places special emphasis on the supportive technology available for reading in an RTI program.

Chapter 6. Mathematics Difficulty or Mathematics Disability? RTI and Mathematics (Dolores T. Burton and John Kappenberg)

Low achievement in mathematics is documented by international comparisons of students' performance in mathematics and is a matter of national concern. This chapter examines the difference between mathematical difficulty and dyscalculia and how an RTI program, with careful attention to fidelity of implementation, can assist in the diagnosis and remediation of mathematical difficulties.

While there are several definitions of dyscalculia, they all share three elements: (1) the presence of difficulties in mathematics, (2) some degree of specificity to these difficulties (i.e., the lack of across-the-board academic difficulties), and (3) the assumption that the difficulties are caused in some way by brain dysfunction. The chapter describes examples of different learner characteristics that can help the teacher in applying error pattern analysis and diagnosing dyscalculia within the RTI model for mathematics. Differences among the three tiers are demonstrated using case studies. Technology resources specific to mathematics and RTI are provided for further study.

Chapter 7. Response to Intervention and Positive Behavior Support (C. Faith Kappenberg and John Kappenberg)

One of the most important applications of RTI is use of positive behavior support (PBS) and other interventions for problems with student behavior and classroom management. Teachers cannot accurately evaluate learning unless behavior is stabilized; PBS provides the knowledge and skills for teachers to do this, and RTI can become a bridge linking it to classroom instruction within a common framework. This chapter presents practical information essential to the use of PBS in stabilizing student behavior in both general education and inclusive settings.

The chapter begins with a thorough review, written for a teacher's perspective, of PBS theory and practice, including reference to its mandated use under IDEA regulations and its role in each of the RTI tiers. It includes an analysis of the challenges teachers and supervisors face in balancing their requirements for academic success with the need to reduce disruptive behavior in order to achieve that goal. Examples of functioning programs in actual schools are included.

This is followed by a presentation of the skills needed to analyze student behavior and develop effective responses, including teacher- and team-friendly tools for effective PBS. The chapter concludes with specific tips on how to implement PBS in each of the tiers of RTI and information on locating additional training for schools and districts.

Chapter 8. Emerging Agendas in Collaboration: Working With Families in the RTI Process (John Kappenberg and Helene Fallon)

Collaboration and teams are central to the RTI process and are discussed in chapters 3, 9, and 10. One critical, but often neglected, area of collaboration is the parent–professional relationship. This chapter serves as a resource for teachers who are beginning to work with RTI and need practical ideas on how to work with parents in ways that are truly collaborative, rather than merely supportive.

It begins with a review of provisions in NCLB (2001) and IDEIA (2004) that require specific forms of parent–professional collaboration and then describes alternative approaches designated as the *client model* and the *consultant model.* Within the client model, professionals assume a position of authority and control, based on their expertise, and parents assume a supportive role in their child's education. In the consultant model, professionals maintain full control and responsibility for the educational process—including RTI—but, wherever possible, parents take on the role of active contributors, providing specialized expertise from their unique experience with the child and insight into his or her behavior. Their role is similar to that of other consultants who contribute to the child's support under RTI, such as psychologists, social workers, and speech therapists; they do not direct the process, but, because of their essential expertise, they are treated as invaluable contributors.

The chapter concludes with extensive review of the research on promising practices in parent–school relationships and organizations that support this research, such as the National Network of Partnership Schools, the IDEA Partnership, and Communities of Practice.

Chapter 9. Leadership: The Role of District and School Administrators in Implementing RTI (Patricia Ann Marcellino and Dolores T. Burton)

This chapter reviews the role and goal of the two top leaders in a district's introduction of RTI: the principal (understood as the *internal change agent*), and the superintendent (understood as the *external change agent*). Although individuals in these roles do not normally work directly within the RTI process, both they and their teachers need to understand that without their leadership, a successful introduction of RTI is nearly impossible. The chapter describes their leadership goals (professional collaboration, consensus building, cross-training, and ongoing communication), and their leadership roles (building manager, instructional leader, political activist, and central evaluator), within a schoolwide or districtwide RTI initiative.

The authors review a two-step process for the introduction of an RTI program, with an emphasis on strategy, structure, supervision, and systems analysis. It includes (1) a needs analysis of the district and school based on the SWOT management technique (strengths, weaknesses, opportunities, and threats), and (2) an explanation of the business management functions using the POLE process (planning, organizing, leading, and evaluating).

The chapter is written with an eye to the needs of teachers, preservice teachers, and teacher educators, as well as administrators, all of whom need to recognize the central role that leadership plays in the process of introducing RTI into a school or district.

Chapter 10. Managing Time: RTI in the Middle and High School Master Schedule (Lydia Begley and Dolores T. Burton)

While resources describing strategies for implementing an RTI program at the elementary level exist, there is little research that focuses on the secondary schools. This chapter includes specific ideas and "how to's" for teachers and administrators that can assist them in implementing RTI in their classrooms and buildings.

The chapter describes potential models for the use of RTI in middle and high school as well as models for how schools can support and organize ISTs around research-based RTI concepts to diagnose learning disabilities. It demonstrates that RTI, although challenging to implement at the secondary level, can work with some minor adjustments to scheduling, flexible staff members, and creative administrators who understand the scheduling process and the need for successful collaboration among members of ISTs. Specific ideas for using technology to monitor student progress at the secondary level are addressed to help teachers keep track of the lowest performing students. A case study is included to demonstrate "theory into practice," and technology resources are provided for further assistance for implementation.

Epilogue: Why Implement RTI?
(Dolores T. Burton and John Kappenberg)

The epilogue reviews the reasons to implement some of the ideas presented in this book and provides some concluding thoughts of the authors.

Progressing With Progress Monitoring

2

Harold J. Dean and John Kappenberg

Peter is a seven-year-old boy in second grade, in a class of 22 students. He is described by his teacher, Ms. Rodriguez, as a "typical second grader, but with some reading difficulties." During kindergarten screening, Peter was flagged for knowing a limited number of letter sounds in the alphabet. As kindergarten progressed, he made gains but never made it to mastery for kindergarten-level phonemic awareness and phonics skills. While he loved looking at books and talking about what he saw, Peter was unable to move into reading more than one- to two-word phrases.

Throughout first grade, Peter read consistently below grade-level expectations within guided reading, always several levels below his peers in regard to leveled texts. His first-grade teacher referred him to the committee on special education, and while testing found his IQ to be in the average range, it did reveal weaknesses in reading and written language skills. Peter was not classified as requiring special services, and he remained in the first-grade general education setting. While he enjoyed looking at books during free reading time, he did not enjoy and tried to avoid guided reading, as he was limited to a selection of books that were cognitively beneath him but that he was unable to master due to his deficit in reading skills.

The year Peter started second grade, the teachers in his elementary school had received professional development over the summer on the use of data to drive instruction within the response to intervention (RTI) model. Benchmarking, progress monitoring, and intervention plans were covered, and benchmark assessments were administered to students over the first few weeks of school. A note from Peter's mother described how he "fell out of love with books" over the last year and how difficult it was to get him to read or even look at books; he refused to read "baby books."

Ms. Rodriguez recognized Peter's frustrations during the benchmarking. The testing allowed precise identification of the literacy skills that were challenging for Peter. Based on these data, Ms. Rodriguez determined a target for Peter to achieve by the end of the first marking period; she grouped Peter with students who were having difficulty with similar skills and designed lessons specific to those skills. This small-group instruction aimed at individual student needs was provided in addition to the regular reading instruction from the core curriculum. Peter's progress toward mastery of those skills was monitored over a period of weeks to determine if the strategies Ms. Rodriguez was using were appropriate for him. As this approach, known as progress monitoring, *continued, Peter gradually achieved higher scores in reading and, more significantly, began to enjoy the process of reading.*

T his chapter offers a brief overview of progress monitoring (PM) and its role in the RTI model. The first, and most important, question to ask is, "How can a good teacher help Peter before he falls 'out of love' with books?" PM is an approach to instruction that systematically reviews instructional strategies and outcomes in a way that helps us to systematically monitor the needs of the student. This enables us to target specific skills and help students reach identified goals before they develop a history of failure that impacts their interest and ability in a subject.

THE RELATIONSHIP BETWEEN PM AND RTI

RTI is a federally mandated approach to serving students identified as "at risk," meaning students not likely to succeed in an academic program without some additional intervention of targeted instruction and curriculum. RTI is a three tiered process that implements and evaluates these interventions (Fuchs & Fuchs, 1997). PM is a method of gathering evidence that informs the RTI process.

The Problem With Assessments

End-of-the-unit tests used in typical school curriculums do not give enough data to effectively evaluate the progress of students at risk. For example, a teacher may spend two or three weeks covering a unit of a math curriculum, such as developing a process skill or mastering a content area such as addition and subtraction of fractions with unlike denominators. A class of 30 students may spend three weeks on the unit, after which they are given a unit test. If the test reveals that some students haven't mastered the material, several weeks of class time may be necessary to repeat the instruction, or the teacher may have to move on to cover the next chapter.

Most traditional unit tests given in schools are considered outcome assessments. They provide a bottom line, end-of-unit evaluation, an overall "How did everyone do?" These types of tests are important and, of course, we would never expect to dispense with them. But they do not provide enough information and data to monitor students who do not succeed during the early or middle stages of instruction. These students are failing, but their problems do not come to light until the very end, after a great deal of time has been lost, and a great deal of frustration may have built up within both the students and their teacher.

What Is PM?

PM provides a systematic method to assess student achievement at frequent, sometimes daily, intervals (Office of Special Education Programs, 2008). Looking forward to its graphing elements, described later in this chapter, PM can also be predictive, allowing teachers to answer questions such as whether a specific student will reach an intended outcome if he or she continues to progress at the current rate.

As required by U.S. Department of Education standards, which require that instructional strategies be based on peer reviewed research, the strategies used in PM are supported by research and implemented with fidelity. The process is a scientifically based practice for assessing student performance; it is designed to provide the data that teachers need to determine objectively how their students are progressing toward a goal within a given time frame (Deno, 2003; Espin & Deno, 1993).

From a student-centered perspective, it also helps identify those at risk of failure. Used with the required frequency and duration, it sets up clear checkpoints every week, every two weeks, or every month, so that no student continues to fail because of instruction that is not effective for his or her learning needs. The more frequently assessments are given, the more data a teacher has to understand how a student is progressing and what type of intervention may be needed when the progress is not on target (Fuchs & Fuchs, 1997; Torgesen, 2005).

From an academic perspective, PM evaluates the effectiveness of the instruction in two ways. First, it tells how the *students* are doing in relation to curriculum goals. Second, it reveals how effective the teacher's *instruction* has been (Council for Exceptional Children, 2007). In this sense, PM is not just for struggling students; it is a technique to help evaluate all students, because again, as mentioned in Chapter 1, in RTI, the first tier includes the entire inclusive classroom. Because it includes all students, Tier 1 may be a point at which the curriculum or teaching methods, not the students, are found to be in need of remediation. PM helps reflective teachers assess their own teaching strategies, and it ensures that any students who are having difficulty are identified and receiving appropriate interventions. PM facilitates this identification and then provides the targeted information needed to assist struggling students through Tiers 2 and 3 of the RTI model. It is a tool that can be administered either individually or to an entire class depending on the level of intervention in RTI Tiers 1, 2, and 3.

Curriculum-Based Measurement

Curriculum-based measurement (CBM) provided the tools that led to the ideas behind data-driven instruction in earlier works, such as *Dynamic Indicators of Basic Skills* (Shinn, 1985) and *Toward a Technology for Assessing Basic Early Literacy Skills* (Kaminski & Good, 1996), and it was introduced into curriculum for secondary English language arts (Espin & Deno, 1993), English language learners (Baker & Good, 1995), deaf learners (Chen, 2002; Devenow, 2002), and general education intervention (Fuchs & Fuchs, 1997).

The key to CBM is graphing a large number of results of student performance measures that, in aggregate, reveal the academic progress of individual students (Deno, 2003). CBM provides data that fill in the gap between how the student performed when the unit began and how he or she did after it was completed, usually weeks later (Shinn, 1995). The charts it produces zoom in on day-to-day performance, telling the teacher and the parent how the student is progressing and revealing areas in need of intervention when that need appears, not days or weeks later.

These measurements are closely aligned with the curriculum, so they give critical insight into not only the learning process and gains of the student but also the teaching process of the educator and his or her classroom methods. They have the potential to reveal both what individual students need and to provide information on what the teacher and the program may need to do differently.

Even though the procedure is scientifically based, it is not intimidating in practice. It is a simple process of gathering and charting data. Each day, or as frequently as possible, the student performs a brief specific skill related to the goals of a curriculum unit (solving three to five math problems or reading several words, for example), and the teacher records the results on a chart. The record keeping is no more complex than keeping track of mileage for a car.

After a period of time, several days or no less than once a week, the teacher reviews the data and makes a judgment about whether the progress shown on the graph, if continued, will allow the student to reach the goal by the end of the unit. The teacher can see, visually and graphically, where individual students are in terms of required skills and how they are progressing (or regressing) in relation to where each needs to be by the end of the unit.

The Administration of PM

One of the advantages of the PM approach is its ease and simplicity of administration. For teachers, it is less time consuming than other assessments: Most individual measurements can be completed in less than a minute. It is designed to give short, regular, frequent, and intermittent assessments rather than extensive testing data (Baker & Good, 1995; Kaminski & Good, 1996).

It gives immediate feedback in the form of scoring visuals, and data are highly relevant to the student's grasp of curriculum elements and progress toward unit goals. It keeps all stakeholders up to date on the current state of the student's work, rather than providing only the final summative conclusions of the wait-to-fail model.

Data are also helpful for parent–teacher conferences. When parents ask, "How is it going?" PM allows the teacher to take out a very detailed graph on which both teacher and parent can see exactly how the work is progressing. It is a very parent-friendly model.

Data from PM are also helpful to teachers and administrators as curriculum-based measures. Focused precisely on what is happening in the classroom, and measuring the exact skills and content that the curriculum requires the student to know and be able to do, this information can inform curriculum mapping and revision efforts. It is not testing for the sake of testing; it is testing of the specific abilities that students need to be successful; it is also a reflection on the sequence of instruction.

The Process

PM involves three components: determining student levels, monitoring student progress, and adjusting instruction based on data.

The first step of the PM process is to determine the current level of student performance in relation to the learning goals for a particular curriculum unit: Where is the student now? Where does he or she need to be by the time the unit is completed?

Step 2 is monitoring the ongoing rate of learning as the unit progresses, and also what is called "administration," meaning the way the instruction is carried out. The key concept with administration is fidelity of instruction, which refers to the degree to which the teacher's instruction is consistent with the standards required by the research-based curriculum and instructional strategy. This is extremely important for data collection and management, since variations in the way instruction is implemented make it difficult to determine whether student performance is the result of the student's individual response to the instruction, or of the instruction itself. The most careful assessment process can be rendered ineffective if the teaching is not carried out with fidelity to the program. If the program is designed for weekly, twice-weekly, or daily assessment, then the assessments must be given consistently at exactly those intervals. If the curriculum calls for six vocabulary words to be mastered each day for 14 days, the assignments and assessments must follow this precise pattern. Variation in the process effectively nullifies the significance of any data that it produces.

The final stage of the PM process is to adjust the instruction, which is traditionally called "intervention," when a data trend indicates that the student will not achieve the unit goal under the current conditions. The adjustment may be in either the instruction, if the student is not responding to the intervention, or in the goal itself, if it is evident that the difficulties are too severe to be corrected by any other means. Usually, the goal has been set too high, but at times the performance trend may indicate that the student is not sufficiently challenged and the goal should be adjusted higher.

Recall Peter, from the case study that opened this chapter:

> *During the first six weeks of small-group, individualized intervention for Peter, Ms. Rodriguez noticed some gains in his performance on curriculum-based measurements and PM assessments. But she realized that at the rate he was progressing, Peter would not reach the target that was set before the intervention. A review of the data revealed that Peter responded well initially, but his progress waned when an additional strategy was introduced to the group. Ms. Rodriguez responded by regrouping students based on their rate of progress after the new strategy was introduced. An alternative strategy was taught to Peter and his progress monitored. The next six weeks saw Peter's rate of progress accelerate as he moved more rapidly toward his marking period goal.*

Basic Steps of PM

PM includes six basic steps (Iowa Department of Education, 2006), shown in Table 2.1:

Table 2.1 Basic Steps of Progress Monitoring

1. Define the behavior.	Describe the measurable skill that is the goal of the curriculum unit, and the change in the student's behavior needed to reach the goal in the set time. (See Qualities of Behavior Within Progress Monitoring, Table 2.2.)
2. Select the measurement strategy.	Define the method used to monitor the student's work.
3. Establish a baseline.	Describe the student's level of performance before the instruction, or intervention, begins.
4. Create a goal.	Describe the measurable level of performance required for mastery of the curriculum unit.
5. Develop a chart.	Define the method for plotting data to illustrate the student's progress throughout the unit.
6. Create a decision-making plan.	Develop a strategy for deciding what form of data will be collected and how often, how it will be analyzed, and what critical evidence will be accepted as indicators that a change of intervention is needed.

1. Define the behavior.

Behavior is the skill, ability, or aptitude that is being monitored and is the most important element of both the PM and RTI models. It can include any area of the academic spectrum—from reading and literacy to mathematics, sciences, and social studies as well as behavioral issues. Table 2.2 describes the qualities of behavior within PM.

Table 2.2 Qualities of Behavior Within Progress Monitoring

Within progress monitoring, behavior must be	
1. Observable and verifiable	It cannot be tinged with elements that extend beyond actual behavior, such as the observer's knowledge of

(Continued)

(Continued)

Within progress monitoring, behavior must be	
	a student's past success or difficulty, a belief in the student's capabilities or limitations, or other nuance and idiosyncrasies. As with any scientific process, two or more different observers should be able to report the same measurement. If possible, both the teacher and an outside observer in the classroom should see and report the same specific level of skill. This means that the behavior being observed should be as objective as possible: a correct answer to a math problem or an identification of different types of sentences, rather than a more subjective capability, such as the student's interpretation of a cartoon. The behavior must be clearly observable and objectively verifiable.
2. Measurable	It should be a skill that can be easily counted and charted over a sequence of time, and one that can reveal stages of growth toward a measurable objective, not just success or failure to reach the summative goal. An assignment to memorize an entire monolog from a play in a specific period of time does not allow for measuring improvement during the memorization process: At the end of the period, the skill is either completely accomplished or not. But memorizing two lines a day over the course of eight days is readily measurable and reportable as progress.
3. Alterable	The skill in question must be something that the student has the capability to master. The skill being monitored has to be alterable through a set of interventions that are available within the academic program. When several interventions produce little or no improvement, it may be time to refer the student to a more professional evaluation of the difficulty. This is one of the key elements of the overall RTI process.

Within progress monitoring, behavior must be	
4. Specific	The behavior to be modified should not involve more than one specific skill. The goal of "passing third-grade math" is too complex and involves too many individual factors to serve as a PM measurement. PM would involve setting a series of more discrete goals within the third-grade curriculum, such as "demonstrate the ability to multiply two-digit fractions." This would allow the teacher to develop a diagnostic assessment, which would determine why the student may be having difficulty with fractions, which specific skills or prerequisite skills are lacking, and what new intervention might improve the student's behavior.

2. Select the measurement strategy.

This is the procedure or tool to be used for collecting the data within the PM process. Determining the strategy should be the work of the full RTI team and the teacher working in collaboration. This is critical, because later on, if decisions need to be made on which new interventions to introduce, all participants need to have been familiar with the plan as it was originally developed. As in most phases of the process, both PM and the overall RTI model benefit from a team approach. Table 2.3 presents the important questions that need to be answered during the decision-making process for determining a measurement strategy.

Table 2.3 Questions and Decisions in the Development of a Measurement Strategy

1. How will data be collected?	This includes the measurement tools that will be used, the frequency of measurement, and the duration of the assessment. These are the ground rules so that the teacher has guidelines on specific skills and measurements of the PM assessment. The rules help assure fidelity of application within the process.

(Continued)

(Continued)

2. What material will be used to collect data?	These would include the resources needed to record the student's behavior and skills, such as notes taken in class, homework, tests and quizzes on paper or in a computer, or notes taken by the teachers to record verbal or other forms of student behavior.
3. In which settings will data be collected?	In the RTI format, there may be several settings for data collection depending on who is working with the student. Traditionally the most common setting would be the classroom, resource room, or other school-based location where student services are provided. In some cases, the skill being measured might require an out-of-school setting or multiple settings. The important points for validity of the PM process are that the setting be explicitly designated and that all data are collected there. Adjusting to unplanned changes of setting can dramatically alter students' behavior and performance.
4. Who will be responsible for data collection?	This is a procedural need, and it may vary depending on which of the RTI tiers is involved. In the first tier, responsibility for the data collections is usually that of the classroom teacher.

A sample form used by an RTI team is shown in Figure 2.1.

Figure 2.1   Progress Monitoring Decision Worksheet

Progress Monitoring Decision Worksheet	
Tier: _____	
Student's Name : _____	
Skill: _____	
How will data be collected?	
Measurement tools	
Frequency	
Duration	
What materials will be used to collect data?	
In which settings will data be collected?	
Who will to be responsible for data collection?	

As you progress through the tiers, as more people start working with a particular student, and as new interventions are introduced, different individuals may become accountable for specific areas of PM and data collection. The worksheet should be revised for each tier.

These are the preliminary first steps before PM can begin. They set the foundation for the remainder of the process.

3. Establish a baseline.

A baseline is the starting point for improvement. It is a statement of a student's level of performance in the skill to be measured before any intervention is introduced. It is the basis for assessing factors such as the goal to be achieved, problems to be addressed in reaching the goal, and rate of growth that can reasonably be expected from the intervention or interventions. A key element in setting the baseline is that it be measured in exactly the same format as will be followed throughout the PM.

The baseline is the starting point of the chart, with the performance standard as the final point. These become the fixed positions on the chart, along with the gap that separates them (both in performance level and time), as the process begins. From this point, the teacher will systematically collect and plot data on performance, filling the time line from the starting point to the goal and evaluating progress to determine whether alternative interventions are necessary.

An inaccurate baseline is among the greatest threats to a successful PM program. Therefore, one of the most critical elements in establishing a baseline is that it be the result of multiple measurements, not a single trial. On any given day, a student's performance may be markedly different from that on another day, usually below the true level, giving a false negative, but occasionally above it, giving a false positive. The only way to eliminate these disparities is through a minimum of three to five repeated measures that can then be averaged.

In addition, using multiple measures to establish a baseline may alert the teacher to important difficulties. If the performance varies widely prior to any intervention, this may indicate a condition that cannot be addressed by a purely academic approach and that calls for further evaluation within the larger RTI framework.

4. Create a goal.

The baseline is one end of the PM graph; the goal is the other. It tells all parties—the teacher, the student, the parent, and the PM team—where the student should be by the end of the academic unit and after a predetermined period of intervention.

The elements of goal setting, based on the acronym SMART and identified by Doran (1981), are shown in Table 2.4.

Table 2.4   SMART Goals

S. Specific	A goal should identify a clearly defined and described behavior.
M. Measurable	A goal must be observable, objective, and responsive to the measurement tools available during the PM process. Once the process begins, the measurement tool cannot be changed.
A. Ambitious	A goal must represent a balance that challenges without overwhelming the student and realistic in relation to the student's current baseline performance, known response to the work, and other aspects of his or her individual history. It should never be determined solely by external standards such as school, state, or national norms for a particular subject and grade. These should be used only when other factors in the student's profile indicate that they are appropriate. For example, if a student's baseline performance in reading is 16 words per minute, and the established level is 40, this would probably not be an appropriate objective as an initial goal for progress monitoring. For this student, an ambitious goal would be, perhaps, 30.
R. Realistic	A goal needs to be manageable within the time frame of the instructional unit and, most important, appropriate to the available resources. This can become an issue when districts and teachers attempt to have students achieve externally mandated goals in settings that do not provide adequate resources. In these cases, the teacher and PM team may need to brainstorm alternative goals until the shortages are remediated.
T. Terminal	A goal must have a deadline. Assigning a finishing date requires that the teacher pace the instruction, adjust interventions as needed, and review the process in the end.

Table 2.5 shows formats that may be used for developing goals in the areas of reading, spelling, mathematics, and writing. The chart illustrates

patterns that goals might take in various subject areas. The elements include a specific behavior or skill to be mastered, a time frame for demonstrating the skill, and an exit criterion, defined by some measurable activity, that can be expressed numerically in a graph: the student will read X number of words, will write X number of correct letters, will record X number of correct digits, will recite X number of total words. Specifying these objective outcomes is essential in determining whether an intervention has been successful.

Table 2.5 Sample Goal Formats

Reading: In (#) weeks, **(Student name)** will read (#) words correctly in (#) minutes from randomly selected grade (#) passages.
Spelling: In (#) weeks, **(Student name)** will write (#) correct letter sequences and (#) correct words in (#) minutes from randomly selected grade (#) spelling lists.
Math: In (#) weeks, **(Student name)** will write (#) correct digits in (#) minutes from randomly selected grade (#) math problems.
Writing: In (#) weeks, **(Student name)** will write (#) total words and (#) correct writing sequences when presented with randomly selected grade (#) story starters.

5. Develop a chart.

After setting a goal, the next step in PM is developing the chart. This is just a visual representation or graph that assists in monitoring the learning process so that obstacles can be identified and addressed. A visual form of representation can be useful in determining when a student is progressing well and when there is need for a new form of intervention. Charts also reveal whether it is likely that the goal will be reached within the required time frame. Compared with simple columns and rows of numbers, charts provide invaluable help for every aspect of data interpretation. Charts also document progress over time, which is at the heart of PM.

A key component of the PM chart is the structured assessment interval, which is predetermined. It specifies exactly how often an assessment is to be given, sometimes including which time of day when the team believes this level of consistency is important for a particular student.

The sample that follows in Figure 2.2 illustrates these techniques. This simplified example plots the number of sight words Peter is able to read in a one-minute period of time during the days between December 1, 2009, and March 31, 2010. If increasing the number of sight words is the goal, it is easy to see a pronounced improvement over time, as well as a brief period of decline and recovery, which might prompt an observer to ask whether any assignable cause would account for it. In addition to the

Figure 2.2 Peter's Number of Sight Words Read Correctly Per Minute

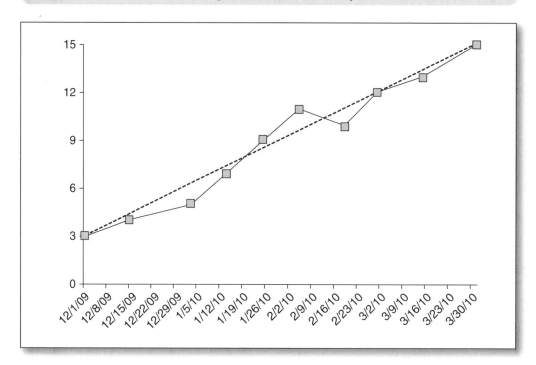

lines connecting discrete observations, a trend line is drawn, which further clarifies the rate of improvement. However, as the later illustrations show, a number of additional elements have to be introduced for a chart to meet the needs of PM.

The next two samples, shown in Figure 2.3 and Figure 2.4, introduce these additional components.

In this example, the target skill for Peter was phoneme fluency, and this illustration charts the reading skill of phoneme segmentation fluency over an entire semester from January through June, with June as the target date and 40 phonemes as the goal. In this case, the first four points serve as the baseline level of performance; the teacher determined this median score from three trials served as the starting point. For clarity, a heavy vertical line is drawn separating these baseline readings from subsequent trials. It was determined that Peter had a realistic potential to raise the score to the level of 40 phonemes between January and the end of the semester in June. To add visual clarity, a line is drawn connecting the baseline position in January with the goal level in June. This is called the *aimline,* and it depicts the approximate trend that the data points will need to follow if the student is to reach the goal at the projected time. Serious deviations from this line are an indication that some new intervention, either alternative instruction or resetting the goal, will be necessary.

Figure 2.3   No or Inadequate Response to Intervention

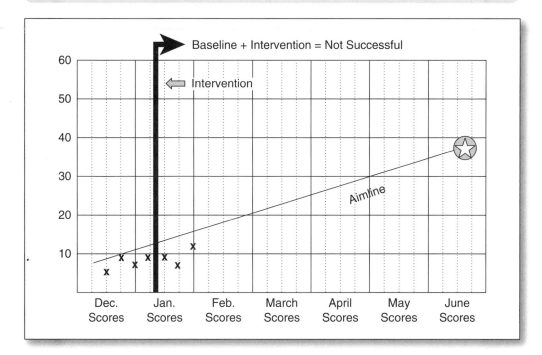

The chart in Figure 2.4 shows Peter's progress through February and March.

Figure 2.4   Positive Response to Intervention

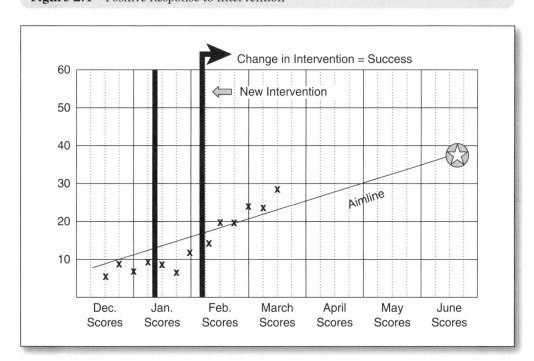

Again, the baseline points are separated from the intervention trials by the left-hand [heavy] vertical line. During February, the first three testing measures show virtually no improvement above the baseline, and at this point the teacher and the team (if a team approach is used) have concluded that the current rate of progress will not bring the student to the goal by June. The initial approach to teaching the student, the first intervention, is not succeeding, and some new intervention needs to be introduced. Note that the decision to change an intervention is always shared among the teacher and PM team if available.

After the decision for a change is made, the next step is to select the new research-based intervention. This intervention may be different from the first in curriculum, materials, time on task, teacher/student ratio, and/or instructional strategy. In Peter's case, a change was made to small-group instruction with a different curriculum. In the example above, the effect of the second intervention is dramatically positive, showing significant improvement in the student's performance. As long as this trend continues, the student is on track to achieve the goal by June. However, if the performance average were to fall below the aimline, the teacher and team would again meet to decide whether some additional intervention is needed. The student then would move to Tier 3 with a different curriculum, materials, time on task, teacher/student ratio, and/or instructional strategy.

6. Create a decision-making plan.

The next step is the decision-making plan. This addresses questions such as the following: How will the charted data be analyzed? How frequently, or after how many data points are collected, will the teacher and team meet to review progress—every week, every two weeks, every month? How often will the data be collected and charted? When should an analysis occur? Standard research protocols will apply to all cases, such as the need for a minimum of six data points to support a valid analysis. There must always be enough data (three to six points) to verify a trend, rule out anomalies or outlier incidents, and draw meaningful conclusions.

Another element of the plan is a strategy for deciding when conditions might indicate the need to change an instructional goal. In the previous example, the teacher and/or team might have decided that, after the first three points fell below the aimline, perhaps both the intervention and the goal would need to be changed. Alternatively, if the student's response had been positive but significantly below the aimline, the teacher and team might have concluded that the intervention was working, but, for this student, the goal had been set too high and needed to be lowered. These alternatives and possibilities need to be planned prior to the start of the PM program.

Recall Peter again:

> As Peter met his goal for the first intervention period, another benchmarking assessment was administered schoolwide. While Peter was still not at a mastery level, he had made considerable progress. Ms. Rodriguez set another goal, as intervention was still required. The same model of goal setting, intervention, monitoring, and adjusting was followed throughout the year. As Peter's literacy skills grew, his love for books returned. He recognized his growth just as much as Ms. Rodriguez did, taking pride in the charting of his progress and working toward his goals.
>
> While Peter will likely require a less intensive level of intervention in the third grade, since he did not master all of the skills required within the current curriculum for second grade, he did demonstrate growth through his responsiveness to intervention. Using the data from Peter's second-grade benchmark and PM assessments, his teacher will be able to place him in an appropriate intervention level upon entering the third grade, and will have background data on which interventions Peter responded to best, as well as on the skills for which he still requires support. This would not have been possible without a thorough assessment of individual student strengths and deficit skill areas, a data-based plan for intervention, and monitoring of the response to those interventions.

The Benefits of PM

PM provides a wide range of advantages over traditional instruction for both the teacher and student. Its regular assessments give systematic and reliable feedback on instruction at a level not possible without the PM process. PM data feedback is not only reliable, but just as important, it is far more current than traditional summative assessment. Depending on the design of a particular protocol, it can give feedback on a range of skills, including assessment of prerequisite skills for the target outcome. All this, in turn, provides the raw material that makes data-based decision making possible. For teachers and administrators, who face growing requirements of high-stakes testing and accountability, the introduction of more numerous and reliable data on student performance is a huge advantage. Knowing which students are struggling, and in which specific areas of the curriculum, lowers the level of guesswork, allows for faster response, and leads to fewer disappointments at the end of the school year.

In addition, PM introduces a common approach to instructional planning and evaluation that makes teacher-to-teacher collaboration far more accessible. The data from PM provide teachers with new resources with which to compare results of classroom techniques across curriculum disciplines and subject levels. In addition to being able to report on the success or failure of a particular intervention, a teacher is able to explain exactly why a problem developed or a success was achieved.

For the students, the advantage is the introduction of much clearer expectations. Since the program is focused on individual students, PM should involve them in both the goal setting and the charting process. In addition to giving a much clearer picture of their goals, it provides the added incentive of sharing in their development and day-to-day monitoring. They see both what is expected and how they are doing in reaching their goal, a proven motivational incentive. Teachers in a PM program report a spirit of involvement and excitement among students as they check their "score sheet" from day to day. The students are often as concerned as the teacher when results fall off, and are stimulated when they see improvement. Students become collaborators in their own education and see the teacher as a coach rather than purely an authority figure.

PM in a Nutshell

In comparison with traditional programs of summative assessment, PM is more effective in serving educational needs, as summarized in Table 2.6.

Table 2.6 Benefits of Progress Monitoring Over Summative Assessment

1. Analysis of instruction	Determines (1) how well students are benefiting from instruction and (2) areas in which instruction can be improved.
2. Balance of evaluation	Focuses equally on students and instructional practices. It can help a reflective teacher in evaluating the success of students, as it monitors how each is doing and how the instruction is affecting them.

3. Analysis of data	Provides data as charts rather than numbers, which are faster and easier to interpret and for students and parents to comprehend.
4. Motivation of students	Collecting data on their own performance and seeing the data displayed visually in charts inspires most students to want to see the numbers and aimlines increase toward the target goal.
5. Speed and simplicity of use	Compared with summative assessments, PM is faster, simpler, and less time consuming. Even though the teacher monitors more frequently, it is less time consuming, because each instance may take no more than one or two minutes and provides information for midcourse corrections in instruction, which may prevent more time-consuming remediation at a later date.

Back to RTI

PM is a tool designed to support the nationally mandated RTI approach to education. And, as the title of the program indicates, its goal is to base instruction, not on the former wait-to-fail approach, but on the response of the student to the instruction, from the very beginning. Embedded in this approach, from the beginning and throughout, are the questions, "How is the student responding to the intervention? How is the student responding to what the teacher is doing?"

PM is an ideal tool to provide the data and documentation to answer these questions. It reveals how students are responding and provides data that, when properly analyzed, can improve instruction both for individual students and for all students. It may begin with an analysis of an individual's response to a particular intervention, but experience has shown that the insights gained from these individuals regularly result in improvements to instruction at all three tiers of the RTI protocol. Even though RTI is a somewhat regimented triangle of tiers, no teacher works with just one student, and the insights gained through PM at one level are easily adapted to the others.

 TECH BYTE

MONITORING STUDENT PROGRESS USING CHARTDOG 2.0

PM uses data to assess students' academic performance and evaluate the effectiveness of instruction. The heart of PM is data, and the soul of data is the graphic presentation that delivers its message and meaning. In light of this, one of the most important steps to introduce PM in practice is to find fast, easy, and reliable methods to transform student performance data from numbers on tables—which are sometimes difficult to interpret—to lines on graphs, which tell a story that even the youngest student can comprehend immediately. Consider another sample student, Tanya, who is having some difficulty in her mathematics class. We will use Tanya's posttest scores on a five-problem probe, measuring ability to multiply two-digit numbers by two-digit numbers in Tier 1 to create a graph in the software program *ChartDog 2.0*. We will measure her progress by comparing expected scores after instruction with her actual scores to create a picture of Tanya's rate of learning. Based on these measurements, instructional strategies can be adjusted as needed.

ChartDog 2.0 (www.jimwrightonline.com/php/chartdog_2_0/chartdog.php) is an online resource for producing fairly sophisticated line graphs easily. This section of the chapter will help you use *ChartDog 2.0* to produce a line graph that describes a series of scores for Tanya over a four-week period. Before starting, you should have access to a computer and the Internet. We will use the scores in Table 2.7 for our graph.

Table 2.7 Tanya's Scores

Week	Number Correct, Expected Score (Observation 1)	Number Correct, Actual Score (Observation 2)
Week 1	3	0
Week 2	4	1
Week 3	5	1
Week 4	5	2

Start by accessing the URL for *ChartDog 2.0*. In the pull down box that appears, change the 20 to 4 (since you have 4 data points—weeks 1 through 4), and click on the "Open *ChartDog!*" link. You will see a single scrollable page arranged in three sections. Section 1 is a menu of chart options, including titles for the chart, names for the horizontal and vertical axes, and symbols to be used in designating data points. (See Figure 2.5.)

Figure 2.5   Screenshot of Data Entry Table in *ChartDog 2.0*

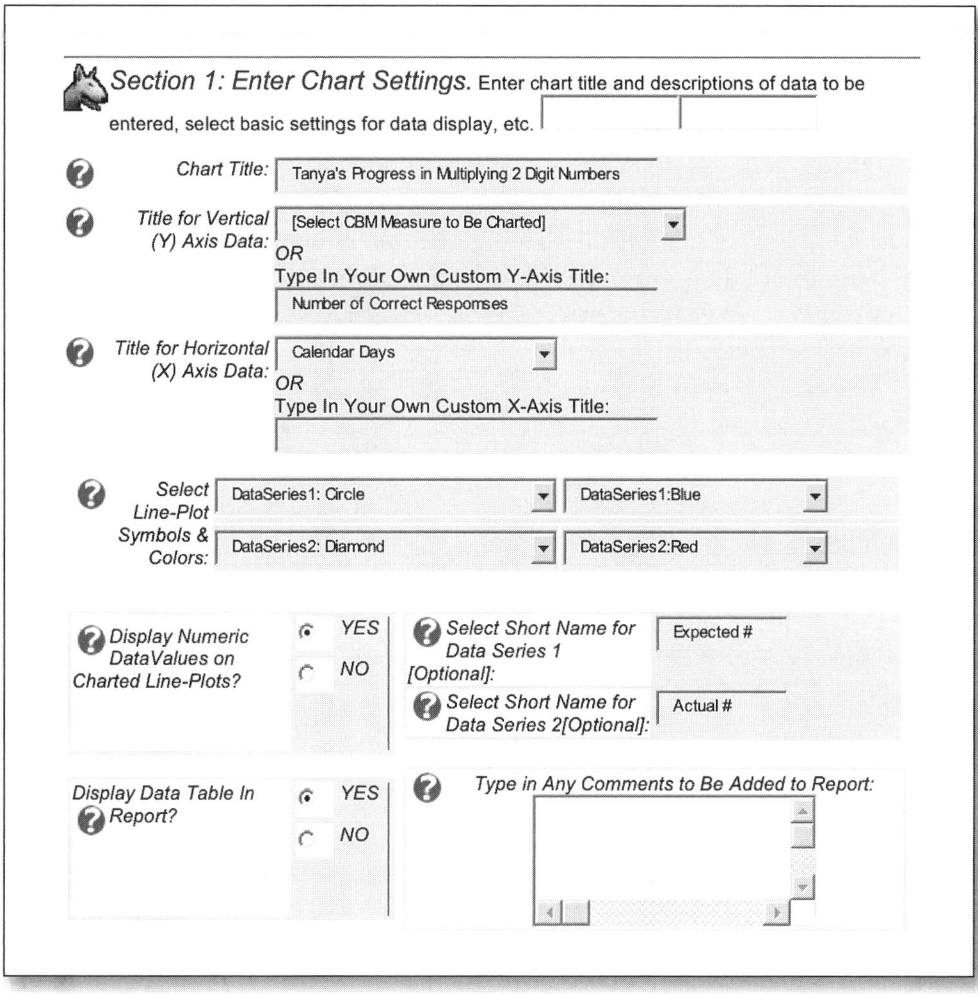

Section 1: Enter Chart Settings. Enter chart title and descriptions of data to be entered, select basic settings for data display, etc.

Chart Title: | Tanya's Progress in Multiplying 2 Digit Numbers

Title for Vertical (Y) Axis Data: | [Select CBM Measure to Be Charted] ▼
OR
Type In Your Own Custom Y-Axis Title:
| Number of Correct Responses

Title for Horizontal (X) Axis Data: | Calendar Days ▼
OR
Type In Your Own Custom X-Axis Title:
|

Select Line-Plot Symbols & Colors: | DataSeries1: Circle ▼ | DataSeries1:Blue ▼
| DataSeries2: Diamond ▼ | DataSeries2:Red ▼

Display Numeric DataValues on Charted Line-Plots?   ⊙ YES   ○ NO

Select Short Name for Data Series 1 [Optional]: | Expected #

Select Short Name for Data Series 2[Optional]: | Actual #

Display Data Table In Report?   ⊙ YES   ○ NO

Type in Any Comments to Be Added to Report:

Section 2 allows selection of one through four data series for presenting regression lines and computation of mean values, all of which are optional and may not be appropriate for a first-time user.

Section 3 is the place for data entry.

Enter Tanya's scores from Table 2.7. Figure 2.6 shows what your data values look like once entered into *ChartDog 2.0.*

After data are entered, the final step is to click the link labeled "Create Chart!" which will produce the finished product. The resulting graph, shown in Figure 2.7, contains a line representing the information relating to Tanya's actual scores, as well as a line representing the expected scores. An examination of the two lines clearly demonstrates the discrepancy

Figure 2.6   Screenshot of Data Entry Table in *ChartDog 2.0* (Completed)

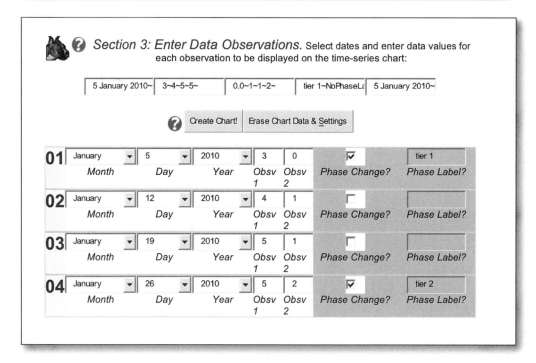

between Tanya's expected learning rate and her actual performance, indicating a need to move Tanya to Tier 2 intervention.

Teachers with busy schedules may find this resource to be useful. In addition, the simplicity of its design allows it to be used by both teachers and most students from the elementary grades and higher, who can easily learn to chart and understand the data from their own work.

RESOURCES

National Center on Response to Intervention. (www.rti4success.org)

This is the website of the national center; it includes information on resources, research and literature, tools and interventions, training and events, and professional development and technical assistance opportunities, as well as links to state-related RTI resources.

Figure 2.7 Screenshot of Graph Generated by *ChartDog 2.0*

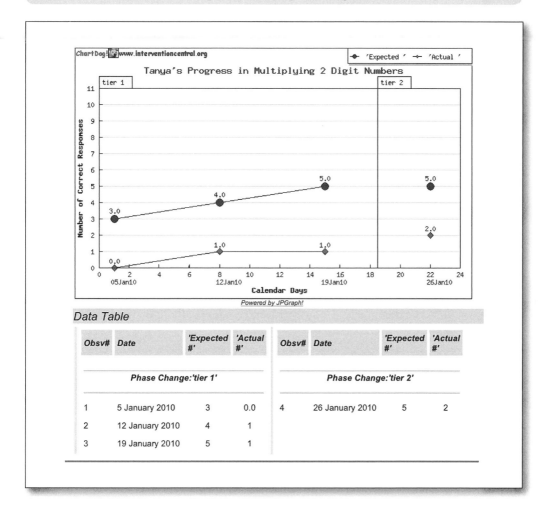

National Center on Student Progress Monitoring. (www.studentprogress.org)

Funded by the U.S. Department of Education, this website includes a resource library, a technical review of PM tools, and general information on the role PM plays in successful schools and data systems.

Fisher, D., & Frey, N. (2010). *Enhancing RTI: How to ensure success with effective classroom instruction and intervention.* Alexandria, VA: ASCD.

This book details the role of assessment in the RTI model, specifically PM. Discusses why to collect data, which data to collect, how to interpret the data, and how to use the data within the RTI model.

Other Resources

For school districts or service providers in the initial phases of RTI, below is a list of some of the other resources that may be helpful.

- Research Institute on Progress Monitoring, www.progressmonitoring.net
- Oregon Reading First Center, http://oregonreadingfirst.uoregon.edu
- State of Iowa Department of Education, www.iowa.gov/educate
- University of California at Riverside, www.extension.ucr.edu/academics/certificates/response_to_intervention.html
- Response to Intervention Action Network, www.rtinetwork.org
- DIBELS (Dynamic Indicators of Basic Early Literacy Skills), dibels.uoregon.edu
- LARS (Literacy Assessment Reporting System) (User-ID restricted), lars.esboces.org

GLOSSARY

Aimline: the expected rate of progress for a student to achieve in order to close the learning or behavior gap by the end of a designated instructional or intervention period.

Baseline: a measurement of a student's current level of knowledge, performance, or behavior commonly gathered at the start of PM to determine growth or response to a newly introduced instructional strategy or intervention.

Benchmark assessment: a formative measurement of student performance given at set intervals throughout a school year, commonly administered in the fall, winter, and spring of an academic year.

Curriculum-based measurement: an approach to measuring the academic growth of individual students through the use of a specific set of procedures intended to evaluate the effectiveness of the instruction they are providing.

Diagnostic assessment: a measure administered when a screening identifies a general deficit in knowledge or skill to determine exact areas of focus for individualized instruction or intervention.

Fidelity of assessment: the adherence to research- or evidence-based protocol or guidelines that were followed for the delivery of a specific assessment or measurement tool; administering an assessment in a manner or conditions different than intended affects fidelity.

Fidelity of instruction or intervention: the adherence to research- or evidence-based protocol or guidelines that were followed for the delivery of a specific instructional strategy or intervention; altering how a strategy or intervention was designed to be delivered affects fidelity.

Outcome assessment: a measurement of total learning for a particular area of study, most common in classrooms as unit tests, standardized assessments, and state assessments.

Progress monitoring: the systematic measurement of student growth over a period of time, commonly used to determine the effectiveness of an instructional strategy or intervention, or a student's responsiveness to an instructional strategy or intervention.

Screening: a type of assessment to identify which students *may not* meet designated goals based on present levels of performance or knowledge.

Trend line: the rate of growth or progress a student exhibits across a period of time under PM to monitor responsiveness to instruction or intervention; used as a comparative to an aimline to predict success of goal attainment.

The Instructional Support Team (IST) **3**

A Foundation of the RTI Process

*Arlene B. Crandall, Erin E. Ax,
and Dolores T. Burton*

Ava Howard is a first-grade student at West Elm Elementary School. Ava's current scores on her district's universal screening tool placed her in the bottom tenth percentile compared to other first graders at West Elm. Below is a list of Ava's strengths and weaknesses as reported by her first-grade teacher.
Strengths:

- *Ava has a lot of background knowledge and uses grade-level vocabulary.*
- *She knows consonant sounds.*
- *She is a sweet girl who responds well to positive reinforcement.*
- *She is social and enjoys working with students and adults.*
- *She seeks to please people.*
- *She can work independently for up to 30 minutes.*
- *She is a visual learner and a concrete thinker.*

Weaknesses:

- *Ava has weak sight-word vocabulary.*
- *Her knowledge of vowel sounds is weak.*
- *She is weak in fluency, below Level 1 reader.*
- *She has trouble retaining bits of information.*
- *She makes frequent trips out of the classroom (e.g., drinks, bathroom, etc.).*
- *Her parents are divorced, and though both parents have her best interest in mind, schoolwork and interventions are not a priority for the parents.*
- *Ava's older brother has been classified with a learning disability.*

A va's story is an example of concerns that cause schools to convene a building instructional support team (IST) to help their students. The definition of IST that will be used in this chapter emphasizes a team of school professionals, including teachers who meet to problem solve the learning needs of students in school. Different states may have different names for teams with this function. In a three-tier RTI model, teams can be used to make decisions at the Tier 1, 2, or 3 level. If these teams are designed well, with consistent procedures, they are integral in supporting the change process necessary for successful implementation of RTI.

At the Tier 2 and 3 levels, the team focuses on instruction and a specific intervention that can support small-group or individual learning. This can be a step in transforming building faculty and administration to think diagnostically about how children learn.

THE INFLUENCE OF SPECIAL EDUCATION LAW

The implementation of Public Law 94–142 (Education for All Handicapped Children Act, 1975) and all subsequent revisions mandated special education services and procedures for students who struggled to learn. Almost immediately, this law began to exert an influence far beyond the special education areas of American schools. Building teams consisting of educational professionals from various disciplines found themselves becoming an integral part of the process for special education classification.

At this time, the essential question asked by building teams was, "Based on the evidence available, can this student be educated in a regular education classroom, or does this student need a special education setting?" The location of a special education service (self-contained class, resource room, related service) within the building was seen as the answer to the student's learning problem. The special educator would provide a different type of instruction and, therefore, would be able to reach the hard-to-teach student. The learning needs of the student were translated to the definition of a disability. Saranson and Doris (1979) referred to this pattern as "a search for pathology" at the point of referral.

A team working with Ava at this point in history would review her extensive list of weaknesses and look for information to support the presence of a disability. This direction would be encouraged by the fact that her brother is already classified as a student with a learning disability. Ava's combination of weak retention, difficulty retaining information, and lower levels of vocabulary, fluency, and vowel knowledge suggests gaps that could be interpreted as a disability.

Prereferral Teams

In some ways, the building-level team became the gatekeeper for the referral to special education. Some teams were renamed as *prereferral teams*, with the intent to have the team focus on supporting the teacher in applying interventions in the classroom before a special education referral was made. The prereferral team was the beginning of a change from crisis/failure intervention to early intervention at the academic level.

Graden, Casey, and Christenson (1985) described the redirection of the prereferral team's function to early intervention by utilizing the stages of consultation. These included (1) request for consultation, (2) consultation, (3) observation, and (4) conference. Research on the effectiveness of prereferral teams was inconsistent, and at times the teams did not appear to be effective (Graden et al., 1985).

> The prereferral team would review the description of Ava's learning, and through consultation and observation design a classroom intervention to address her reading needs. Many schools simply provided remedial reading programs in a kind of one-size-fits-all approach to support struggling students.

Piersel and Gutkin's (1983) research on factors that affect resistance to consultation was a key tool for analyzing the school systems where prereferral teams were not effective. They noted several variables that affect the level of resistance in a building. Of the several variables that they discussed, one of the most interesting was the concern that consultation could reveal a system-level need in the building. When teams did the work of prereferral, they often revealed some systemic needs in the general education domain, such as the need to develop curriculum and instructional skills that make learning more accessible. This research on team functioning was one of the early connections between system theory on resistance and the reasons that teams were ineffective in impacting student learning.

> Ava's profile is the perfect example of a student case whose needs could raise some systemic questions about reading instruction. Her cluster of needs in vocabulary, phonics, and basic skills calls into question how she is being instructed. What happens in the classroom when a student does not keep up with peers? Is instruction adjusted to the needs of the struggling student? Is there an analysis of Ava's needs? Are basic skills taught to automaticity?

Instructional Consultation Teams

As the approach of school consultation gained momentum, Sylvia Rosenfield (1989) developed a different form of teaming called *instructional consultation teams.* In this model, teachers are key members of the team. The component stages of this process include contracting, problem identification and analysis, intervention design, intervention implementation, intervention evaluation, follow up/redesign, and closure. This is a strength-based model that focuses on the skills of the student and on how an intervention could be built upon those skills. The other team designs tended to focus on the weaknesses of the student in order to make the case that the student qualified for such services as remedial reading support or special education. This significant change was a major step toward the current RTI model.

In this model, the strengths in Ava's learning profile would be a key part of the problem analysis. If Ava can learn her consonant sounds, why not her vowels? How can an intervention be designed that uses her current skills? What measure would help to best monitor her progress?

Mainstream Assistance Teams

Another model of the school-based team began to emerge at a time when the number of students in special education services was dramatically increasing. The mainstream assistance team (MAT) was developed by Fuchs, Fuchs, and Bahr (1990) to address the needs of difficult-to-teach students in an effort to help them learn rather than refer them to special education. The distinctive features of this model included the following:

- use of a multidisciplinary team, following written scripts in order to implement the steps of behavior consultation with fidelity,
- use of the data to find the most effective and efficient use of consultation, and
- outcomes measured by student performance and teacher behavior as well as teacher referral rate to special education.

The key components of (1) outcome measures and (2) teacher behavior that reflects fidelity of implementation are important precursors to today's RTI model.

Ava's meeting in this model would have focused not only on the specific intervention as well as measurement of progress, but also on monitoring the fidelity of intervention implementation. What teacher behavior should be observed during intervention implementation? What skills does the teacher need to implement the intervention?

The Problem-Solving Model

The RTI literature suggests that using the problem-solving process is the most effective building team model (Batsche et al., 2006). The problem-solving model parallels the scientific process (see Table 3.1). The pattern of analyzing the student's learning needs and matching them with a well-constructed intervention brings a level of precision to the work of building teams.

Table 3.1   Steps in the Problem-Solving Model

1. Define the problem—describe the learning needs in a way that is objective, quantifiable, and measurable.

2. Analyze the problem—review the information presented by the teacher to drill down to the specific skill gap or deficit that is impeding the learning.

3. Design and implement an intervention plan—choose a research-based intervention that will target the learning needs of the student, record who will implement it, and determine the frequency and duration of the intervention and the frequency of data collection.

4. Evaluate the learning impact of the plan—review data gathered during the implementation to determine if the intervention increased the student's targeted skill.

THE IST AS A VEHICLE FOR THE PARADIGM SHIFT NEEDED IN RTI

Implicit in an RTI model are research-based instruction and intervention matched to students' needs, collection of screening data on all students, progress monitoring of some students, and use of all data to make decisions about students (Batsche et al., 2006). If an RTI model is to be successful, a shift in understanding needs to occur in four specific areas: (1) how assessment results are used, (2) how curriculum is used, (3) how remedial or skill-building instruction occurs, and (4) how services are delivered to students. At Tiers 2 and 3, teams need to consistently address essential questions such as the following: What are the learning needs of the student? What evidence does the team have about the learning needs of the student? What skills does the student have, and how do the educators move the student to the next step of learning? These questions begin a different type of discussion at the meeting.

At the Tier 2 and 3 levels, this might be a significant change in perspective for many school staff members. It breaks the thinking pattern that believes the specialists (reading teacher, resource room teacher, etc.) can better serve the struggling student than the classroom teacher. IST supports the paradigm shift toward classroom teachers implementing differentiated instruction (RTI Tier 1) and small-group learning (RTI Tier 2) rather than removing students for services by "experts."

Before a school embraces the early intervention perspective of IST, assessment is often seen as a means to determine what is wrong with the child, with an eye toward "fixing" the child. Assessment reports often discuss student weaknesses as key to the problem solving. When a team changes to an early intervention model of IST, assessment tools are used to identify student strengths. Data describe what a student currently knows in order to identify the next steps in learning. This shift in thinking sets the stage for the RTI assessment structure of universal screening and progress monitoring.

The common understanding of curriculum before the focus on early intervention is captured in the phrase "one size fits all." The pace of instruction is geared toward the middle of the class, and a common set of materials is used by all students. When considering early intervention, curriculum is understood as something that is molded by instructional methods. Differentiated instruction becomes the norm as defined by Tier 1 in the RTI model.

These may look like simple changes, but they are actually profound shifts in how a school functions and how its faculty supports the evolution toward an RTI model. If the faculty is analyzing where the gaps in the student's learning are, they are introducing the practices needed for an RTI model. If they are looking at evidence of improved learning from an intervention developed by the IST, the faculty is preparing to learn and implement curriculum-based measures and progress monitoring.

IST Members

Core IST members should be few in number, and each member should have at least a moderate level of collaboration skills. Too many members in the core team can lead to ineffective problem solving. A group consisting of six to eight members is generally sufficient to make decisions and coordinate activities (Jennings, 2009). Core IST members should include, at a minimum, a facilitator, a scribe, and a time keeper. Other members may be invited to participate based on their knowledge and expertise. Ava Howard's IST summary sheet (Table 3.2) illustrates the composition of a small but well-balanced group.

Table 3.2 Ava's Instructional Support Team Membership

Instructional Support Team Summary Sheet	
Name: Ava Howard	Grade: 1st/Williams
IST Members: • Facilitator: Dr. Dale, school psychologist • Scribe: Ms. Protus, speech-language pathologist • Time Keeper: Mrs. Shelly, West Elm assistant principal • Referring Teacher: Ms. Williams, Ava's first-grade teacher • Invited Teacher: Mr. Slott, Ava's kindergarten teacher • Reading Specialist: Mrs. Blard The reading specialist (Mrs. Blard) and Ava's kindergarten teacher (Mr. Slott) were invited to join the Core IST, since Ava's referral dealt with a primary reading challenge.	

School staff who are invited to join the IST should be selected based on their knowledge of and expertise with either the referred student's strengths (e.g., last year's teacher) or intervention planning in general, based on the student's referral needs (e.g., a reading specialist for a student with decoding challenges). Expertise can include strong knowledge of curriculum and instruction, excellent classroom management skills, ability to differentiate, and knowledge of classroom assessments, particularly formative assessment. Without task-relevant experts, the IST is ineffective or inefficient, because the knowledge base necessary for critical problem solving is not available.

Roles and responsibilities of IST members

Roles must be clearly defined for core team members as well as invited guests. Collaborative problem-solving teams function more effectively when all members know each other's responsibilities. Roles may be assigned to core group members for a set period of time (one month, one semester, one year, etc.), and should be based, not necessarily on job function, but on individual expertise. For example, while the active participation of a school administrator is essential for IST functioning, the school administrator does not have to serve in the role of team facilitator. If a special education teacher is not knowledgeable about specific academic interventions, or is not a particularly collaborative individual, it is not necessary for that person to be a core IST member simply because of her or his certification.

As mentioned above, three roles are key to the functioning of the team: IST facilitator, scribe, and meeting time keeper. These roles are assigned to the participants. In some schools, specific professionals are regular members of the team due to the needs of the population. It is not unusual for elementary schools to have a reading teacher as a regular member, because a child's reading ability is often a key reason for referral to an IST. At the secondary level, the school counselor is often a regular member, because of the amount of information these individuals have about the ongoing academic performance of each student.

IST facilitator: The IST facilitator runs the meeting and is responsible for its organizational process as well as enhancing communication and collaboration among team members. At the beginning of the meeting, the facilitator should review the agenda and also the problem-solving process for new and returning team members. The facilitator should establish, clarify, and check the process; ask good, probing questions; encourage participation; set an efficient pace for the meeting; and bring the group back on track if necessary.

IST scribe: The scribe is the record keeper for the team. If there are required forms, including minutes or entries in an online documentation database, the scribe completes them during or after each meeting. Ideally, the scribe will record statements on a chart board or electronic whiteboard so that the entire team can focus on the key points of discussion.

Meeting time keeper: Since most IST meetings occur before, during, or after school, members often must work within a strictly allotted time frame. The time keeper's role is to maintain the pace of the meeting so that there is adequate time for intervention planning.

Other core members who may be different individuals include the following:

Referring teacher: The teacher who referred the student should be in attendance. It is necessary for the teacher to be present in order to clarify the concerns and respond to questions about how the student learns in the classroom. It is not sufficient for another individual to report from a form completed by the teacher.

A second classroom teacher: It is helpful to have the perspective of an additional classroom teacher to assist in designing interventions that are classroom friendly.

School administrator: An administrator provides two critical elements to the work of the team: first, a perspective on the potential impact of IST actions on the overall school operation, policy, and precedent; and second, the symbolic benefit of participation by a member of the leadership team in the group's decisions.

Academic interventionist (e.g., reading specialist, math specialist): Appropriate academic interventionists should be invited based on referral concerns.

Behavioral interventionist (e.g., school psychologist, school social worker, school counselor): Appropriate behavioral interventionists should be invited based on referral concerns.

Invited guests based on referral concern: Any teacher or staff member in the school may be considered a consultant to the IST, depending on needs and circumstances. For example, the school nurse can be an invited guest/ interventionist in the event that a student has a medical or medication history.

Parents: Parents should be notified whenever their child is being discussed at IST meetings and should be included in intervention planning. Unlike committees on special education (CSEs), for which federal law mandates parent participation, parent involvement in the IST process is optional. Some ISTs always invite parents as members, while others inform parents of IST interventions after the meeting. However, any educational process focused on a struggling student that does not include the parent is missing one of the most important elements of the program; it is never recommended that parents be excluded from any decision-making process that involves their child.

Student: When developmentally appropriate, students should be included in intervention planning for them, so they can share their perspectives on their strengths and challenges. Minimally, students should be interviewed about the referral concern, as well as their strengths and challenges.

Nurse: The nurse should be invited to IST meetings when a student has medical involvement or history that is pertinent to the referral.

Speech-language pathologist (SLP): If a student receives speech or language services or is suspected of having an articulation deficit or language-based reading problem, the SLP should be invited.

Occupational therapist (OT): If a student receives occupational therapy or is suspected of a fine- or gross-motor delay, the OT should be invited.

English as a second language (ESL) teacher: If the student receives ESL support, the ESL teacher should be invited to the meeting.

The IST Meeting

In order for IST meetings to run effectively and efficiently, several important steps should occur. Prior to the start of the school year, the administration should decide when and for how long the team will meet. The decision must balance both logistical needs, such as teacher contract hours, and broad program concerns, such as fidelity of implementation to the role-based IST process. Generally, efficient and effective IST meetings take around 30 minutes per student for complete intervention planning.

Before the meeting

Before the IST meeting, the referral form must be completed by the referring teacher(s) and submitted to the administrator, coordinator, or other person responsible for referral intake. The form should have information on all interventions that were implemented prior to the IST referral as well as data on the effectiveness of the interventions in meeting the student's needs. Table 3.3 contains an example of a completed form.

It is essential that the completed referral form be submitted three to five days before the scheduled meeting so that all IST core and invited members can review it prior to the actual meeting. One of the most common causes of breakdown in the IST process is poor decisions made as a result of little background given to the team before the meeting.

Once the IST referral is submitted, the person responsible for referral intake (administrator, coordinator, etc.) must review the form to determine who should attend the meeting. For example, if the referral concern involves a second-grade student who reads fewer than 30 words correctly on a fall RCBM benchmark assessment, the reading specialist, as well as any other teachers with expertise in differentiating reading groups, might

Table 3.3   A Sample IST Referral Form

West Elm School Elementary IST Form

STUDENT INFORMATION:

Pupil's Name: Ava Howard   Date: December 12, 2010

Age: 6   Date of Birth: February 2, 2004   Grade: 1

Referred by: Ms. Williams   Teacher(s): Ms. Williams, Mrs. Dottie (TA)

Number of Days Absent: 0   Tardy: 4   Early Release: 2

Has the student always attended West Elm? Yes: _X_   No: _____

If no, please list what district and how long attended: _____

Does the student or the family speak a second language?: Yes: _____   No: _X_

Is English spoken in the home? Yes: __X__   No: __

Is the student an English Language Learner?: Yes: _____   No: _X_

How long ago did he/she come to the U.S.?:   n/a

From what country did he/she come?:   n/a

Special Needs (if known): _____ vision   _____ hearing   _____other (explain)

_____

_____

_____

_____

_____

_____

To your knowledge, has the child been evaluated outside of school—educational, medical, psychological, and/or speech/language testing, and other results? Please list:

No, she has not been evaluated outside of school.

To your knowledge, has the child been referred to the IST this school year or in prior years? If yes, please provide the outcome if known.

No, she was not brought to the IST in kindergarten, but her teacher implemented Tier 1 interventions in the classroom.

REASON FOR CONCERN:

Ava is a sweet student who has a strong desire to please. She seems to forget information from one day to the next and can't keep up with the class. Unfortunately, her parents are having a difficult time. Ava has weak reading skills. Her DIBELS scores fell in the intensive range for PSF, NWF, and DORF. She is not progressing in reading and continues to read on Level 1. I am worried that she will slip further behind in class. Ava needs a double dose of foundations. She needs AIS support and may possibly need a CSE evaluation.

Describe the foundational skills this student demonstrates in the area of concern:

Ava knows her consonant sounds, can use grade-level vocabulary in spoken language, and can work independently for up to 30 minutes.

How does the student approach/react to the area of concern? (i.e., daydreaming; refusal to work; bathroom/nurse; will not attempt; distracts others, etc.)

Ava tends to withdraw from participating in class and frequently asks to be excused to go to the bathroom. She has become less inclined to interact with other students as the term progresses.

CURRENT LEARNING PROFILE:

Assess this student's learning style. (How does this child seem to learn best?)

__x__ visual   ____ auditory   ____ kinesthetic (tactile)

Please describe this student's *strengths* (i.e., reading, written language, oral expression, etc.)

Ava performs in the average range in math. She enjoys working in math groups and responds well to manipulatives. She has good background knowledge and does a great job telling stories and with spoken vocabulary.

CURRENT ACADEMIC PROGRAM (Check all that apply):

__x__ remedial writing   ____ remedial math   __x__ remedial reading

____ double dose Fundations   ____ leveled literacy intervention

(Continued)

(Continued)

____ resource room   ____ speech therapy   ____ occupational therapy

____ physical therapy   ____ counseling

____ multisensory reading (Wilson)   ____ other (explain)

PERFORMANCE DATA: (attach most recent report card)

State Assessments: not applicable for this grade

Reading Benchmarks: DIBELS PSF – 22 (well below benchmark),
DIBELS NWF CLS – 17 (well below benchmark)

Grades/assessments related to area of concern: DRA Level 1

What interventions and strategies have you implemented in order to address the area of concern (i.e., manipulatives, small groups, cooperative groups, reteaching, etc.)?

I've moved Ava's table to be close to me. I checked in with her frequently and had her repeat directions back to me. She has a table buddy who clarifies directions to her.

I also work with Ava one on one during reading groups. I conference with her and occasionally one other student every day. I've modified her books choice and book baggie. I put her on starfall.com every other day.

Describe communication with the parent regarding the area of concern. Please include the date and outcome of that communication.

I speak with Mrs. Howard often. I try to call home every week. Every night Mrs. Howard is supposed to sign Ava's reading log, although that rarely happens. I told Mrs. Howard about the IST during a phone conversation yesterday (December 11th), and she is in full agreement with the need for a referral.

Please bring work samples of the student and those of an average student from your class, and a current report card. YOU WILL BE NOTIFIED OF THE DATE YOUR STUDENT WILL BE DISCUSSED.

---

be invited. If this were the only apparent problem, the school social worker, nurse, and OT would not be invited.

During the meeting

The facilitator should begin by introducing both the team's general problem-solving process and the student's specific referral concern. This should be a brief summary, since all IST members are expected to have reviewed the referral prior to the meeting. As the facilitator leads the team through the problem-solving process, the scribe takes notes that are visible to all team members. The time keeper keeps track of the time allotted to each of the steps in the problem-solving process. Core and invited members should be active participants in the meeting. The meeting should follow a systematic process in which the referral concern is discussed, strategies are brainstormed by the team, one strategy is selected, and a specific action plan is written.

First, the facilitator invites the teacher to introduce the major concern regarding the student's learning, including both strengths and weaknesses in the area of concern. The objective is to build an understanding of the student's foundation of knowledge, learning, and school skills. Some of the key questions asked and answered may include the following:

- "Describe the student's strengths and interests."
- "What does the student's learning look like?"
- "What can the student do even in the area of concern?"
- "Describe the learning concern. Try to be as objective and specific as possible."

Team members ask clarification questions in order to "see" the student's struggle in learning. If there is more than one area of concern, the team must identify a single *priority* concern. (It is important that the priority concern be unified and focused, rather than diluted among competing goals. For example, if a student is having difficulty in reading and math, the team should look for a common root cause and address it, rather than developing two distinct interventions.)

Once the single priority concern is identified, the team should brainstorm interventions. At this stage, any ideas that match the student's learning needs are acceptable. The team will need to develop several response strategies, each aligned with the specific priority concern. This prepares the group to adjust to the outcomes of the interventions they have designed. Those that do not produce the desired result—a fairly common event—will need to be replaced quickly, and this should not require that the team reconvene and start the process from the beginning.

After several alternative strategies have been identified, the next step is to select no more than two strengths-based strategies. It is essential that the teacher select one or two strategies that are doable in the classroom; otherwise the intervention will not be implemented with fidelity. Though the team can brainstorm interventions, the teacher must be the one to select the specific strategy. More than two strategies can overwhelm the student or teacher, creating an ineffective intervention.

The final step in the meeting is to write an instructional support plan (ISP) and transfer it onto the instructional plan form, such as the one illustrated in Table 3.4.

Table 3.4   A Sample Instructional Support Plan Form

Instructional Support Plan for Ava, Tier 1		
Academic Behavior Concerns:		
1. Phonics		
2. Sight words		
Suggested Intervention (WHAT)	*Person Responsible (WHO)*	*Goal Score/Date (WHEN)*
Double dose Fundations 4 times per week for 30 minutes	Mrs. Blard	
Sight word flashcards Daily 5 minutes	Mrs. Williams	
Weekly foundation tests	Mrs. Williams	
Dolch sight word list, pre/post tests	Mrs. Blard	

One strategy that has been found effective is to photocopy a calendar to the back of the ISP. The classroom teacher notes—with handwriting, starring, or a smiley face—the date and time when each intervention occurred. It is necessary for team members to leave the meeting with a concrete action plan so that all members know their responsibilities. Intervention responsibilities are determined and documented. Finally, a method of measuring or evaluating the effect of the strategy should be determined before the meeting closes.

In closing the meeting, the facilitator reads agreed-upon interventions to confirm agreement of the group. A follow-up date, six to ten weeks later, should be set for the IST to meet and review progress of the student. Finally, the team should assign a case manager to follow up with the classroom teacher and anyone else with assigned responsibilities.

After the meeting

After the meeting, the referring teacher implements the strategy that he or she has decided upon. Two critical supports need to be provided to ensure that the strategy is as successful as possible: (1) The teacher needs a contact person so she or he can ask questions and have continued support, and (2) fidelity of implementation needs to be ensured in order to have a real measure of success or struggle. These functions can be filled by a "case manager" who is assigned to the student by the principal. Who fills this role is not critical, but a case manager needs to be part of any good implementation plan.

The meeting process

Many building teams have become adept at designing procedures and forms to support the structure of a meeting, but they may not be familiar with the process of a group thinking together, which is critical to the success of meetings. Meetings can become hierarchical and not collaborative. Unless all members contribute to the problem-solving process, important information about the student's learning needs and strengths may not surface, limiting the list of possible interventions.

Each of the roles described earlier was originally designed to improve meetings in the corporate world (Doyle & Straus, 1993). Using a facilitator to guide the discussion and a scribe to create a team memory are critical steps to focus the team on the instructional needs of the student.

The skills of facilitation should be learned by all core members. The actual role of facilitator should be rotated to avoid slipping into the perception of a single individual as superior to other team members in either expertise or judgment. The entire group needs to know and practice the key skills of facilitation so that there is group support for the focus on instruction. All members need to listen actively, paraphrase to check for understanding, stay on track, ask questions to clarify student descriptions, synthesize ideas, and help to summarize the work of the team (Bens, 2005). Stephen Covey's maxim, "Seek first to understand, then to be understood" (Covey, 2004, p. 235), should drive all group discussion.

ISTS, RTI, AND A NEW PARADIGM OF SCHOOL RESPONSIBILITY

If the RTI model is going to become part of how a school functions, the culture of conversation at IST meetings needs to focus on instruction. Social-emotional issues need to be given to the school professionals such as school psychologists, school counselors, or social workers who can help the family.

Within an RTI process, the goal of the IST is to intervene following an early intervention model aimed at stopping the cycle of failure immediately at its *educational* source. Other sources of stress in a student's life are addressed through a school/parent/community partnership to find the appropriate services to address the social-emotional needs of the student.

This practice also keeps the focus of the classroom teacher on the instructional needs of the student.

During the past 40 years, school professionals have come to understand that they have full responsibility for the irreplaceable role that only they *do* play in the learning process. Few would disagree that the parent and home play an important role in the success of a child. Yet during the hours the student is in the classroom, the teacher is the child's major source of learning and academic success. Given this reality, neither the teacher nor the school can allow influences beyond the classroom to be accepted as the reason for failure inside the classroom. The growth of the RTI model, with its reliance on ISTs, comes from recognition of this responsibility for the success of each child—such as Ava—regardless of circumstances that the school cannot control.

 TECH BYTE

USING GOOGLE DOCS TO GATHER AND SHARE INFORMATION

The information gathered and interventions shared by ISTs need to be available to staff as students progress from year to year in the school and district. There are a few commercially available documentation systems that support this work. *Google Docs* (http://docs.google.com) is one free resource available to document meeting minutes and intervention plans.

Google Docs (Figure 3.1) is available by signing up for a free google.com account. You can create a new document or edit an existing document, presentation, spreadsheet, form, or drawing.

Figure 3.1 Screenshot of File Menu in *Google Docs*

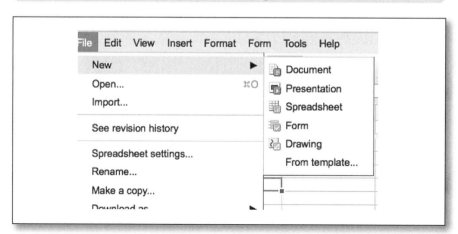

For the purpose of IST meeting minutes, a document is the best tool (see Figure 3.2).

Figure 3.2 Screenshot of Sample Document in *Google Docs*

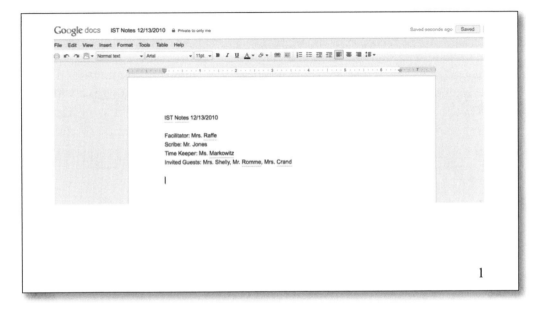

For progress monitoring, an intervention after the IST, the spreadsheet (Figure 3.3) may be the most appropriate tool.

Figure 3.3 Screenshot of Sample Spreadsheet in *Google Docs*

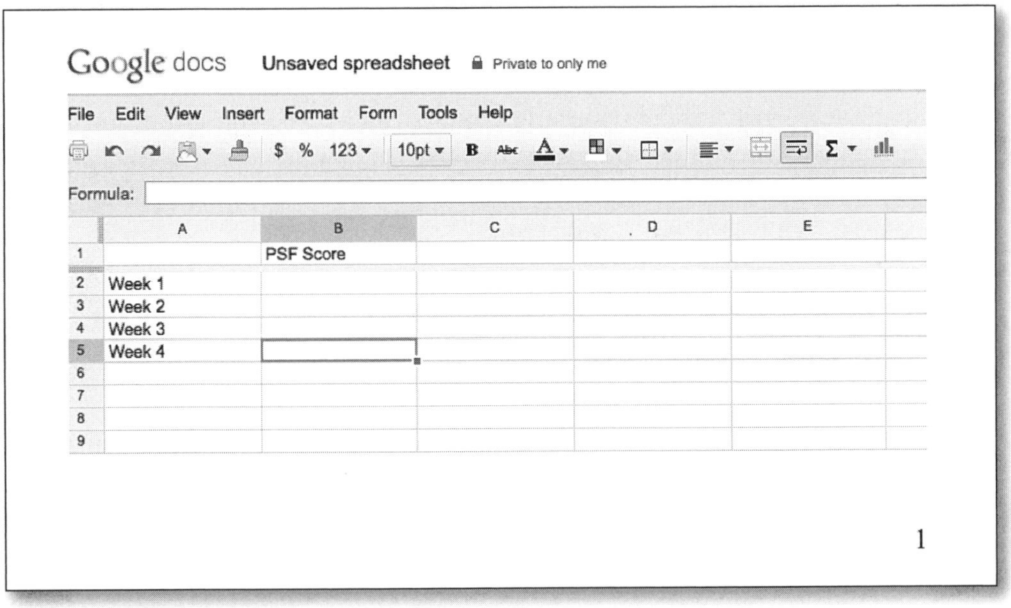

Files created in *Google Docs* are dynamic and collaborative. For example, the person who creates the document or spreadsheet can choose to invite other participants to view and edit it (see Figure 3.4).

Figure 3.4 Screenshot for Sharing Files in *Google Docs*

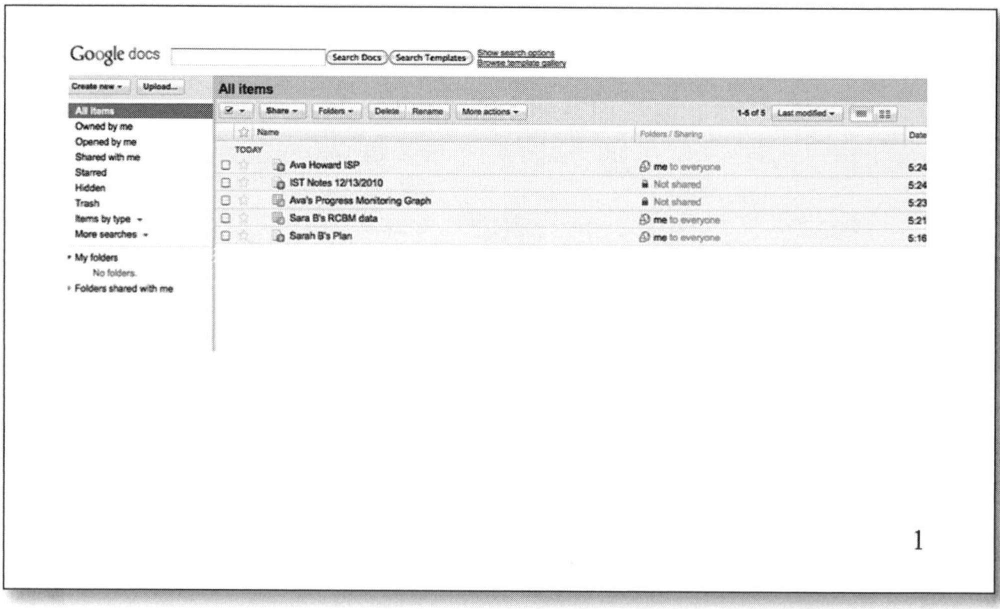

Every participant in an IST should have access to the ISP. If one of the steps called for a speech-language screening, for example, the SLP would be able to edit the *Google Docs* document when the screening was completed. All IST members would then receive an e-mail that the document had been changed and the SLP had made the alterations. Thus, *Google Docs* helps to streamline the case manager's role, since all members of the team are continually alerted whenever anyone updates the plan.

RESOURCES

There are a number of resources for ISTs to use for intervention strategies. The team should use sources that focus on research-based interventions and share the background of the research. Without strong, research-based interventions, you just have another version of remedial support with no real path for measured improvement.

Bender, W. N., & Shores, C. (2007). *Response to Intervention: A practical guide for every teacher.* **Thousand Oaks, CA: Corwin.**

This publication includes extensive resources for strategies, a clear overview of RTI, and numerous resources for diverse learners.

Big Ideas in Beginning Reading. (http://reading.uoregon.edu/)

This website offers specific information on the big ideas of reading, including concepts and research, instruction, and assessment ideas. Other resources include curriculum maps for kindergarten through third grade and "Consumers Guide to Evaluating a Core Reading Program K–3: A Critical Analysis."

Chapman, C., & King, R. (2003). *Differentiated instructional strategies for writing in the content areas.* **Thousand Oaks, CA: Corwin.**

This publication includes information for teachers and IST members describing the developmental stages of writing as well as strategies for diagnosing writing difficulties. Ready-to-use charts and checklists are also included in this book.

Florida Center for Reading Research. (www.fcrr.org/)

This research-to-practice focused website offers research studies and research reviews on specific curricula and instructional strategies. There are hundreds of take-and-make activities for each of the big five ideas of reading for grades K–1, 2–3, and 4–5 appropriate for small groups and individual students.

Gregory, G. H., & Kuzmich, L. (2005). *Differentiated literacy strategies for student growth and achievement in grades K–6.* **Thousand Oaks, CA: Corwin.**

This publication includes numerous strategies for literacy instruction. It includes teacher-friendly materials such as summary chart of developmental readiness for reading and writing, questions starters for each level of Bloom's taxonomy, and strategies for English language learners.

Kemp, K. A., & Eaton, M. A. (2008). *RTI: The classroom connection for literacy: Reading intervention and measurement.* Port Chester, NY: Dude.

This publication has extensive classroom-based strategies for reading instruction divided by the big five categories. The strategies are designed as lesson plans; there is also a framework for observing student learning to diagnose targeted needs.

Reading Rockets. (www.readingrockets.org/)

Reading Rockets has helpful information on reading development and reading interventions for administrators, teachers, and parents in the form of podcasts, presentations, articles, and easy-to-implement strategies.

Vaughn, S., & Linan-Thompson, S. (2004). *Research-based methods of reading instruction grades K–3.* Alexandria, VA: ASCD.

This is a book of evidence-based reading strategies, delineated by area of reading, that are easy to read, understand, and use. Each of the big ideas of reading is broken down and explained, and then specific strategies are provided.

GLOSSARY

Data-based decision making: Tiered intervention decisions within an RTI model are made based on student performance data. Data-based decision making is used at each tier of the RTI model. At the Tier 1 level, universal screening data should be used to assess the effectiveness of core instruction/curriculum and to identify students who are at risk compared to peers or national standards. At the Tier 2 and Tier 3 levels, progress monitoring data should be used to assess effectiveness of intervention. Data should be used to increase or decrease intervention support.

Instructional support plan (ISP): An instructional support plan is an action plan developed for an individual student by the instructional support team. The ISP should include one to three specific, observable, and measurable goals and specific interventions to meet those goals; identification of the person or people responsible for the intervention; progress monitoring tools; and dates or deadlines for meeting or reassessing the goals.

Instructional support team (IST): The IST is a collaborative and multidisciplinary team in a building that meets on a regular basis to discuss schoolwide, gradewide, and individual strengths and challenges. The IST evaluates data, plans interventions, and makes decisions using data. At the individual student referral level, the goals of the IST are to (1) solve individual student challenges using a strength-based model and (2) increase the problem-solving skills of the referring teacher.

Intervention: Interventions are instructional strategies that are targeted to address the student's specifically identified skill deficit. Interventions can be delivered in small groups or individually. Interventions should be validated as effective through independent, empirical research studies (i.e., research based and/or evidence based).

Problem-solving model: The problem-solving model follows a systematic approach to identification and intervention. Steps of problem solving are the following: (1) Define the problem, (2) analyze the problem, (3) design and implement an intervention plan, and (4) evaluate the learning impact of the plan.

Referral: Teachers who are concerned about an individual student's academic or behavioral progress should submit a written referral form to the building-based IST. A referral form includes information on the student's strengths and weaknesses as well as his or her educational history and interventions implemented prior to IST involvement.

ACRONYMS

A number of acronyms had been used in this chapter. The acronyms are short forms of the following phrases.

AIS: academic intervention services (a New York State service for students in danger of failing the state assessments)

CSE: committee on special education (the New York State term for multidisciplinary team)

DIBELS: (Dynamic Indicators of Basic Early Literacy Skills), http://dibels .uoregon.edu

DORF: DIBELS oral reading fluency

DRA: developmental reading assessment

IST: instructional support team

LARS: literacy assessment reporting system

NWF: nonsense word fluency

OT: occupational therapist

PSF: phoneme segmentation fluency

RCBM: reading curriculum based measures

SLP: speech-language pathologist

WUF: word use fluency

Literacy Instruction: Tier 1   **4**

Lynn Burke and John Kappenberg

It was September... the beginning of another school year. Ms. Ward was excited about meeting her new class of third graders. Eight-year-olds are old enough to reason with, yet they're still young enough that they "play." Ms. Ward had decided to incorporate into her reading/language arts instruction an approach she had just learned, and she was looking forward to the challenge. She felt cautiously optimistic that it might at least help to bridge the gap for the students who continued to struggle with the process of learning to read, spell, and write. Every year, that group of brave but very weary academic warriors tried hard to believe Ms. Ward's optimistic reassurance that "this year it will all fall into place." Then, as the year progressed and nothing got better for them, Ms. Ward shared their disappointment and growing frustration, as she watched them use every ploy they could think of to avoid having to read in front of their peers, and as they continued to do poorly on spelling tests despite having studied all week with their very worried parents.

Ever since her school had begun using RTI, to monitor progress and ensure adequate individual academic growth for all students, Ms. Ward saw her understanding of teaching begin to change. Previously, she had engaged in the kind of teaching she had experienced as a student, which hadn't been challenged by what she had learned in college: Assess background knowledge of the students; present, to the best of your ability, the information that your students need to learn; do some form of postinstructional testing; give each student a grade; and proceed to the next unit of instruction. But, it had always bothered her when kids "didn't get it"... especially the ones who chronically didn't get it. Those students needed the lessons repeated that they had failed to master, but, somehow the system had teachers feeling pressured to maintain a steady instructional pace that would get all the students through the entire core curriculum by the end of the academic year. On her own and through experience, Ms. Ward had slowly begun to expand and deepen her understanding of the fact that not all children learn in the same way or at the same rate. This new insight was accompanied by an awareness of the need to increase her repertoire of instructional skills.

At first, RTI presented intimidating challenges. The data gathering seemed overwhelming; so, initially, RTI was "one more thing for teachers to do," and, "yet more forms for teachers to complete." As she and her colleagues became more familiar and comfortable with the process, they began to grasp the significance of the data being accumulated for each student and started to see the potential for achievement that results from appropriately modifying instruction. It became evident that the variety of learning needs among any group of students mandates flexibility and variety of instruction if every student is to achieve to his or her best potential.

As Ms. Ward sees it, RTI had the potential to significantly change education, because it shifted the focus of education. It was no longer enough for the majority of students to be assessed as having acquired, retained, and developed the ability to utilize the curricular information to which they were exposed. Now, all students were expected to make learning gains commensurate with the expectations for the students of a particular age and/or grade. Education was becoming more learner focused, and the educator's responsibility was changing. It was no longer enough to present "the information" that needed to be learned. Rather, the teacher was responsible for engaging each student in activities and endeavors that provoked active exploration and discovery, resulting in the learner constructing an understanding of the knowledge and information being studied. "Funny," thought Ms. Ward, as she reflected on her thinking. "RTI makes sense." Ms. Ward found that her teaching was becoming even more gratifying and rewarding . . . and that felt good!

The more she learned, the more she wanted to know and understand about the pedagogy or instructional strategies that improve educational outcomes. Because, in a highly industrialized and technology-based culture such as ours, where reading is the cornerstone on which all future learning is based, Ms. Ward continued to be amazed that the public education system in the United States had only recently begun to question seriously why so many people fail to learn to read at a proficient level. Why hadn't she been exposed to the discrepancy between instruction and achievement in any of her preservice college work? Why were her colleagues and she having to work so hard to learn different instructional approaches for teaching reading after just having completed their college educations? She reflected on what she was now learning, and kept digging deeper and deeper.

ORAL LANGUAGE AND THE BRAIN

Ms. Ward learned that oral language is a hardwired, brain-based ability, rather like an instinct, and that it is found in every society. Human beings, like many other animals, tend to live in groups. To function effectively, group members must be able to communicate. Human beings use oral language to communicate; this practice is unique to our species and universal among its members (Pinker, 1997).

Interestingly, within every known society, oral languages are learned in the same manner: by responding to modeling, accompanied by incremental developmental use and growth. Babies listen to the words spoken around them and attempt to imitate the discrete sounds within those words. Adults in all societies instinctively respond to these efforts by exaggerating the fundamental *vowel sounds* of their language when "talking with" infants; this form of language is often referred to as "motherese." When born, an infant has the ability to discriminate even subtle phonetic differences among the *phonemes* (i.e., speech sounds) endemic to *all* languages. However, by the age of eight to ten months, babies' brains have neurologically eliminated all phonemes not heard on a daily basis; that is, babies retain only the phonemes that they actually hear in the language that is used for oral communication on a daily basis within their immediate environment (Fernald et al., 1989).

Ms. Ward wondered how an infant knows what a word is. We do not speak in a sequence of discretely pronounced words. Rather, in conversational speech, the words seem to "bleed," one into the next, with only subtle, often imperceptible pauses between words. We rarely say, "Come . . . here." We are more likely to pronounce something that resembles "comeer." Neuroscience has learned that infants begin responding to the organizational aspects of their native language while the babies are still preverbal. They notice the order of sounds within a word as well as the emphasis pattern of syllables within that word. In English, unlike many other languages, content words most often have an accented first syllable, or a strong–weak accent pattern, for example, MO-ther, FA-ther, BASE-ball, FAM-il-y. Infants quickly discern that an accented syllable probably indicates the beginning of a new word (Stanovich, 1994).

That information particularly fascinated Ms. Ward because of the difficulty she experienced when teaching her third graders about accent patterns of words, which is among the more difficult concepts to teach to third graders. The auditory difference between PRES-ent and pres-ENT eludes them. By eight years of age, youngsters know what constitutes a word; the adaptive importance of recognizing syllable patterning, so important in infancy when they are first deciphering their native language, has diminished dramatically. The vast field of oral language acquisition is fascinating, and further research may eventually result in the ability to determine in early infancy a person's potential for future difficulties with learning to read and write. For now, what is already known about oral language acquisition gives us insight into our understanding of the process by which children learn to read, an endeavor that is always preceded by learning spoken language.

Understanding this new information impacted Ms. Ward in many ways. When teaching, the unavoidable impact of individual differences among learners and the significance of cultural competence must be considered. She realized how inadequate her knowledge of her native English language was, and she recognized the importance of acquiring a firm knowledge base from which to teach language arts. An educator must have thorough knowledge and understanding of the content being conveyed to students, as well as of the myriad factors that impact each student's perspective on the content and the student's ability to assimilate it to a point of mastery. It was becoming increasingly clear that RTI is much more than accumulating data about a child's learning success. To implement RTI with fidelity, teachers must become masterful at analyzing and subsequently identifying the various factors that may be negatively impacting successful learning, and then they must be able to make knowledgeable selection among instructional approaches and interventions that may eliminate or diminish the impact of the confounding variables, thus facilitating masterful learning.

WRITTEN LANGUAGE AND THE BRAIN

Unlike oral language, which is universal, written language develops only when a culture becomes sufficiently large that one-to-one or small-group communication is no longer adequate, or when social complexity mandates the communication of abstract concepts, such as laws. Written language is the transcription of the sounds or phonemes of speech (i.e., oral language) using a visual symbol code. Worldwide, known written languages vary significantly in format, utilizing a variety of different types of symbols (Buckley, 2003). Here, we will restrict discussion to the symbolic system used to codify English: the Latin or Roman alphabet. It consists of 26 letters that are used to represent the 44 discrete sounds of the English language. The letters are used singly and in combinations, forming *graphemes* that represent (*spell*) the 44 phonemes (sounds) of spoken English. English is an alphabetic language that has very manageable numbers of both phonemes (the smallest units of sound in a language) and graphemes (the spellings of those phonemes). The seeming complexity of the English language results from the lack of one-to-one correspondence between sounds (phonemes) and letters (graphemes), as described in Table 4.1.

Table 4.1 Examples of Lack of One-to-One Phoneme/Grapheme Correspondence in English

Variant Spellings of Specific Sounds	
Sounds	*Variant Spellings*
long a	a (baby), a_e (ape), ai (maid), ay (say), ea (steak), ei (vein), eigh (eight), ey (they)
long e	e (she), e_e (here), y (silly), ea (meat), ee (sheen), ie (piece), ey (key), ei (ceiling), i (obedient)
long i	i (silent), i_e (five), ie (pie), igh (sight), y (my), y_e (type)
long o	o (coma), o_e (slope), oe (toe), oa (boat), ow (snow)
long u	u (music), u_e (use), ew (few), ue (rescue), eu (feud)
/oi/	oy (boy), oi (boil)
/ou/	ou (loud), ow (crowd)
Variant Pronunciations of Specific Graphemes	
Ea	eat, bread, steak
Ie	pie, piece

For decades, the incorrect assumption in education was that since children learn oral language through exposure and modeling (a well-established principle of linguistics), they also learn to read and write through exposure and modeling (Hiebert, Pearson, Taylor, Richardson, & Paris, 1998).This error was accompanied by a simplistic, and subsequently disproven, model of intelligence: namely, that people who tested higher on standardized intelligence measures could and would learn to use written language more effectively than less gifted people. As a corollary, it was presumed that people with lower intelligence could not learn to read and write at a higher than "as needed" level, if at all. In addition, intelligence was believed to be fixed. However, recent developments in neuroscience have established that intelligence is remarkably malleable and very capable of change, adaptation, growth, and even decline. (The "use it or lose it" adage is verified by science.) Experience alters intelligence (Wilson, 2011).

Specifically, we know that for the overwhelming majority of people who have normally functioning senses and average or above average intelligence, yet have trouble learning to read, the difficulty does not result from either a dysfunction of their senses or a lack of intelligence. Rather, the difficulty is rooted in a processing difference that occurs within the brain. Drs. S. E. and B. A. Shaywitz (Yale University) demonstrated this utilizing functional magnetic resonance imaging (fMRI), during which a subject's brain functioning is observed before, during, and after the subject engages in language-based activity. They found distinct differences in neurological functioning between the brains of people who acquire written language skills with ease and those who struggle with the process (Shaywitz, 2003).

READING INSTRUCTION: THE GAP BETWEEN KNOWLEDGE AND PRACTICE

In the 21st century, our information-based society has become critically dependent on literacy as an essential tool for survival. Reading and writing are no longer optional skills in either the work place or daily living. Without the ability to read and write at a highly proficient level, the chances of living a fulfilling, productive life are very seriously compromised. In fact, the ramifications of failing to master written language skills are so extreme that the National Institution of Child Health and Human Development, part of the National Institutes of Health, has declared it to be both an educational problem and a national *health* crisis (Lyon, 2002).

Reading is a complex skill that includes all elements of the English language: phonology and phonemic awareness, sound-symbol association, syllable knowledge, morphology, syntax, and semantics. A scientifically based reading research (SBRR) program, as delineated by the National Reading Panel (NRP), has five essential elements of instruction: phonemic awareness, phonics, fluency, vocabulary, and comprehension (NRP, 2000). One might expect that the vast body of new knowledge steadily being amassed about how people learn, and, more specifically, how they learn to read, would produce improvements in both the process and outcomes of reading instruction. Yet, that is not always happening. As is often the case, scientific advances, like recent developments in the neuroscience of reading, have greatly outpaced the ability of complex bureaucratic systems, like public education and institutions of higher education, to adapt.

As a teacher struggling within the system, Ms. Ward was frustrated, and she kept digging. Slowly, it was beginning to make sense. From the 1930s through the 1950s, phonics-based reading instruction was replaced by what was then seen as a "reading for meaning" instructional approach, called the "look-say" method. Lists of frequently used words were memorized, and readers used context clues to figure out new words. In 1955, Rudolph Flesch reasserted the need for reading instruction to return to the inclusion of a strong phonetic base in his book, *Why Johnny Can't Read,* and the "reading war" began to emerge between the proponents of reading for meaning and those who advocated phonics instruction. The late 1960s saw the emergence of the "whole language" approach to reading instruction, in which learning to read was promoted as a "natural process" that does not involve drill work but, instead, focuses on the use of authentic literature. The reading war raged for the next 30 years, until test scores began to clearly indicate that far too many students were failing to master the skills of reading and writing.

In 1997, the U.S. Congress authorized a thorough assessment of "the status of research-based knowledge, including the effectiveness of various approaches to teaching children to read" (NRP, 2000). In 2000, the NRP released the report, discussed earlier, *Teaching Children to Read: An Evidence-Based Assessment of the Scientific Research Literature on Reading and Its Implications for Reading Instruction.* That analysis resulted in instructional conclusions that, at a minimum, provide an evidence-based starting point for assessment of what is currently being done with regard to reading instruction in a given educational setting.

While taking a position with regard to any particular instructional program was beyond the scope of the NRP's deliberations, throughout the report, positive reference was made to instruction that is *explicit, systematic,* and *cumulative.* Most significantly, the panel recognized that the intensity and duration of instruction needed for mastery of the wide range of language elements *varies among students.* The NRP was the first federal agency to explicitly recommend that the need for individual evaluation is best fulfilled by regular progress monitoring, as outlined within the method now known as response to intervention (RTI).

Reading the NRP report left Ms. Ward alarmed by the inadequacy of her preparation to teach reading, despite having taken the majority of her college coursework in elementary education. She kept exploring for information and soon found the website for the National Council on Teacher Quality (NCTQ), where she read *What Education Schools Aren't Teaching About Reading and What Elementary Teachers Aren't Learning* (NCTQ, 2006). That report details an investigative study conducted by NCTQ aimed at discerning what preservice teachers are being taught about reading instruction. The NRP report helped to catalyze federal legislation that resulted in the No Child Left Behind Act of 2001.

In spite of all of this, a decade later, the educational performance of American students in the area of reading remains a problem of significant magnitude. In 2005, performance on the National Assessment of Education Progress (NAEP) indicated that 38% of all fourth graders read below a basic level. That is about the same level of reading performance that had been reported for the previous 25 years, despite the fact that, during that same time, we have dramatically increased our knowledge of how people learn to read (NCTQ, 2006).

READING AS A COMPLEX SKILL

We now know that reading probably comprises the most complex skill set a person ever learns. This conclusion is based on validated scientific research into, and an ever expanding knowledge base and understanding of, both the physiology and psychology of learning. Prior to this, educational pedagogy was based largely on theory, philosophy, and tradition. Today, drawing on discoveries in a wide variety of scientific fields, including neuropsychology and neurobiology, we have a more validated understanding of what needs to be done to successfully teach people to read. Based on a preponderance of validated research, these are the major elements of effective reading instruction:

- Content must be organized in a *logical sequence* that builds cumulatively.
- Students must master the skills of *phonemic awareness:* the ability to hear, separate, and manipulate the individual sounds, or phonemes, that compose a spoken word. This results in readiness to learn the relationship (*phonics*) between the sounds of spoken language (phonemes) and the letters of written language (graphemes) that are used to represent those sounds.
- *Phonetic knowledge* establishes an understanding of the fact that the phoneme–grapheme correspondence is fixed and predictable (the *alphabetic principle*).
- *Explicit instruction* assures that nothing is inadvertently omitted from the sequence of knowledge essential to the mastery of skilled reading, spelling, and writing.
- *Effective instruction* provides opportunities for students to apply what they are learning until the essential knowledge and skills are mastered.
- Once students can reliably *decode* (read) and *encode* (spell) words, it is essential that they develop the ability to read text accurately and quickly (*fluency*). A person can perform only one cognitive task at a time. Therefore, fluent reading, which is automatic and without

conscious attention to the underlying aspects of the process, is an essential precursor to reading comprehension. If a reader has to work at decoding more than an occasional word, the meaning of the text gets lost in the effort of decoding.

Table 4.2 shows the progress from phonological awareness to semantics. All of these reading elements are *skills,* and as with all skills, they are perfected by practice, practice, and more practice—to the point of mastery.

Table 4.2 The Progress From Phonological Awareness to Semantics

Semantics	• Understanding the meanings of words, phrases, and sentences • Using words appropriately when speaking
⬆	
Syntax	• Rules that govern the ways words combine to form phrases, clauses, sentences
⬆	
Morphology	• Internal structure of words • Modification of word meaning through the use of morphemic elements (e.g., prefixes, suffixes, affixes)
⬆	
Six Syllable Types	• Syllable: a word or part of a word with one vowel *sound* • Type of syllable determines the particular sound represented by a letter (e.g., no, not, note, noble, north)
⬆	
Sound–Symbol Association	• Representation of a language's sounds (phonemes) with an alphabet's letters (phonics) • Systematic, reliable correspondence of specific letters to specific sounds
⬆	
Phonological Awareness	• Realization that spoken words are made up of smaller, discrete units of sound

"Now I get it," thought Ms. Ward. "*I was able to learn with whole-language instruction, because I've always been a naturally good reader and speller. But some of my friends hated to read out loud, and when they did, it was slow and hard to understand. They usually did poorly on spelling tests, too. I knew they were smart, but, they just couldn't get good grades in school.*" Ms. Ward knew then that she was on the right track. She, like a great many aspiring teachers, hadn't been taught the *science* of reading, but she was learning it now, on her own. She was learning it because she could see that she needed to know more if she hoped to break the cycle of ineffective reading instruction and better meet the needs of all of her students, particularly the ones who struggle with learning to read and write.

Ms. Ward had spent the summer learning a multisensory structured language (MSL) approach to reading and writing instruction, and it made so much sense. She acquired written language skills easily, often just through exposure. So, when her students questioned her, she had great difficulty explaining *why* certain words were spelled in particular ways, or *how* they could tell when to do things like "change the 'y' to 'i' and add 'ed.'" Ms. Ward usually didn't know why or how; she just "knew" the correct spelling of the word and when to "change the 'y' to 'i." MSL was teaching her "why" and "when," which is why she was excited about incorporating it into her language arts instruction.

The five basic building blocks of the MS approach are shown in Table 4.3.

Table 4.3 Multisensory Structured Language Instruction

Five Elements of Instruction	
Simultaneous and multisensory	Uses all pathways in the brain: visual, auditory, tactile/kinesthetic.
Systematic and cumulative	The sequence must begin with the easiest and most basic elements; it must progress methodically to more difficult material. Each step must be based on those already learned.
Direct and explicit	The inferential learning of any concept cannot be taken for granted.
Diagnostic and prescriptive	The teacher must be adept at prescriptive or individualized instruction.
Analytic and synthetic	Whole to parts in spelling. Parts to whole in reading.

READING INSTRUCTION IN AN RTI FRAMEWORK

The things Ms. Ward was learning engaged her interest, and she began to actively apply that new knowledge to the work she was doing with her students. Analyzing the sounds they heard and deciding how to spell the word, and conversely, synthesizing a word from the individual graphemes in an unfamiliar word, stretched and honed their higher order thinking skills.

Ms. Ward had mapped out a beginning strategy that would provide more instructional time in the specific elements that RTI screening would indicate were weaknesses for specific students. She knew, too, that she had to learn new ways of presenting the same material, both to better meet the learning needs of each individual student and to keep the learning environment new and interesting for everyone in the class.

Ms. Ward began using her new approach by creating a spelling program based on teaching her students to "listen for the sounds in words" (phonemes) and then "write down the sounds that you hear" (graphemes). Ms. Ward knew from experience that the majority of her third graders would not accurately know phoneme/grapheme correspondences for all 44 phonemes. Through her spelling lists, she would teach her students about the six different syllable types. A syllable is a word or part of a word with one vowel sound. For the vowel letters, each of which represents more than one sound, the syllable is the context that determines which sound the vowel will represent. Table 4.4 shows the six types of syllables.

Table 4.4 Six Syllable Types

Syllable Type	Description	Vowel (V) or Consonant (C)	Example
Closed	• one vowel letter, followed by one or more consonants • vowel sound is short	VC	cat
Open	• ends in one vowel letter • vowel sound is long	V	go
Vowel-consonant-e	• one vowel letter, followed by one consonant + silent *e* • vowel sound is long	V(ce)	rope

(Continued)

(Continued)

Syllable Type	Description	Vowel (V) or Consonant (C)	Example
R controlled	• one vowel letter, followed by the letter *r* • vowel sound is not long or short	V(r)	car for her fir fur
Consonant-le	• always a final syllable • has one consonant, one silent *e* • preceding syllable is either closed syllable (short vowel sound) or open syllable (long sound)	–C(le)	bubble Bible
Vowel teams	• two vowel letters	VV	steam boil

When Ms. Ward learned about the *diagnostic/prescriptive* component included in the MSL approach, she thought it sounded much like RTI's formative assessments. She had begun to understand the importance of using formative as well as summative assessments in evaluating her students' growth and struggles with reading.

Progress monitoring was becoming more useful to Ms. Ward, because she had a better understanding of how the results of ongoing assessments would drive the course and pace of instruction. While teaching a linguistic concept, Ms. Ward envisioned tracking student progress through daily analysis of words used and on weekly spelling assessments, using that information to make decisions about scaffolding the efforts of her struggling learners while progressively challenging the more capable spellers.

Response to *intervention* was originally called response to *instruction.* Within that context, RTI mandates what "best practice" teaching should be: screening to determine learner needs; instruction by experienced, highly qualified teachers; consistent use of SBRR methodology and materials; ongoing formative assessments given during instruction to facilitate instructional adjustments; and periodic summative assessments that indicate how well the students have learned the material taught. The results of each assessment determine what the teacher does next—with the group as well as with individual learners.

For students who totally grasped the material, the teacher's next step would be to facilitate those students using and applying what they have learned. For those who learned the material pretty well, the teacher would first reflect on the teaching to see if the program/curriculum was taught with fidelity. Then, the teacher would, perhaps, reteach the material, adapting instruction according to his or her best judgment about the changes needed, helping the students better understand the area(s) that had caused them difficulty.

Often, failure to thrive in an educational setting results in the student being moved to progressively smaller instructional groups (e.g., resource room instead of the mainstream classroom), and/or reduction of the quantity of work for which the student is responsible (e.g., 10 instead of 20 spelling words, of the same type as the rest of the class). Ms. Ward felt confident that the sequenced lessons of MSL would present a broader range of intervention strategies. MSL seemed very compatible with RTI.

For students who clearly didn't understand the material, the teacher would make a more fundamental instructional change, perhaps covering less information during each session, doing more Socratic questioning, using an alternative instructional approach to better engage the students. Reassessment would reflect the relative success of the revised efforts. Sometimes, multiple interventions would be needed before any measurable improvement was recorded.

MSL had introduced Ms. Ward to a language reality about which she had never previously thought, and which has the potential to correct instructional difficulties rooted in a misunderstanding of terminology. Students, particularly young ones, often confront abstract concepts, taught by teachers who use equally abstract language. For instance, vowels can represent sounds traditionally labeled "short" and "long." The origin of these labels is lost in history, but the problems they create for many students live on. When students first learn about phonemes, were the teacher to use more concrete labels, the concept might be more easily grasped. Skilled reading does not require accurate labeling of vowel sounds; it requires knowing *how and when* to use them.

MSL labels vowel sounds more descriptively. Long vowel sounds are called "say your own name sounds" because the sound is the equivalent of the letter name (e.g., a long *a* says /a/ as in *ape*). Short vowel sounds are called "signal sounds," and students are taught a physical signal for each short vowel sound, which serves as a mnemonic that helps them distinguish among sound differences that are difficult to discriminate. In teaching with concrete labels, the teacher would use the "signal sound" and "say your own name sound" vowel labels, and would gradually, over time, pair the use of these "reminder" labels with the more conventional labels of "short" and "long" vowel sounds, progressively decreasing the use of the reminder labels. As scaffolding is gradually removed, students usually emerge from instruction using conventional vowel labels.

When Ms. Ward thought about that concept, she wondered if it was equally true in other subject areas. Students are so often faced with abstract ideas (e.g., "participatory government," "subject–verb agreement," "the commutative property of multiplication") that are difficult to understand, and these ideas are given abstract labels, making it even more difficult to grasp the concept. For example, teaching multiplication is a major focus in third grade. From a language standpoint, Ms. Ward realized that a phrase like "four times three" may be difficult for a third grader to grasp, since it expresses a concept that can't be visualized . . . What does "times" mean to a third grader? She was anxious to see if changing her terminology to something like "four . . . three times" or "three groups of four" would make the concept easier to grasp.

This relatively minor shift in language usage might be just the instructional alteration that could make a difference in learning ease for some students who are more concrete in their language development—not an uncommon characteristic among third graders (and some students of all ages, to be sure). For these students, this change might enable them to benefit from mainstream classroom instruction; it is a change that would harm no one and might, potentially, help many students. Ms. Ward couldn't wait to see.

Similarly, when learning the pedagogy of handwriting instruction (an important aspect of MSL instruction), Ms. Ward had been struck by the small instructional changes that could yield significant gains in student achievement. For instance, writing on a chalkboard is very different from writing on a whiteboard. Chalkboards offer the writer more resistance, resulting in greater muscular/neural feedback. For some students, that increased feedback results in a better sense of where their hand is and in what direction their hand is moving.

Likewise, Ms. Ward was astounded when she learned about the neurological ramifications of being left-handed in a right-handed world. How effectively can a right-handed teacher teach handwriting to a left-handed student if the teacher doesn't understand the neurological implications of dominance? Lefties are neurologically wired to move from their midline toward their dominant left hand. They instinctively want to move in the opposite direction from what is required for successfully reading and writing English.

Ms. Ward couldn't help but wonder why she hadn't learned anything about handwriting or neurology during her college education. But, she could clearly see the difference that her new knowledge and awareness were going to make in her teaching effectiveness. Such insights were help-ing Ms. Ward formulate a clearer understanding of RTI, and effective teaching that facilitates successful learning.

Before teaching anything, academic or otherwise, the instructor must look at the end product, the result of the instruction, *diagnostically.* The maxim for physicians—diagnose before you prescribe—applies equally to education. Instructors must "factor analyze" the task they wish to teach; that is, think about all of the variables involved in performing the task or learning the material. They are then in a position to select and manipu-late, during subsequent teaching and relative to individual learners, one variable at a time, followed by assessing whether or not the result is improved performance. This, of course, is simply the application of tradi-tional scientific method to the activities of teaching and learning. As edu-cation becomes more scientific and validation oriented through the use of RTI, data will drive instructional improvement. The fundamental question will change from "What do I need to teach the students," to "What can I change in my teaching that might improve a student's learning?"

THE PRESENT AND FUTURE OF RTI IN READING

Using RTI, new instructional options become available to the educator, who can make systematic, incremental, data-driven changes in day-to-day classroom activities, and then assess the impact of those changes on individual student achievement, as well as the achievement of an entire class. But, before any of this can be done effectively and without resist-ance, the educator needs to understand *why* RTI holds such great poten-tial for improving teaching and learning. Among other things, RTI is a bridge that links the elements that general and special education have in common. Almost every educator would agree that the goal of schooling is to generate learning in *individual* students, and that this goal is best meas-ured by the performance of individuals, not aggregate statistical groups. Yet for generations, educators have relied on the paradigm of evaluating their success primarily on the reporting of *group* results, rather than the outcomes of individual students. This filters down to teachers as a gener-alized pressure to think and act on behalf of aggregate collections of stu-dents, rather than individuals. (This is in contrast to most of the other "helping" professions, such as medicine, psychotherapy, and social work, where practitioner emphasis is primarily on the individual client or patient.)

With the advent of federally mandated special education regula-tions in 1975, for the first time, national standards were set in place that reoriented the focus from an emphasis on classroom outcomes to a focus on the individual child—in special education. The centerpiece of this change was the individualized education program (IEP), which federal law mandates for every special education student. Until now, general education had not been directly impacted by these changes.

It is no coincidence that the first movements toward the application of scientific data gathering for individual student performance—which would eventually become known as progress monitoring and be embedded in RTI—began just a few years later, in the late 1970s. But since these approaches were directed at the entire student population, not just special needs students, they were not widely received at first.

During the 1980s and 1990s, general education (with its whole class instruction orientation) and special education (with its focus on the learning success of each individual student) tended to remain separate. But with the passage of the federal No Child Left Behind legislation in 2001, and the reauthorization of the Individuals with Disabilities Education Act in 2004, U.S. schools were told, from the highest levels of their federal and state governments, that *all* students are entitled to an education formulated around the results of individual diagnostic evaluations and rooted in scientifically recognized approaches, and that the most widely accepted format for this was the process that had become known as RTI. Thus, the requirement that educational practice be driven by the needs of individual students, as well as by the more generalized needs of groups of students, has made its way from special education to general education, and all students stand to benefit.

This change in educational focus represents the most significant paradigm shift in education in the past 50 years. It is a change that has the potential to result in far better educational outcomes, driven and documented by data rather than beliefs, experienced in a greater comfort level for all learners, and reflected in increased gratification experienced by educators, who see that they can, in fact, be successful with a broad range of learners.

 TECH BYTE

THE INTERNATIONAL CHILDREN'S DIGITAL LIBRARY

The mission of the International Children's Digital Library (ICDL) Foundation is "to support the world's children in becoming effective members of the global community—who exhibit tolerance and respect for diverse cultures, languages and ideas—by making the best in children's literature available online free of charge." The foundation's goal is to build a collection of children's books that represents outstanding historical and contemporary works from throughout the world, representing every culture and language. The site contains digital books in many languages and free resources for teachers and parents.

Below is one idea for using the site that was suggested in the "Using the Library" section of the site (http://en.childrenslibrary.org/books/activities/index.shtml).

Digital Story Time: If you have a standard computer projector, then try using it the next time you read a book to children (whether in a library's story time hour, in school, or at home). Simply hook up the projector to your computer, find a book in the ICDL and read with the large projected display. This has the advantage of making illustrations (and words) large enough for everyone to see—and the technical nature of the display is often engaging. To make it work as well as possible, be sure to maximize your browser window (on Windows, try ->Full Screen). And once you get to the book pages within ICDL, click on the ⊚icon, which will reduce the size of the navigation icons—making more room for the page image.

Literacy Intervention: Tiers 2 and 3

5

Sarah McPherson and Dolores T. Burton

> *Reading instruction in Ms. Cohen's second-grade class includes phonics, phonetics, oral reading, vocabulary, and comprehension. She uses a reading series adopted by the district for basic literacy development. The series includes exercises to develop decoding, vocabulary, and comprehension skills in basal readers; workbooks; and accompanying computer software programs aligned with the skills. The reading performance of all the students is carefully monitored to ensure that they meet the curriculum benchmarks for reading.*
>
> *A few students, such as Jonathan, struggle with meeting the benchmarks and following the rules. Fortunately Ms. Cohen is implementing RTI in her classroom. Analysis of Jonathan's performance data alerts her that he needs Tier 2 intervention for reading, which may also improve his behavior. Ms. Cohen follows the student, environment, task, and technology (SETT) framework for guiding her implementation of the RTI process.*

Basic literacy skills are the cornerstone for successful learning in American schools. Development of literacy skills begins at birth with the introduction of language, vocabulary, and books that connect symbols to meaning. Most children enter school with a 3,000- to 5,000-word vocabulary, a working concept of sentence structure, and a framework for understanding the relationships among sounds, symbols, and meaning (Child Development Institute, n.d.). However, educators face enormous challenges for those children who enter school with limited prerequisite literacy skills. For most children, literacy instruction works quite well, but for many others, strategic approaches, such as explicit skill-based instruction, progress monitoring, and response to intervention (RTI), are required to address the complexities of the child's lack of prior knowledge, experiences, and abilities. In this chapter we will address RTI for all children struggling with traditional literacy instruction in general education classrooms.

LITERACY AND LEARNING DISABILITIES

The term *literacy* encompasses skills in reading, writing, speaking, listening, and language. We can look to the recent development of Common Core State Standards for English Language Arts and Literacy in History/Social Studies, Science and Technical Subjects, coordinated by the National Governors Association Center for Best Practices (NGA Center) and the Council of Chief State School Officers (CCSSO), as an example of the breadth of literacy. Literacy is the use of language for communication, whether for gaining information from text or from oral language, or written or spoken expression. Each area of literacy addresses specific skills; these include phonics, phonetics, fluency, vocabulary, and comprehension in reading; writing includes letter formation, use of standard language for expression of thought, and mechanics of grammar and punctuation; speaking and listening involve vocabulary, comprehension, and use of standard English-language grammatical conventions. These skill areas are intertwined but are often separated for instructional purposes. Subsets of specific skills in each area are benchmarked according to age and grade level with increasing developmental complexity throughout the grades. Assessments are designed to measure student achievement and progress in meeting the benchmarks for each subset.

A child's difficulty acquiring adequate literacy skills is sometimes associated with a specific learning disability (SLD). As a result of the increased number of children identified with a learning disability and the possibility of misdiagnosis, the 2004 reauthorization of the Individuals with Disabilities Education Act (IDEA) revised the procedures for identifying students with SLD with the stipulation that the child has been "provided with learning experiences and instruction appropriate for the child's age or state-approved grade-level standards" (U.S. Department of Education, 2004). The legislation goes on to require data to demonstrate that, prior to or as part of the referral process, the child was provided appropriate instruction in a regular education setting, delivered by qualified personnel (U.S. Department of Education, 2004).

According to Dr. Sheldon Horowitz (2009) at the National Center for Disabilities, "The term specific learning disability refers to one or more of the basic psychological processes involved in understanding or using language, spoken or written, and affects a person's ability to listen, think, speak, read, write, spell, or do mathematical calculations." A child diagnosed with SLD has neurological processing difficulties that interfere with how he or she learns. The child with SLD will, in all likelihood, continue to have difficulties in school unless special education services are provided for reading, writing, and/or mathematics.

Since 1975, the number of children identified with SLD has doubled, and more than 50% of students receiving special education services are classified with SLD (Council for Exceptional Children, n.d.). These numbers are alarming and raise concerns about whether a neurological condition causing learning disabilities exists in these children, or whether their difficulties in reading, writing, and mathematics are due to lack of appropriate instruction. IDEA addresses these concerns with the call for evidence-based instruction and RTI performance data. The anticipated outcome of the legislation is to reduce the number of students misclassified as SLD while improving the instruction provided to all students.

Several myths prevail about reading and literacy development that add to the complexity of RTI and appropriate instruction for all students.

Myth #1: IQ is a predictor of reading ability.

A discrepancy between IQ and reading achievement levels may be due to a variety of causes, including lack of opportunity to participate in preschool or home literacy development activities, unidentified language or learning disabilities, or the fact that English is not the child's and parents' native language. This lack of exposure and opportunity, rather than intelligence, impedes an individual's reading/literacy development (Feldman, n.d.; Snow, Burns, & Griffin, 1998).

Myth #2: Parents' reading habits determine a child's reading achievement.

Opportunities for early language experience, access to books and written materials in the home environment, and parents' or caregivers' modeling of reading habits influence development of reading habits (Friederici & Thierry, 2008; Gresham, VanDerHeyden, & Witt, 2005). However, a child's capacity for or interest in reading is not solely determined by the parents' reading habits. In fact, a child may have a learning disability, or, conversely, children whose parents may not provide a rich literacy environment at home may have the cognitive ability and motivation to learn to read very well.

Myth #3: Most reading difficulties are the result of perceptual problems.

Perceptual problems due to poor eyesight from compromised visual processing or neurological dysfunctions are causes for some children to have difficulty learning to read, but not all. Corrective lenses usually can accommodate poor eyesight. Neurological dysfunctions are more complicated. Dyslexia is the term used for the perceptual problems that result in difficulty or inability to read (Hudson, High, & Al Otaiba, 2007). Dyslexia occurs more often in individuals with a genetic predisposition for dyslexia, and this suggests it has genetic origins rather than being the result of environmental conditions, with the accompanying implications for literacy development (Fisher & DeFries, 2002; Grigorenko, 2001).

Myth #4: Reading and learning difficulties are best identified in second or third grade.

Prior to 2004, the legal requirement was that a child's performance must be at least two years below grade level for the child to be eligible for special education. This policy, known as the discrepancy or wait-to-fail model, was based on the difference between a child's expected performance based on IQ and his or her actual performance (Torgesen, 2004). It allowed, and in fact required, a child to experience continuous failure for a minimum of two years, losing valuable instructional time that might have been used for remediation, and left both the teacher and child with an almost impossible task of recovery. RTI calls for early intervention, so evaluation can occur much earlier.

RESEARCH FINDINGS

We will now explore some of the recent literature to help us understand developments in the areas of early literacy and school readiness.

School Readiness and Literacy

Children who enter kindergarten with poor language and literacy skills tend to persistently perform poorly in early grades, and often the poor performance continues into adolescence. Conversely, children who have strong literacy skills when they arrive at school learn to read earlier and develop better literacy skills that continue throughout the higher grades, providing a solid foundation for academic success.

Much of early *language* learning (in contrast to the process of reading) begins at home, with parents as the child's first teacher. Some parents use language extensively, talking and reading to their children to develop vocabulary and awareness of meaning in text, thereby building early experiences relating text to sound and meaning. However, other children have limited opportunity to learn literacy skills at home. Their parents may not talk with them or read to them, which limits their acquisition of literacy skills prior to entering school. To help these children, preschool programs, such as Head Start, Even Start, and public prekindergarten, have been established to provide children with additional opportunities to learn literacy skills and improve their school readiness (Puma et al., 2010). These programs have proven successful in helping children catch up with some of the literacy skills they haven't learned at home.

The U.S. Department of Education recently commissioned the National Center for Educational Research's Institute of Education Sciences (IES) to study the effects of preschool curriculum on school readiness. The IES report issued in 2008 indicates that few curriculum programs have significant effects on school readiness (Preschool Curriculum Evaluation Research Consortium, 2008). The learning that occurs in the home environment—parents using language with their children—is the most critical aspect of literacy development for young children. Many children who enter school with limited language skills are at risk for lack of achieving academic success, regardless of their exposure to preschool programs. These students will need more supportive interventions for successful literacy development, such as those provided by RTI.

RTI IN LITERACY INSTRUCTION

The American school curriculum is based on the expectation that all children will learn to read in primary grades. Reading entails phonics, phonetics, fluency, vocabulary, and comprehension. At the kindergarten level, competencies include knowing letters, sight/sound relations, phonemes, basic sight words, and understanding of print text. The skills are practiced, and scaffolding is provided as complexity increases. As a whole, research shows that as many as 30% of students find reading a "formidable challenge," approximately 60% find it "challenging," up to 20% find it "relatively easy with instruction," and extremely few find reading "effortless" (Parks-Recore, 2008).

For the teacher, the realities behind these percentages can be overwhelming in a classroom where the primary focus is literacy instruction. The challenge is to provide quality, evidence-based instruction that increases opportunities for all students to learn. One of the most essential elements of RTI is to systematically and universally assess the progress of all learners to ensure that those with persistent difficulties are identified and receive appropriate support.

Assessment

Prior to IDEA 2004, the legislation defined specific learning disabilities as a discrepancy between the academic achievement level that would be expected for a child of a given IQ and the child's actual achievement level. A discrepancy of two years behind grade level was defined as valid evidence for referral to special education services. In other words, the system systematically waited for a child to fall below grade level, that is, to fail, and for the gap to increase to two years, before implementing even an *evaluation* process—let alone remediation—to determine if the child had specific learning disabilities such as dyslexia, dysgraphia, and dyscalculia. The lack of instruction at the appropriate level resulted in the loss of opportunities to learn. This wait-to-fail approach led to overidentification of children with SLD, when, in fact, their problems might have stemmed from their having been inappropriately taught (Fuchs & Fuchs, 2006).

Assessment Under IDEA 2004

Recognizing this, the 2004 reauthorization of IDEA included new language specifically prohibiting any requirement that schools use a discrepancy model for referral to special education services and requiring evidence-based instruction to meet the learning needs of *any* child experiencing difficulties in reading and writing.

IDEA 2004 became a powerful endorsement for the use of RTI as a recognized example of a "scientific, research-based intervention." The fact that it had been known and used for decades in general education was an additional strength, since the legislation now strongly encouraged schools

> to develop and implement coordinated, early intervening services . . . for students in kindergarten through grade 12 (with a particular emphasis on students in kindergarten through grade 3) who have not been identified as needing special education or related services but who need additional academic and behavioral support to succeed in a general education environment. (Pub. L. 108–446, §613(f)(1), as cited in NASDSE/CASE, 2006)

Although the law did not specifically require the use of RTI, the Department of Education has strongly promoted RTI for more than a decade. The 2002 report of the President's Commission on Special Education presented the recommendation: "Incorporate Response to Intervention. Implement models during the identification and assessment process that are based on response to intervention and progress monitoring. Use data from these processes to assess progress in children who receive special education services" (President's Commission on Excellence in Special Education, 2002, p. 21).

LITERACY INSTRUCTION USING THE THREE TIERS OF RTI

Literacy instruction is focused on reading, writing, speaking, and listening. It is aimed at explicit, structured, and sequential development of early literacy skills, such as, phonics, phonetics, fluency, vocabulary skills, and comprehension. Strategies for developing these skills include modeling, scaffolding, and providing opportunities to manipulate and practice sound/letter relationships, word patterns and meanings, text configurations, and contexts. Practice, accompanied by timely corrective feedback, ensures that children develop and eventually master reading skills with fluency and automaticity. Explicit instruction in comprehension may be needed when the difficulty is with reading comprehension rather than with phonics and phonetics. RTI is applicable to all literacy skill areas—comprehension instruction may be specifically targeted for students who can decode words, but cannot comprehend the meaning of the words or reading passage. Children with strong literacy skills also develop metacognitive strategies for learning, independent reading, critical thinking, and problem solving, all of which are necessary for academic success in higher grades.

The Classroom Setting

General education teachers may use a variety of flexible grouping configurations, including whole groups, pairs, and individuals, in their classrooms. Groupings may match students performing at the same level or at heterogeneous performance levels. Classrooms may be arranged with learning centers serving as reading and writing stations. There may be collections of leveled printed books, audio recordings of books and players for them, computers and websites for games and practice exercises, electronic books, e-readers with speech-enabled text on mobile readers, board games or games to play on an iTouch or iPad, and/or writing and drawing materials. This wealth of resources, including technology, can support literacy development for all children.

Scientific Research, Evidence, and Data-Based Education

In 1997, Congress and the National Institute of Child Health and Human Development (NICHD) commissioned the National Reading Panel to identify research that could be implemented in the classroom to support early literacy. The report (2000) provides evidence of research-based practices to meet national requirements, including the following:

- Phonemic awareness and phonics instruction
- Fluency
- Comprehension, which addresses vocabulary and text comprehension
- Teacher education and reading instruction
- Computer technology and reading instruction

A recent project of the New York State Department of Education Office of Vocational and Educational Services for Individuals With Disabilities (VESID), Special Education Services, developed a *Quality Indicator Review and Resource Guide for Literacy* (www.p12.nysed.gov/specialed/techassist/LiteracyQI). The quality indicators for literacy were categorized by levels, as listed in Table 5.1. Resources, performance

Table 5.1 Quality Indicators for Literacy

Quality Indicators for Literacy	
Level	*Quality Indicators*
Early Literacy Instructional Practice	• Phonemic awareness • Phonics and decoding • Fluency • Vocabulary • Reading and listening comprehension • Written expression • Spelling and handwriting
Adolescent Literacy (Middle Level)	• Direct, explicit comprehension instruction • Reading across the curriculum • Motivation and self-directed learning • Intensive writing
High School Literacy	• Direct literacy instruction across disciplines in all content areas • Reading to learn information (opposed to learning to read) • Motivation and self-directed learning • Writing embedded in the content areas

assessments, and benchmarking protocols were included for each quality indicator listed. These evidence-based quality indicators are recommended as the necessary elements of high-quality literacy instruction at each of these general education levels.

RTI Tier 1 for Reading: Universal Screening

Instruction for all children is considered Tier 1 of RTI. The teacher monitors *all* children through periodic and systematic universal screening, meaning that all children are assessed for their progress in literacy skills. The National Center on Response to Intervention defines universal screening as

> brief assessments that are valid, reliable, and evidence-based. They are conducted with all students or targeted groups of students to identify students who are at risk of academic failure and, therefore, likely to need additional or alternative forms of instruction to supplement the conventional general education approach. (National Center on Response to Intervention, 2010)

The classroom teacher usually conducts these assessments, although others such as special educators, speech and language professionals, and paraprofessionals may participate in the process. Teachers also may use informal assessments such as letter naming, letter-sound fluency, phonological blending, word identification, and informal reading inventories. Universal screening should occur for all children in the early grades three times per year (fall, winter, and spring) so that teachers have ample opportunity to target children who are struggling.

RTI Tiers 2 and Tier 3 for Struggling Readers

RTI Tier 2 for Reading

Tier 2 is supplementary instruction to Tier 1, geared for only those students having difficulty. It consists of supplementary instruction for building foundation skills, scheduled at more frequent intervals and with more time allotted to it. Using the results of the universal screening, teachers can identify those students with deficiencies in specific literacy skills and assign them Tier 2 interventions. Tier 2 involves remediation of specific skill deficits. Students requiring remediation are placed in small groups (ideally four to six students), often with a specialist. For example, supplementation strategies for vocabulary development may include graphic organizers, games, and activities with auditory and visual cues. Instructional time increases, and Tier 2 instruction is given in addition to the regularly scheduled instruction to provide opportunities for additional practice to develop mastery and fluency. The teacher, or support person assisting in Tier 2, may administer weekly assessments to monitor student progress. Some software that may be used for intensive instruction at Tier 2 may generate reports that inform the teacher or support person of the students' progress toward mastery of target skills. The information from frequent systematic progress monitoring provides information to guide the instruction and to reinforce instruction with corrective feedback.

In addition, progress monitoring in Tier 2 provides evidence of whether even more intensive interventions are needed. Children who make adequate progress will return to Tier 1, and monitoring will resume at that level. Children who fail to make progress at Tier 2 in the small group, with additional time, increased frequency, and additional targeted instruction, will be placed in Tier 3 for individualized instruction.

RTI Tier 3 for Reading

Tier 3 offers more intense instruction for those who continue to have difficulty after a reasonable amount of time in Tier 2. The Tier 3 instruction is supplemental, remedial, and one-on-one in the areas of the individual student's deficiencies and includes systematic documentation of details of the intervention implementation and results in student performance (Gersten et al., 2008). Strategies in Tier 3 address individualized target skills with increased direct instruction, time on task, and frequency of instruction. Typically a reading specialist or special education teacher provides the intensive Tier 3 instruction and administers the assessments for determining progress at this level. The frequency of assessment is determined by the schedule for the targeted one-on-one instruction, but it may be administered as frequently as each session. Again, software reports, if used, may generate adequate assessment data for progress monitoring. Whoever is providing the instruction administers the assessment and analyzes the data for adequate progress at Tier 3. The tutoring may be effective, and the child may revert to Tier 2 or perhaps even to Tier 1. However, if the child fails to meet benchmarks at Tier 3, the RTI data are used to support the recommendation for an evaluation for special education services.

LITERACY INSTRUCTIONAL TOOLS FOR RTI

How does a teacher organize instruction to support all children in their struggle to learn to read? One effective approach is Zabala's (1998) four-step SETT framework.

S represents the *student.* What the student brings to the learning is critical to the RTI process. This is a diagnostic process and involves analysis of the student's background, abilities, characteristics, performance, and appropriate grade/age-level progress.

E is the *environment.* This is an analysis of the classroom where learning is expected to take place. What does the classroom look, feel, and sound like? What furniture and equipment are available and how is it arranged? What is the classroom culture and climate? What other environmental factors may affect learning such as time of day, temperature, lighting, noise, and so forth? What classroom management strategies are used? All these factors affect the student's ability to learn, to concentrate, and to be engaged, and are therefore critical to a student's successful learning.

T stands for the *tasks* the student is expected to be able to do. The tasks are the general education age/grade-level expectations in the curriculum, instruction, and assessments. The opportunities for practicing skills, and the assessments used to measure them, should be carefully aligned so that the student's performance reflects what he or she actually knows and is able to do.

T represents *technology* to support learning. Technology resources can enhance the teaching and learning process in RTI in many ways.

Let's return to Jonathan and see how he progresses through RTI using the SETT framework shown in Table 5.2.

CONCLUSION

IDEA 2004 legislation calls for a fundamental shift in our thinking about reading difficulties, and part of this shift is an understanding that in most

Table 5.2 Jonathan's Progress Using the SETT Framework

Student: *Jonathan is a seven-year-old second grader in a general education classroom. He has trouble decoding words while reading, often miscuing letters, sounds, and diagraphs. This affects his fluency, vocabulary skills, and reading comprehension. He is easily frustrated with his inability to read fluently and comprehend what he reads. His attention span is quite short, and he often distracts others when he is off task and angry with himself.*

Strengths:

- He exhibits strengths in recalling stories and decodes some one-syllable words.
- He is alert and active, and he likes to do things with his hands.
- He responds to questions when asked.
- When working in a small group, he tends to stay focused and actively participates.
- He is outgoing and friendly.
- He enjoys working one-on-one with the teacher.

Weaknesses:

- He is below grade level in sight words, decoding, spelling, vocabulary, and oral expression.
- He is often frustrated with reading, loses interest easily, and distracts other students with angry outbursts.
- When he encounters an unknown word, he skips over the word and does not attempt to sound it out.
- He has difficulty following written and oral directions.
- He is much slower in completing written work than other students.
- He is easily distracted and needs occasional reminders to stay on task.

Environment: *Twenty-four students are in Ms. Cohen's second grade. The classroom is arranged with tables of four students, an interactive whiteboard is at the front of the room, and four computers are in the back of the room. Ms. Cohen uses six centers for reading, listening, writing, art/illustrating, word games, and computers. Students move with their table group through the centers at times specified in the daily schedule; 15-minute intervals are allotted at each center. The students are generally well behaved and on task. However if there is misbehavior, such as talking too loudly, not cooperating with peers, or disobeying class rules, there is a time-out chair on the side of the room opposite the door.*

Task: *Ms. Cohen has identified that Jonathan's major difficulty is decoding according to second-grade benchmarks. She assigns him to Tier 2 intervention and consults Ms. Robinson, the reading specialist, on how to address this area of difficulty. Ms. Robinson recommends additional resources and materials based on the Orton-Gillingham reading method for decoding words using tactile and kinesthetic exercises.*

(Continued)

(Continued)

Technology: She also recommends that Ms. Cohen use StarFall, an animated software program with multisensory games for decoding phonics and recognizing letter combinations to supplement the instruction, providing Jonathan additional practice with decoding. Jonathan is placed in a small group for oral reading with Ms. Cohen and three other students who are struggling with decoding. She administers weekly probes to monitor their progress in decoding words and fluency in oral reading.

After four weeks of Tier 2 intervention and weekly monitoring, Ms. Cohen determines that Jonathan continues to fall behind in oral reading fluency and comprehension due to his inability to decode accurately.

Jonathan is moved to Tier 3 intervention. The reading specialist schedules 30 minutes three times per week to work one-on-one with Jonathan on decoding strategies and oral reading. The additional time with Ms. Robinson increases his opportunities to develop decoding skills, oral fluency, and comprehension. Ms. Robinson uses additional materials to reinforce the decoding strategies used in Tier 2 and engages in reciprocal teaching strategies for increasing comprehension. Ms. Robinson's approach is to combine decoding practice with comprehension strategies to maintain Jonathan's interest and motivation while decreasing his frustration with the difficulties he has decoding.

Reciprocal teaching strategies include interactive questioning between Ms. Robinson and Jonathan to check for comprehension, such as "What do you think is going to happen?" "Why do you think [the character] said [or did] that?" "What has already happened in the story?" Using these techniques, Jonathan and Ms. Robinson discuss the reading by summarizing, questioning, clarifying, and predicting to check for comprehension.

Ms. Robinson also has a parent conference with Jonathan's mother and shares with her some things she can do with Jonathan at home, such as review his decoding homework exercises, allow him to play StarFall games on the computer, and read with him daily. These extra few minutes engaged in reading activities will increase Jonathan's opportunities to develop skills to become a more proficient reader. Ms. Robinson develops a checklist for Jonathan's mother to help her record the reading activities and time Jonathan spends doing them.

Ms. Robinson continues with the weekly progress monitoring for several more weeks. Slowly Jonathan is making progress toward meeting the benchmarks. By continuing to work with Ms. Robinson and at home with his mother, he may have gained sufficient skills to return to Tier 2 at the beginning of the next marking period.

cases, reading problems are not attributable to conditions within the child. More often, the problem lies with the instruction, and therefore the instruction needs to be improved. According to Mellard (2004), the major features of RTI for literacy can deliver this needed improvement by providing high-quality, research-based, individualized reading instruction.

Reading proficiency depends on effective instruction to develop a solid foundation in the basic skills: phonics, phonetics, fluency, vocabulary, and comprehension. Assessment of classroom performance is critical for reading instruction to ensure that target benchmarks are met. Tier 1 is based on universal screening of all students to identify the 20% to 30% who struggle to meet the age/grade-level benchmarks for attaining basic reading skills.

For those who need the more intensive intervention of Tier 2 and Tier 3, continuous monitoring is required to check progress toward meeting the benchmarks. If the new intervention is effective, skills develop, and student learning improves.

 TECH BYTE

SCREENING TOOLS

The National Center on Response to Intervention has reviews of screening tools on its website, www.rti4success.org. The screening tools chart lists commercial screening systems with information about their technical rigor, efficiency, cost, and implementation requirements. Each commercial tool is reviewed and rated according to area (math or reading), classification accuracy, generalizability, reliability, validity, disaggregation of valid and reliable data for diverse populations, and efficiency of administration. This tools chart provides educators and families with information useful for selecting screening tools.

One popular commercial screening tool developed by the Center on Teaching and Learning at the University of Oregon is called *Dynamic Indicators of Basic Early Literacy Skills* (DIBELS) (www.dibels.org/) for kindergarten through sixth grade. DIBELS is validated as a reliable research-based criterion-referenced early literacy universal screening assessment for identifying struggling readers to target for Tier 2. The DIBELS measures the five domains of early literacy: phonological awareness, alphabetic principle, fluency with connected text, vocabulary, and comprehension. Each measure in DIBELS has been thoroughly researched as a reliable and valid indicator of early literacy development. These measures have been found to be predictive of later reading proficiency, and so they can be useful for identifying children who are not progressing as expected. The DIBELS assessment system includes benchmarks in these reading domains for determining student progress. Therefore, when used in RTI Tier 1, the DIBELS assessment provides systematic universal screening. The benchmark probes are designed for assessing progress in the five skill domains three times per year—fall, winter, and spring—for each grade level, kindergarten through sixth grade. The DIBELS measures provide critical formative assessment information to consider along with other indicators of student progress, such as teacher assessments and observations, state standardized test results, and other evidence that may be available relevant to a child's progress in developing literacy skills.

AIMSWeb (www.aimsweb.com) is widely used for universal screening. It has benchmarks for assessing all students three times per year and for progress monitoring in general education. For measurement based on a reading curriculum, the probe is the child reading a passage aloud for one minute. The oral reading fluency score, which is determined by the number of words read with accuracy, serves as a reliable and valid measure of reading achievement. The assessment is quick to administer and straightforward to measure. Early literacy is probed in kindergarten and first grade with assessments of the child's abilities in letter naming, letter sounds, phoneme segmentation, and pronouncing nonsense words. Other probes assess comprehension, spelling, and written expression. Comprehension is assessed through multiple-choice cloze tasks that students complete while reading silently. The spelling probe is the number of correct letter sequences the child can produce for grade-level words dictated aloud for two minutes. Students are assessed for written expression by having them produce a writing sample in three minutes from an appropriate story starter. *AIMSweb* provides all the assessments in Spanish as well as English. Further details and supporting research on the validity and reliability of these measures can be found at the *AIMSweb* website.

RESOURCES

Center for Implementing Technology Education. (www.cited.org/index.aspx)

The Center for Implementing Technology Education (CITEd) maintains a portal that provides links to evidence-based resources for integrating technology to support student learning. The site is organized by category of educators: teachers, administrators, technology coordinators, and other professionals. Topics include English language learners, differentiated instruction, evidence-based practice and IDEA, strategies and modifications for using technology for writing, differentiation strategies that use increasing amounts of technology, and progress monitoring systems.

International Reading Association (IRA). (www.reading.org)

Professional associations such as the International Reading Association (IRA) provide extensive resources for literacy instruction and RTI. The

IRA's commitment to literacy and research-based reading instruction is evident in the professional development resources published on their website as well as in an extensive reference list of articles published in reading research literature. The IRA established a Commission on RTI that produced *Response to Intervention: Guiding Principles for Educators From the International Reading Association* (2009).

IRIS Center for Training Enhancements. (http://iris.peabody.vanderbilt.edu/)

The U.S. Department of Education Office of Special Education funds the IRIS Center for Training Enhancements project. The purpose of the IRIS Center is to provide high-quality resources for teacher preparation programs and professional development providers pertaining to research-based practices for inclusion. The IRIS Center provides nine learning modules on RTI, including one that specifically addresses kindergarten through third-grade reading instruction.

Reading Rockets. (www.readingrockets.org)

The U.S. Department of Education Office of Special Education provides a major grant to WETA to fund *Reading Rockets* and a Spanish version, *Colorin Colorado* (www.ColorinColorado.org). This site provides parents, teachers, administrators, librarians, and other professionals with extensive research-based information on reading instruction, classroom strategies, ways to support struggling readers, and RTI.

ReadWriteThink. (www.readwritethink.org)

The IRA and the National Council of Teachers of English cosponsor Verizon Thinkfinity, *ReadWriteThink*. This website provides teachers, students, and parents with free online resources. The materials from a series of five webinars on RTI for language literacy can be found on the *ReadWriteThink* site; these include an overview of the IRA principles on RTI, differentiated instruction, systemic and collaborative assessment, and language diversity.

RTI Action Network. (www.rtinetwork.org)

The National Research Center on Learning Disabilities has developed the RTI Action Network to provide information and support professional development about RTI for educators and parents. It presents basic information and references, approaches for getting started, essential components, resources, and connections to experts in the field for pre-K, K–5, middle school, high school, and higher education personnel as well as parents and families.

Mathematics Difficulty or Mathematics Disability?

6

RTI and Mathematics

Dolores T. Burton and John Kappenberg

> *Melissa is a shy, pretty, fifth-grade student with long brown hair and a pleasant smile. Her reading scores are on grade level. She has struggled with mathematics throughout elementary school and avoids answering questions in mathematics class, as she is afraid she has the wrong answers. Mrs. Thomas, her teacher, notices in September that even when Melissa is given more time to do her mathematics word problems, she still cannot complete assignments, and the work that is completed is not correct. Mrs. Thomas knows that more difficult work is yet to come and is concerned that because mathematics is a cumulative subject, Melissa will continue to fall behind and not be able to catch up.*

Mathematics difficulties like Melissa's are widespread in the United States as well as in other industrialized nations. Low achievement in mathematics has been documented by international comparisons of students' mathematics performance, such as the 2007 *Trends in International Mathematics and Science Study* (TIMSS), and is a matter of national concern (Gonzales et al., 2008). Many students with and without learning disabilities encounter learning problems with mathematics in the upper grades, and sometimes this is due to an insufficient understanding of the basic mathematical concepts that were presented in the primary grades. A survey of 743 algebra teachers associated with the National Mathematics Advisory Panel report (Hoffer, Venkataraman, Hedberg, & Shagle, 2008) identified key deficiencies of students entering an algebra course, including aspects of whole number arithmetic, fractions, ratios, proportions, and word problems. When students struggle with foundation concepts, such as the ones cited in this study, it is impossible for them to learn to do more complex mathematical problems and understand more abstract mathematical ideas.

In 2000, the National Council of Teachers of Mathematics (NCTM) published *Principles and Standards for School Mathematics*, which continued the call for a change in focus of curriculum from memorizing rules and procedures to an increased emphasis on mathematical reasoning, understanding, comprehension, and problem solving (Remillard, 2000). The standards provide an outline or guideline that states what students should know and be able to do in four grade-bands: prekindergarten through Grade 2, grades 3–5, grades 6–8, and grades 9–12. The standards were created in an effort to emphasize that students should not simply memorize mathematics algorithms without understanding the process, and should be successful in communicating which process or strategy they used in order to accomplish the task. The NCTM mathematical reform represents a goal of increasing expectations for students' performance in mathematics for all students. The six principles for school mathematics outline the basic components of high-quality instruction in mathematics and provide guidelines for teachers and educators to use to assess their instructional programs. They are described in Table 6.1.

Table 6.1 Six Principles for School Mathematics from *Principles and Standards for School Mathematics*

Equity	Excellence in mathematics education requires equity—high expectations and strong support for all students.
Curriculum	A curriculum is more than a collection of activities: it must be coherent, focused on important mathematics, and well articulated across the grades.
Teaching	Effective mathematics teaching requires understanding what students know and need to learn and then challenging and supporting them to learn it well.

(Continued)

(Continued)

Learning	Students must learn mathematics with understanding, actively building new knowledge from experience and prior knowledge.
Assessment	Assessment should support the learning of important mathematics and furnish useful information to both teachers and students.
Technology	Technology is essential in teaching and learning mathematics; it influences the mathematics that is taught and enhances students' learning.

Source: NCTM (2000).

Principles and Standards for School Mathematics (NCTM, 2000) contains a description of content standards. The standards describe what students should know and be able to do in five content areas: numbers and operations, geometry, algebra, measurement, and data analysis and probability. The document also provides resources for teachers to assist their students in reaching the process standards. The process standards are described in Table 6.2.

Table 6.2   Five Process Standards for School Mathematics

Problem Solving	Students require frequent opportunities to formulate, grapple with, and solve complex problems and to reflect on their thinking during the problem-solving process so that they can apply and adapt the strategies they develop to other problems and in other contexts.
Reasoning and Proof	Students who reason and think analytically tend to note patterns, structure, or regularities in both real world and mathematical situations. Students should see and expect that mathematics makes sense.
Communication	Mathematical communication is a way of sharing ideas and clarifying understanding. Listening to others' explanations gives students opportunities to develop their own understanding and explore ideas from multiple perspectives.
Connections	Mathematics is an integrated field of study, not a collection of separate strands or standards. When students connect mathematical ideas, their understanding is deeper and more lasting.
Representations	Mathematical ideas can be represented in a variety of ways: pictures, concrete materials, tables, graphs, number and letter symbols, spreadsheet displays, and so on. Instruction should help students create representations to capture mathematical concepts or relationships.

Source: NCTM (2000).

Instruction that incorporates the guidance provided by these principles and standards will facilitate the creation of classrooms where all students can learn. This is consistent with goals of implementing RTI, which is to enable all students to reach their potential in mathematics by learning with research-based instruction and meaningful assessment.

One approach to ensure all students learn and reach their potential was identified by Howard Gardner (1983) in his seminal work, *Frames of Mind: The Theory of Multiple Intelligences.* His initial work identified seven intelligences (now there are eight): linguistic and logical-mathematical were the intelligences measured most often on psychological tests; the other five were spatial, bodily-kinesthetic (including large and small motor skills), musical, interpersonal, and intrapersonal (self-knowledge). His theories focused on individual students' different strengths and the challenge for teachers to teach to those strengths. His work was a call to educators to create new strategies for instruction and new forms of assessment to address each student's broader spectrum of abilities (Kornhaber & Krechevsky, 1995). This framework can be used in implementing RTI in all three tiers, as the teacher and team decide on appropriate interventions for a student. Adams (2000) created a matrix identifying seven of the eight intelligences and activities that address the process standards identified by the NCTM. Table 6.3 describes suggested activities that are aligned with each intelligence.

It is estimated that 6% or 7% of the general population have a specific mathematical disability (Fuchs & Fuchs, 2005). More than 50% of students with identified learning disabilities have IEP goals in mathematics (Lerner, 2003). Policymakers look to RTI in the hope that it (a) will encourage and guide practitioners to intervene earlier on behalf of a greater number of children at risk for school failure, and (b) will represent a more valid method of LD identification (Fuchs & Fuchs, 2005).

To help Melissa, Mrs. Thomas must determine if Melissa's challenge with mathematical word problems is due to a specific learning disability (SLD), dyscalculia, or some other cause. One way *dyscalculia* is defined is as a difficulty in understanding and coping with quantitative or spatial information, in particular a reduced ability to understand or apply core mathematical processes. It can result in a difficulty in handling sequences of information or processing numerical data. There are several definitions of dyscalculia, an SLD. However, all definitions have three common elements: the presence of difficulties in mathematics, some degree of specificity to these (i.e., a lack of across-the-board academic difficulties), and the assumption that these are caused in some way by brain dysfunction (Rourke & Conway, 1997).

Educators knowledgeable in the difference between mathematical difficulty and dyscalculia can assist in the diagnosis and remediation of

Table 6.3 Overlapping of Gardner's Multiple Intelligences and NCTM Process Standards

Gardner Intelligence Type	Problem Solving	Reasoning and Proof	Communication	Connection	Representation
Linguistic—perceiving or generating spoken or written language	• Write stories as context for word problems. • Write about problem solving.	• Express arguments in ways that make sense to others. • Refute/support a mathematics idea.	• Respond to prompts for writing with/about mathematics. • Define terms.	• Write about relationships between mathematical concepts.	• Translate word problems to algebraic expressions and vice versa.
Logical-Mathematical—facility in the use of numbers and logical thinking	• Gather, record, and use numerical data to solve problems. • Calculate to solve problems.	• Generalize mathematical conclusions. • Provide nonexamples.	• Develop and use categories to classify written and oral mathematical information.	• Categorize and classify numbers. • Explore the use of numbers in other disciplines.	• Use technology to represent and sort data. • Represent numbers in various ways.
Spatial—perceiving visual images in one's mind	• Use drawings and diagrams as problem-solving strategies. • Explain a drawn solution.	• Use paper folding and cutting to prove concepts.	• Describe characteristics of two-dimensional shapes and three-dimensional objects.	• Explore the uses of mathematics in architecture. • Describe classroom and school.	• Use diagrams, charts, pictures, and tables to solve problems.

Gardner Intelligence Type	Problem Solving	Reasoning and Proof	Communication	Connection	Representation
Bodily-Kinesthetic—the use of one's body to create products or solve problems	• Use dramatization as a strategy for problem solving.	• Use parts of the body to reason about concepts (e.g., proportion).	• Use body language or charades to convey a mathematical message.	• Investigate connections between body and various restrictions in the world.	• Model division by distribution of objects to people.
Musical—creating and communicating meaning from sound	• Translate problem solving strategies to a musical tune to help recall strategies.	• Compare patterns to songs that have patterned rounds that "never end."	• Listen to counting songs in other cultures and languages.	• Create a mathematics musical in connection with the music program.	• Use objects to model music rhythms. • Explore the sound of concrete objects.
Interpersonal—sensitivity to the feelings and beliefs of others	• Solve problems through cooperative learning. • Lead a problem-solving excursion.	• Collaborate with others to develop arguments and proofs.	• Share communicative roles in cooperative groups.	• Lead peers in discussions about mathematical connections.	• Debate the applicability of various representations.
Intrapersonal—ability to self-reflect analytically to achieve goals	• Set goals for growth in problem solving. • Monitor problem-solving process.	• Use personal and previous knowledge to build a basis for a conjecture.	• Describe feelings and attitudes about mathematics. • Think aloud.	• Consider ways in which mathematics is used in own life.	• Organize thinking according to various representations. • Use different representations.

mathematical difficulties for students like Melissa. RTI is a process that can assist in this determination.

The Individuals with Disabilities Education Improvement Act of 2004 (IDEA; P. L. 108-446) changed the law about identifying children with SLDs. The previous version relied on a severe discrepancy between achievement and intellectual ability to determine whether there was a learning disability; current law uses RTI as a substitute for, or supplement to, the IQ/achievement discrepancy model. Learning disabilities are a particular type of "unexpected" low achievement and are distinguished from types where low achievement is expected due to emotional disturbance, social or cultural disadvantage, or inadequate instruction (Kavale & Forness, 2000). The operational definition attempts to capture the complex and multivariate nature of SLD. The components include a severe discrepancy between ability and achievement; learning difficulties in language, reading, writing, or mathematics that require special education; psychological processing deficits that are associated with academic learning problems; and exclusionary criteria indicating factors that make the learning failure not unexpected.

TEACHING CHILDREN MATHEMATICS USING RTI AS A FRAMEWORK

RTI in mathematics is an assessment and intervention process for systematically monitoring student progress, examining errors for patterns in conceptual or procedural understandings, and making decisions about evidence-based instructional modifications or increasingly intensified services based on the student's need. RTI begins with implementation of scientifically based, schoolwide instructional interventions and promotes intervention at the first indication of nonresponse to traditional classroom instruction. No two students learn the same way. Curriculum and instruction should incorporate alternatives so that all students—including individuals with varying backgrounds, learning styles, and abilities—have access to materials that accommodate their special needs and maximize each student's ability to learn and progress (Rose & Meyer, 2002). A key principle in RTI is the focus on incorporating prevention and early intervention rather than waiting for failure.

The three tiers are characterized by differences in time on task, instructional strategies, curriculums, and teacher/pupil ratio. The first tier (Tier 1) includes universal screening and effective research-based practices implemented classwide in the general education classroom. Student progress for all students is carefully monitored and documented. It is expected that 80% of the general population will be successful.

The 20% that still may experience challenges are then moved to Tier 2, where they receive supplemental small-group instruction (four to six in a group is ideal) for a longer period of time, with different instructional strategies and materials. It is expected that 15% of students will benefit from Tier 2. This instruction can be done by the classroom teacher or other staff if available and is in addition to the regular classroom instruction.

Students that require a greater level of support, increasing in intensity and specificity (usually not more than 5% of all students) are moved to Tier 3. Tier 3 includes one-to-one instruction for increased periods of time with different materials and instructional strategies; it may be done by personnel with additional training. All interventions, whether Tier 1, 2, or 3, should be evidence based. An intervention can be considered to have a strong evidence base if it has been shown to be effective in at least three high-quality studies (Gersten, 2009).

Progress monitoring is a key component of RTI. Monitoring student progress entails collecting repeated measurements of student performance. The purpose of progress monitoring is to provide data that can inform instruction. Measurements are taken prior to intervention (baseline) and throughout implementation of intervention(s). These measurements are graphed to create a visual display of student learning. The instruments for progress monitoring provide a snapshot of a student's understanding and should focus on a single or small number of concepts and problems. They are not meant to provide an exhaustive examination of the student's mathematical ability, but rather to serve as probes, giving the teacher a series of work samples on which to conduct an error pattern analysis, which will help guide systematic and explicit intervention.

Teachers can note any error pattern and determine whether the error pattern indicates a conceptual or procedural nonunderstanding. For example, while doing a division problem, if the student consistently adds or subtracts instead of dividing, or if a student's responses are random guesses, it is likely that the student does not understand the division process (conceptual nonunderstanding). Frequency of measures can vary from every day to once every week or once a month depending on the tier. Teachers should monitor the progress of Tier 2, Tier 3, and borderline Tier 1 students using grade appropriate curriculum-embedded assessments.

Fidelity of implementation is the delivery of content and instructional strategies in the way in which they were designed and intended to be delivered: accurately and consistently. Although interventions are aimed at learners, fidelity measures focus on the individuals who provide the instruction (Gresham, MacMillan, Beebe-Frankenberger, & Bocian, 2000). Teachers must be provided with professional development that models the correct way to implement an instructional strategy and given support from a person trained in that strategy. If an instructional strategy is implemented differently each time the teacher works with the child, it is impossible to ascertain if the strategy is or would be effective for that student. Table 6.4 describes the practices needed to ensure fidelity of implementation, based on the work of Gresham et al. (2000).

Table 6.4   Practices to Ensure Fidelity of Implementation

Linking interventions to improved outcomes
Definitively describing operations, techniques, and components
Clearly defining responsibilities of specific persons
Creating data systems for measuring operations, techniques, and components
Constructing a system for feedback and decision making
Implementing accountability measures for noncompliance

Source: Gresham, MacMillan, Beebe-Frankenberger, & Bocian (2000).

Tier 1 mathematics intervention instruction should be research based and systematic, and it should include procedure, concepts, and word problems on the same mathematical topic. Teachers should use contrasting examples and models and smaller problem sets, and they should ask students how they arrived at their answers. "Intervention materials should include opportunities for the student to work with visual representations of mathematical ideas, and interventionists should be proficient in the use of visual representations of mathematical ideas" (National Center for Education Evaluation and Regional Assistance [NCEERA], 2009, p. 30). Students who have difficulty learning mathematics typically lack important conceptual knowledge, have anxiety about mathematics, and may have visual as well as auditory processing difficulties. Assessment should include grade-appropriate short quizzes or checklists (probes) prior to intervention (as a baseline measurement) and throughout the intervention process. The focus of the intervention should be on a single concept, or on a small number of concepts and problems, and the student's understanding of this focus should be assessed several times over the course of instruction. Assessment outcomes should be graphed. Often, students benefit from seeing the graph of their progress over time.

Tier 2 mathematics intervention involves using different curricula with small groups of students, and it should be conducted by trained and supervised personnel. Effective Tier 2 interventions should be targeted to the student deficit, occur three to five times per week in addition to the time allotted for core mathematics instruction, and last approximately 30 minutes per day (Burns, Hall-Lande, Lyman, Rogers, & Tan, 2006).

Tier 3 math intervention requires individual instruction implemented by a special education teacher or other specialist with more training in teaching diverse populations. It includes some one-to-one work and more intense methods. As with Tier 2, different curriculum materials, different instructional methods, and increased time on task are components of Tier 3 intervention. "This includes providing models of proficient problem solving, verbalization of thought processes, guided practice, corrective feedback, and frequent cumulative review" (NCEERA, 2009, p. 6). A number of national organizations have made recommendations for the implementation of RTI programs in mathematics. The recommendations for the implementation of RTI from the NCEERA (2009) are shown in Table 6.5.

Table 6.5 Recommendations for the Implementation of RTI

Recommendations
1. Screen all students to identify those at risk for potential mathematics difficulties, and provide interventions to students identified as at risk.
2. Instructional materials for students receiving interventions should focus intensely on in-depth treatment of whole numbers in kindergarten through Grade 5 and on rational numbers in grades 4 through 8. These materials should be selected by committee.
3. Instruction during the intervention should be explicit and systematic. This includes providing models of proficient problem solving, verbalization of thought processes, guided practice, corrective feedback, and frequent cumulative review.
4. Interventions should include instruction on solving word problems that is based on common underlying structures.
5. Intervention materials should include opportunities for students to work with visual representations of mathematical ideas, and interventionists should be proficient in the use of visual representations of mathematical ideas.
6. Interventions at all grade levels should devote about 10 minutes in each session to building fluent retrieval of basic arithmetic facts.
7. Monitor the progress of students receiving supplemental instruction and other students who are at risk.
8. Include motivational strategies in Tier 2 and Tier 3 interventions.

Source: National Center for Education Evaluation and Regional Assistance (2009, p. 6).

Now let's take another look at Mrs. Thomas's work with Melissa as she implements the three tiers of RTI.

STRATEGIES TO TEACH
PROBLEM SOLVING IN TIERS 1, 2, AND 3

Tier 1

As a first step, Mrs. Thomas identified the specific concept at which to target intervention, problem solving. She administered a probe—a short targeted assessment—of two different one-step whole number word problems, one each in addition and subtraction; and two different two-step problems, one each in addition and subtraction; to identify Melissa's proficiency in whole number functions as well as one- and two-step problems. Melissa did not correctly solve any of the word problems. Mrs. Thomas then administered a probe to see if Melissa had the foundation skills to solve addition and subtraction problems correctly when the problems were given to her as standalone problems. Melissa could solve these problems correctly, so Mrs. Thomas focused her intervention on the problem-solving skills.

If Mrs. Thomas had found errors in Melissa's computational skills, she would have done an error pattern analysis to drill deeper to diagnose the concepts to address. Mrs. Thomas could use an error pattern analysis checklist like the one shown in Table 6.6 to guide her instruction.

Table 6.6   Error Pattern Analysis Checklist for Addition and Subtraction

Check if Present	Observed Error	Cause to Probe
	The sums of the ones and tens are each recorded without regrouping.	A lack of regard for or nonunderstanding of place value.
	All digits are added together.	Inaccurate procedure (algorithm) and a lack of regard for place value.
	Digits are added from left to right. When the sum of a column is greater than 10, the "unit," or "ones" placeholder is carried to the column on the right.	Inaccurate procedure (algorithm) and a lack of regard for place value.

Check if Present	Observed Error	Cause to Probe
	The smaller number is always subtracted from the larger number without regard to placement of the number.	Either misunderstanding of the importance of place value or a visual/motor deficit that makes the regrouping process difficult.
	Regrouping is used when it is not needed.	Inaccurate procedure (algorithm).
	When regrouping is needed more than once, the correct value is not subtracted from the column borrowed from in the second regrouping.	Inaccurate procedure (algorithm).

Source: Adapted from Mercer & Mercer (1997).

The Tier 1 intervention was direct teaching of problem-solving strategies, 45 minutes a week in the regular classroom. This was accomplished by breaking the class into groups one day a week by ability. Data were collected once a week and examined after six weeks. The probes used were five-question word problems from www.interventioncentral.org.

Mrs. Thomas used a research-based explicit teaching instructional technique. She focused on helping Melissa to identify and use the cognitive processes needed for successful mathematical problem solving, including reading the problem for understanding, paraphrasing the problem by putting it into her own words, hypothesizing or making a plan to solve the problem, estimating or predicting the outcome, computing or doing the arithmetic, and checking to make sure the plan was appropriate and the answer is correct (Montague, Warger, & Morgan, 2000). Melissa did not make adequate progress in Tier 1, so Mrs. Thomas, in consultation with the building team, moved Melissa to Tier 2.

Tier 2

With the assistance of the math specialist and the building team, Mrs. Thomas decided to implement Tier 2 with a different problem-solving strategy, the RIDD strategy—read, imagine, decide, and do (Jackson, 2002). This strategy, like all interventions, should take place in an area free of distractions and large enough to allow for the proper materials and movement needed for the intervention (Riccomini & Witzel, 2010). The strategy was implemented four times a week for 20 minutes. Progress monitoring continued, with probes once a week for four weeks. The RIDD strategy is described in Table 6.7.

Table 6.7 The RIDD Strategy

Read	"Read the passage from the first capital letter to the last mark without stopping." This helps students to focus on entire task rather than reading one line at a time. For younger students, teachers must model this step, since these students may not even be reading yet. Call attention to the first capital and the last punctuation mark of the passage.
Imagine	"Imagine or make a mental picture of what you have read." This technique helps students focus on the concept being presented and provides a self-monitoring procedure. It helps them to link pictures to information, and it facilitates their retention.
Decide	"Decide what to do." Choose the first step in solving the problem, or decide if you need help or should reread the problem.
Do	"Do the work." Complete the problem, and explain how you did the written work.

Source: Jackson (2002, pp. 280–281).

Tier 2 used two research-based strategies: RIDD and the use of visual representations. Effective visual representations, whether on paper or in one's imagination, show the relationships among the problem parts and may be helpful to some students (Van Garderen & Montague, 2003). Unfortunately Melissa did not make progress during Tier 2, so the building team moved Melissa to Tier 3 intervention with different curricula, increased instructional time, and different implementation personnel.

Tier 3

In Tier 3, the schema strategy was used for problem solving. The building math specialist, Ms. Hall, taught with Mrs. Thomas for the first three sessions to demonstrate the strategy so Mrs. Thomas could become familiar with it. Ms. Hall then made visits to the classroom to implement the strategy one-on-one with Melissa 30 minutes a day for four weeks. The instruction focused on Melissa learning to recognize the problem pattern and translating the words into a graphic representation. Melissa was shown how to organize and represent information in the story in diagrams using three types of schema:

1. The Change Schema—Problems include a set of information that indicates change in other information in the problem.

2. The Group Schema—Items are grouped together from various sets.

3. The Comparison Schema—Problems require students to determine and subsequently compare values.

This Tier 3 strategy uses graphic organizers. These have been helpful to some students in mathematics, because external representation may reduce the learner's cognitive processing load and may make more of the student's short-term memory available for engaging in analysis and solution. Miller (1956) has argued that short-term memory (or attention span) has limitations in respect to the amount of information it can hold and retain. A graphic organizer creates a "picture" of the problem to solve, and therefore the short-term memory does not have to imagine the picture and can focus on finding the solution. The schema goes beyond mastery of the algorithm to the semantic structure of the problem (Jitendra, 2002). In a study of gifted students, average students, and students with learning disabilities, successful mathematical problem solving was positively correlated with use of schematic representations (Van Garderen & Montague, 2003). The Tier 3 strategies worked for Melissa, and while Mrs. Thomas will continue to monitor Melissa's work on the core curriculum, Melissa will not be referred for special education screening at this time. Table 6.8 shows Melissa's three-tiered RTI plan.

Table 6.8   Melissa's Three-Tiered RTI Plan

Tier	Who	What	Where	When
1	Mrs. Thomas	Probes are administered to diagnose Melissa's mathematical challenges.	In the general education classroom.	During daily mathematics core instruction **and** 45 extra minutes a week.

(Continued)

(Continued)

Tier	Who	What	Where	When
		Intervention is implemented of explicit instruction in the cognitive processes needed to problem solve, including direct teaching of problem-solving strategies.		
2	Mrs. Thomas	The RIDD strategy—read, imagine, decide, and do is implemented.	In the general education classroom.	During daily mathematics core instruction **and** four extra 20-minute periods each week.
3	Ms. Hall, math specialist	The schema strategy is implemented.	In the general education classroom.	During daily mathematics core instruction **and** daily extra 30-minute periods for four weeks.

Some students with and without special needs have difficulty with mathematics, including comprehending and making generalizations about math skills and concepts (Rivera & Bryant, 1992). In some cases students may have a severe difficulty in reading that affects their proficiency in mathematics when they struggle to read word problems from their mathematics textbooks, handouts, and directions on mathematics tests or assignment sheets (Hughes & Kolsyad, 1994). Educators need to be aware of these conditions, identify the difficulties, and devise strategies that do not include watering down the material, which would be a disservice to all students (Kimmel, Deek, Farrell, & O'Shea, 1999).

While to accurately diagnose a student with dyscalculia multiple assessments must be used, there are specific learner characteristics that when observed may assist teachers to identify the difference between mathematical difficulty and dyscalculia. Table 6.9 is not an exhaustive list of these characteristics, but it may provide some guidance when added to other evidence.

Table 6.9   Clues Observed in Some Students With Dyscalculia

Trouble recognizing printed numbers.
Trouble learning math facts (addition, subtraction, multiplication, division).
Inconsistent computation results in addition, subtraction, multiplication, and division.
May not be able to understand the meaning of some mathematical symbols, such as +, −, ×.
Inability to understand math processes (order of operations, etc.), and basic addition, subtraction, multiplication, and division facts.
Difficulty with time and money concepts.
Difficulty with geographical locations of states, countries, oceans, streets, and so forth.
Difficulty keeping score during games, or difficulty remembering how to keep score.
Trouble with mental math.
Difficulty finding different approaches to problem solving.

CONCLUSION

All teachers, both general educators and special educators, are required to prepare all students in their charge to reach the new benchmarks set by state and national standards, even though all educators may not necessarily have been trained in content, methods, and strategies to educate their diverse learning populations. This chapter is only a short overview that is designed to assist teachers with strategies to help their students reach those benchmarks. The shift in education practice guided by local, state, and federal regulations has resulted in a call to action for all educators to become proficient in research-based instructional practices that will allow all students to learn mathematics. This will enable educators to participate in the accurate diagnosis of students who need special education interventions. RTI is one tool to help educators in that effort.

TECH BYTE

MATHEMATICS-SPECIFIC RESOURCES

National Center on Response to Intervention: RTI and Mathematics

(www.rti4success.org/index.php?option=com_content&task=view&id=1403&Itemid=75)

This site contains a webinar, led by Dr. Russell Gersten, director of the instructional research group and professor emeritus at the University of Oregon, presented on November 18, 2009. The webinar includes an overview of the research related to RTI and mathematics. Dr. Gersten describes specific guidelines for implementation of RTI in mathematics for grades K–7, including effective instructional practices for interventions, and strategies for screening, progress monitoring, and selecting intervention curricula. The site contains the transcript of the webinar as well as a PDF version of the slides used in it. The site was created by the American Institutes for Research, and it is supported by U.S. Department of Education Office of Special Education Programs.

Dr. Lynn Fuchs on RTI and Mathematics

(www.rti4success.org/index.php?option=com_content&task=view&id=1399)

This site, within the National Center on Response to Intervention: RTI and Mathematics home page, features a brief discussion by Lynn Fuchs, a nationally renowned authority in RTI, speaking on the differences between the use of RTI in math and its use in reading.

RESOURCES

RTI Action Network. (www.rtinetwork.org/)

RTI Action Network is one of the largest and most sophisticated sources for response to intervention foundations, strategies, and materials. The home page presents a matrix of five key areas for inquiry (Learn About RTI; Get Started; Essential Components; Connect with Others; and Professional Development). Each of these is plotted across five areas of application (Pre-K; K–5; Middle School; High School; Parents and Families). Within these 25 starting points, a search can uncover hundreds of references and resources for RTI, including mathematics, technology, and their interaction within the RTI framework.

Database of Mathematics Standards. (www.floridastandards .org/Standards/FLStandardSearch.aspx)

This site provides benchmarks by grade level of mathematical skills aligned with the Florida state standards. The site is rich in resources for teachers and is a link off of http://rtitlc.ucf.edu, the site of the RTI-TLC project sponsored and funded by the State of Florida Department of Education. The resources include math games and activities and links to other resources.

Intervention: *I CAN Learn Pre-Algebra* and *I CAN Learn Algebra*. (http://ies.ed.gov/ncee/wwc/reports/middle_math/iclprea/)

This site describes five studies of two software programs, *I CAN Learn Pre-Algebra* and *I CAN Learn Algebra,* that have met the rigorous standards of the What Works Clearinghouse (WWC) for evidence. One study met the evidence standards, and four studies met the standards with reservations. The five studies included 16,519 eighth-grade students from middle schools in California, Florida, Georgia, and Louisiana. Based on these five studies, the WWC considered the extent of evidence to be medium to large that *I CAN Learn Pre-Algebra* and *I CAN Learn Algebra* are effective for increasing math achievement.

The Expert Mathematician. (http://ies.ed.gov/ncee/ wwc/reports/middle_math/expert_math/)

The site describes a study of 90 eighth-grade students in a middle school in St. Louis, Missouri, using the software program *The Expert Mathematician.* The program includes three years of instruction and covers general mathematics, prealgebra, and algebra. The developer describes the curriculum as covering the range of concepts and content areas in the National Council of Teachers of Mathematics Curriculum and Evaluation Standards. One study on *The Expert Mathematician* met the WWC evidence standards.

Response to Intervention and Positive Behavior Support

7

C. Faith Kappenberg and John Kappenberg

Miguel is a 14-year-old boy in the eighth grade who is impulsive, easily distracted, and generally a C student. He is viewed as likeable by teachers and students. His classes range in size from 28 to 36. In the last four months, three of his four teachers have become concerned about his increasing lack of cooperation and rude remarks toward classmates. His achievement tests place him slightly below grade level. A psychological evaluation from third grade indicated a full scale IQ of 95, a verbal IQ of 112, and a performance IQ of 90. His schoolwork is erratic, and homework is rarely submitted.

His social studies teacher, who maintains strict control of him in her classroom, reports that he is maintaining Cs but could be a B+ and A student. Similar efforts by his other teachers to enforce stricter discipline and consequences seem to be making him more defiant. This has caused some tension between his social studies teacher and his other teachers, who have commented that they are being blamed for Miguel's underachievement and deterioration.

Tier 1 formative academic assessment through progress monitoring reveals that Miguel's performance is extremely erratic. Reading comprehension is good and appears to be above grade level. Some of the paragraphs he writes are well written, while others are a jumble of phrases. Math skills are weak, but sometimes he completes word problems better than equations. He has learned most of his social studies content, but class work and homework are often sloppy and incomplete. He is now failing science and has been sent to the dean five times in the past month for rude remarks.

Tier 2 RTI academic interventions, such as moving his seat in front of the teachers and requiring three days a week at afterschool homework help, are not working. Tier 2 progress monitoring shows a slow but continuing decline.

In addition, Miguel has cooperated with informal weekly counseling, but this has generated more disagreement between the teachers who are at odds over "coddling" Miguel, because counseling is "giving him one more excuse to get out of his responsibilities in his classes." Observations that Miguel has been overheard talking more and more about gang initiations and seen hanging out with gang members raises more concerns about at-risk behaviors and an evaluation for oppositional defiant disorder, ADHD, and special education classification. The teachers agree that before they move to Tier 3 academic and positive behavior support (PBS) interventions, a Tier 2 PBS assessment will be coordinated by the school psychologist.

THE RELATIONSHIP BETWEEN PBS AND RTI

RTI and Disruptive Classroom Behavior

One of the most significant aspects of RTI is its application to educational needs outside the purely academic. By embracing comprehensive and scientifically based methods for student behavior and classroom management on an equal basis, RTI forms a single unified framework and skill set. Achieving compatibility of strategies to improve academics and classroom management has long challenged educators. Training teachers to target both areas simultaneously is a dual task that can be huge and daunting. When teaching and behavior management strategies are not compatible, it can be likened to patting your head and rubbing your stomach at the same time. Yet, teachers cannot accurately evaluate learning unless behavior is stabilized.

As a component of RTI, PBS provides the tools that are essential for stabilizing and improving a student's behavior, self-esteem, and relationships in general education classes, as well as in inclusive settings. It is also an essential foundation for a child's preparedness for academic work. As a system within RTI, PBS shifts the burden on the teacher from competency to "manage" the class and "control" the student's disruptive behavior to identifying causes of inappropriate behavior, encouraging positive behaviors, and monitoring interventions.

Positive Behavior Support: PBS Defined

PBS is a form of behavior analysis that has been thoroughly researched in scores of juried studies. It is designed to decrease the most serious and complex challenging behaviors by reducing the likelihood of punishment and aversive techniques, which can have the negative effect of prolonging and even worsening challenging behaviors (Carr et al., 1999). Its essential elements include development of hypotheses, functional behavior assessment (FBA), person-centered planning, collaboration and team building, systems change within schools, and evaluation (Carr et al., 1999)—analogs to the components of RTI, applied to behavior rather than academic achievement.

In contrast to older, more tradition forms of behavior analysis and behavior management, PBS emphasizes analysis, progress monitoring, and interventions that use positive reinforcement and naturally occurring positive experiences in the student's environment. As PBS developed, experts expanded its methods to incorporate principles such as context, a systematic examination of all the potential factors that may influence behavior change (Carr et al., 1999).

PBS is also known as *positive behavior intervention support* or PBIS, suggesting its close linkage to RTI (Sugai et al., 2000). Both terms have been used to describe schoolwide and statewide efforts to implement and monitor comprehensive initiatives in our schools to decrease problem behavior and precursors to violence and to support prosocial behavior. *Schoolwide positive behavior support*, also known as SWPBS (Office of Special Education Programs, Center on Positive Behavioral Interventions and Supports, 2004), employs a series of RTI tiers, or continuum of behavior support strategies of universal supports, for the entire school. This includes targeted strategies for students who have been identified to be at risk, plus intensive assessment and intervention for students who struggle with chronic behavior problems (Mueller & Brewer, 2008).

The transformation of PBS from behavioral science to educational program and policy has had a significant influence on RTI—some of it welcomed, some of it challenging. As PBS and RTI—systems previously unknown in schools of education and foreign to traditional elementary and secondary educators—are adopted by (some would say forced upon) American schools, they are sometimes experienced as encroachment on professional turf; chaotic, unwanted change; a quick fix without adequate training and support; or just the latest fad.

Chapter 1 introduced RTI as a "three-tier composite of academic and behavioral spheres" that, in fact, interact with one another, rather than being parallel but isolated. The illustration shows the RTI process as a three-tier composite of academic and behavioral spheres, and it suggests that these reflect and reinforce one another. This model is based on an understanding, rooted in PBS, that academic performance is a form of student behavior. The two spheres are interdependent and inseparable, meaning that an RTI program needs to evaluate all aspects of a child's performance in school: curriculum work (academics, which is a form of behavior) and social interactions (behavior, which strongly affects academics). PBS is scientifically and nationally recognized as the most effective approach to integrating both spheres of a child's life.

The Evolution of RTI and PBS

While the integration of RTI for academic and behavioral needs is a significant achievement, it is a fairly recent paradigm. The use of PBS as a component of RTI can raise many questions and much confusion. Is PBS part of RTI, or is it a separate triangle? How does it fit in RTI? Is it just for Tier 3? Is it a separate Tier 4? How do we fit the academics and behavior elements of each tier together?

This confusion stems from historic separation of behavior management as the realm of behavioral science and mental health professionals, and academic remediation as the realm of teachers and educators. Also, it is rooted in the assumption by specialists in each camp that, as specialists, they are not required to explain and demonstrate the connection. As a result, there has been a lack of interface between academic and behavioral interventions in the RTI literature (Mueller & Brewer, 2008), and only recently have the two camps attempted to merge. Outstanding books and articles on PBS, and more authoritative publications on RTI, are being published. However even the most recent PBS publications never or barely mention the powerful similarities and parallel processes of RTI and PBS (Mueller & Brewer, 2008).

APPLYING PBS WITHIN AN RTI PROGRAM

Since, as we have seen, student success in academics needs to be understood as a form of behavior, overcoming impediments to learning depends on systematic examination of all the potential factors that may influence the elements of academic success, such as information processing, learning, and classroom behavior. In fact, the link between behavior and academics has long been recognized. Sandomierski, Kincaid, and Algozzine (2007) recently reported as follows:

> Most educators would agree that it is rare to find a student who has behavior challenges who does not also have academic challenges, and many times the behavioral problems originate

because of the student's inability to succeed academically at a level comparable to his/her peers. An analysis conducted by the FL PBS Project of three schools in Florida found that over 80% of all students identified as having severe behavioral problems were also identified by their teachers as having academic problems. If a student has shown a poor response to universal and classroom-level behavioral interventions, his/her academic proficiency should be assessed. (pp. 4–5)

Thus, both RTI and PBS depend on explicit, graphic depictions of the processes that all scientific methods of investigation require.

The Building Blocks for Living and Learning

One effective starting point is the graphic shown in Figure 7.1.

Figure 7.1 Building Blocks for Living and Learning

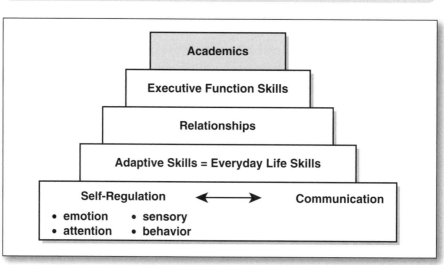

Similar to a Maslow-type hierarchy of needs (Maslow, 1943), this is a series of interdependent stages depicting the growth of capabilities within an individual. In the area of human behavior, the model follows a path similar to Maslow's hierarchy of needs, in which an individual becomes capable of higher order functioning only after lower level needs have been met. In Maslow's frame, satisfaction of physical needs allows for a sense of personal safety and stability; security then makes socialization possible;

interaction with others produces self-esteem; and only when all these needs have been met is a person capable of what Maslow calls "self-actualization," of self-fulfillment.

In the Building Blocks for Living and Learning, growth necessarily starts from a foundation of self-regulation and communication. Only then does one become capable of higher order behavior: adaptive skills, executive functioning, relationships, and finally—only after all of the foundational capabilities have been reached—academic achievement.

But there is an alternative vision of this, shown in Figure 7.1a, that turns the relationships upside down.

Figure 7.1a Building Blocks for Living and Learning, Alternative
Paradigm: A Challenge for Educators and Parents

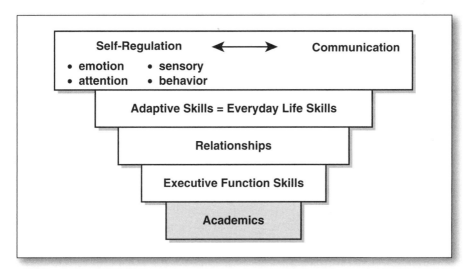

This is the paradigm that educators, parents, and of course, children, often face. Academics is seen as the foundation and purpose of a school's programs. The assumption is that academics can be learned independently of the student's foundational needs, and that these other needs can be carried along and developed within purely academic interventions. In short, academics can carry the full weight of a child's success in school.

Educators and parents of struggling students, who have attempted to work within this paradigm, understand that the results almost always collapse, as shown in Figure 7.1b.

Figure 7.1b   Building Blocks for Living and Learning, Alternative
Paradigm: Collapse

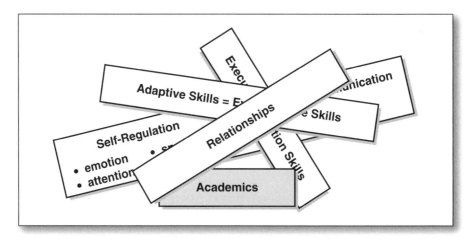

Self-regulation, adaptive skills, executive functions, and relationships come crashing down around an all-consuming emphasis on academics, high-stakes testing, and academic regulations.

Initially, when the authors presented these diagrams, they anticipated resistance from teachers and administrators, since (1) academics, curriculum, and instruction composed such a small portion of the building blocks graphic, and (2) the activities that have been considered foundational to the traditional paradigm of education (academics and learning) are portrayed as totally dependent on elements that are completely beyond pedagogical skills. And while academics held the position at the top of the living and learning hierarchy, as a goal to be attained, it drew the least attention in the graphic.

However, at every training session with educators, the reverse occurred: We received reflective and grateful responses that the magnitude of demands and expectations of a classroom teacher were so thoroughly acknowledged. When we understand the reasons why students have difficulties with behavior, we have a better understanding of the close relationship between PPS and RTI.

At the base of the diagram, the primary foundation block shows the interdependency of behavior (which is profoundly determined by a person's level of self-regulation) and communication (which is the visible expression of self-regulation). It conveys the principle that all behavior communicates a need, and all communication, whether positive or negative, is a form of behavior. You can't teach, and your student can't learn, unless the student's emotions, impulses, and attention are intact. (Every preservice teacher is made aware of this when the supervising teacher presents the time-honored initiation lecture: "You cannot teach a class until the children are orderly and under control.")

After self-regulation, a child needs to master the basic adaptive or daily living skills needed for independent living. These include hygiene, nutrition, functional safety, and the other physical needs in Maslow's hierarchy. They are the basis for what will become personal integrity: a sense that one can demonstrate the ability to control and fulfill the most basic physical needs of life. This, of course, depends on some level of mastery of self-regulation.

When adaptive skills are secured, the next foundation block is the ability to move from regulating one's own behavior to forming productive relationships with peers, teachers, and family—what Stephen Covey calls the move from independence to the higher level of interdependence (Covey, 1989). This refers to the interdependency, self-restraint, and awareness of alternative perspectives that are required to work successfully with others.

And moving up to the next block, executive function skills are equally important for living and learning. The executive functions include higher levels of adaptability to the outside world, such as the ability to shift attention, plan, organize, and think flexibly, among many other skills. They are seen in behaviors such as withholding inappropriate responses, resolving conflicts, flexibility in responding to interpersonal encounters, adjusting a response when it appears to be counterproductive, and testing hypotheses about events and people.

To manage academics, children and adolescents need to master all of these foundation skills. Without capability in the foundation skills, no purely academic intervention within RTI—no matter how successful it may be in national peer reviewed studies—can succeed. The interdependency between behavioral and academic activity becomes all too clear when they are not in sync.

But what happens when a child has not had an opportunity to learn the foundation skills, and educators are compelled to focus on academics and test preparation? What happens if the focus on academic standards forces administrators to sacrifice resources needed for students to master the foundation blocks? This becomes a major frustration and anxiety for teachers and students. And it often creates desperation in parents who have children with learning problems but are offered only pedagogical remedies in school. Many of these parents become a major source of disruption and strain for both general and special education, as discussed in Chapter 8.

In terms of an RTI program, a focus only on academic interventions, to the exclusion of interventions focused on behavioral and foundation skills, can lead to failure that could have been averted. It is the kind of failure that one sees in novice teachers who focus only on teaching the curriculum while ignoring the misbehavior that prevents the class from learning.

One of the major reasons why RTI programs become ineffective is that educational standards and curricula tend to rush past adaptive skills much too quickly for children with complex, multiple learning delays, placing enormous pressure on educators and parents. The dilemma is clear: We are asking so much of our educators.

When we started using the foundational graphics in presentations to educators, we were concerned that we might offend or further polarize professionals, but we soon found that both educators and parents appreciate how these descriptions convey the enormity of the task of educating children. They know that the constraints on both educators and parents come from issues much deeper than personality conflicts and petty disputes. The benefit of this analysis of foundation skills is in at least allowing all parties to be aware of why teaching and learning are so complex, and why an individualized RTI program depends as much on attention to behavior as it does on attention to academics.

FROM BUILDING BLOCKS TO TIERS

Fundamental Principles of PBS as It Relates to RTI

Awareness of the integral role of behavior in academic success calls for a broader understanding of the RTI method than is typically offered. One often-cited description of RTI is "the practice of providing high-quality instruction and interventions matched to student need, monitoring progress frequently to make decisions about changes in instruction or goals, and applying child response data to important educational decisions" (Batsche et al., 2006, p. 6). The focus on the problem-solving, outcome-based aspect of RTI is what separates it from the input-oriented approaches of past generations.

However, the rigorous, intervention-based method of RTI requires that educators recognize the full range of learning areas—academic, behavioral, and foundational—that need to be addressed, and that they have access to a full range of potential interventions for each of these areas. As RTI teachers and teams review the possible responses for a struggling student, it is important to consider which sphere (academic or behavioral) as well as which tier (first, second, or third) is appropriate for a particular child. In this chapter, we are focusing on the role that PBS can play in responding to students like Miguel, whose academic difficulties may be rooted in the behavioral and foundational sphere. Within this sphere, we will consider how PBS might become an effective intervention in each of the three tiers.

Behavioral Intervention in Tier 1

Academic standards for the general education program (Tier 1) are fairly easy to set, and the range of interventions is relatively well known. The skills are readily practiced and measured, the scope and sequence of the curriculum are typically defined statewide, and teachers can download an almost limitless number of lesson plans from the Internet.

With behavior, goals are often harder to define, interventions less well known and tested, success and failure less distinct and quantifiable. An RTI team, such as Miguel's, that works in the behavioral sphere faces a much greater challenge than does one in the academic area.

Traditionally, the only really measurable and quantifiable data on student behavior have come from the official referrals to the principal's office for discipline (often referred to by the color of the paper it is written on: "pink slip" or "blue slip") (Clonin, McDougal, Clark, & Davison, 2007). However, clinicians have long known that these externalized actions capture only a small portion of the negative behaviors that can affect academic success. A much greater number of students suffer from internalized disturbances that may never be revealed unless school professionals are sensitive to the possibility (Nelson, Benner, Reid, Epstein, & Currin, 2002).

One of the great advances of RTI over traditional student evaluation processes (such as the wait-to-fail model discussed in Chapter 5) is its reliance on proactive identification of students who may be at risk, and the use of early interventions that might prevent this. Unfortunately, as recently as 2007, few reliable screening processes existed for intervention in the behavioral sphere of RTI (Sandomierski et al., 2007). Those who understand the importance of behavior to academic success must also understand that they will need to become pioneers in developing and testing methods for identifying the full range of at-risk students and of developing interventions that work.

At the hands-on level, the CHAMPs (Conversation-Help-Activity-Movement-Participation-Success) model by Randy Sprick (2009) is one of a few effective approaches to PBS for a boy like Miguel in the Tier 1, general education setting. It allows general education classroom teachers to design a proactive and positive approach to classroom management that has been proven successful for large numbers of struggling students in a clear, teacher- and student-friendly system of five prosocial behaviors.

CHAMPS allows the teacher to identify the behaviors they want to see and then teach what these behaviors look like in the classroom by giving students specific behaviors to practice. Visual reminders and expectations are posted and reinforced at all times. Teachers and administrators may look to these and a number of other developing practices for Tier 1 general education behavior intervention, but these need to be tested and the results reported.

Behavioral Intervention in Tier 2

When general education interventions fail to improve behavior for students in Tier 1, or when academic interventions do not succeed and clinicians suspect that a hidden foundational issue may be the cause, an RTI team should recommend moving a student to additional support in Tier 2. Here, interventions can be used in a more focused, small-group context, and additional time may be available.

One approach that might be attempted for a child like Miguel, who has given indications of possible gang involvement, would be the "check-in/ check-out" behavior education program developed by Hawken, Pettersson, Mootz, and Anderson (2006). In this case, Miguel would be assigned a positive adult role model, be provided with the structure that may be lacking in his life, be given examples regularly of behaviors that would produce success within his personal frame of values, and receive frequent feedback on both his positive and negative behaviors.

Other Tier 2 interventions the team might choose for Miguel could be a peer mentoring program (if it exists in his school), group counseling, and many of the social support groups that are typically available in secondary schools. The difference that RTI and PBS would make is in the systematic collection of data on Miguel's response to the interventions that the team recommends, as well as in the support of a wide range of stakeholders, including teachers, mentors, professional mental health clinicians, and equally important, input from parents who can report on the effect of interventions outside the school environment.

Behavioral Intervention in Tier 3

If Miguel continues to struggle with his academics in spite of Tier 2 interventions, and after thorough review of clinical as well as educational data, the RTI–PBS team may recommend that he needs the intense intervention of Tier 3. This step would have to include a reanalysis of all the data from Tier 1 and Tier 2, looking particularly for potential causes or interventions that had been overlooked. This is the point at which the team develops the skills practiced by research scientists; their work combines use of the scientific method with creative hypothesis generating and problem solving. Those closest to Miguel—his classroom teacher and parent—should have the largest role in this stage of the process.

The team may elect to do a full functional behavior assessment (FBA) developed by professionals. The FBA will collect extensive data, represented by the acronym ABC, to identify (A) the antecedents that may have precipitated negative behavior, (B) the behavior itself, which may reveal patterns that can lead to understanding the cause, and (C) the consequences of the behavior. This will reveal whether Miguel is gaining reinforcement from negative behaviors more than staff realizes.

This would then lead to the team asking for a professionally developed behavior improvement plan (BIP), which would recommend specific interventions based on the data gathered from the FBA. The team would closely monitor Miguel's full range of behavior and academic performance for a predetermined period of time before making additional recommendations, which could include accommodations under federal Section 504 legislation, classification to a special educational program, or another clinical intervention.

THE FUTURE FOR MIGUEL AND PBS

The encouraging aspect of the RTI–PBS approach is that Miguel, and millions of students like him, may soon have the advantage of a school system that has the expertise to solve his individual learning problems. In recent years, we have learned several important points through our use of PBS and RTI:

1. Academics and behavior are inseparable components of every child's life at school, and they are interdependent spheres within the RTI process.

2. Within RTI, a focus on academic interventions alone is almost guaranteed to be inadequate at best and a failure at worst.

3. Within PBS, the full range of expertise is needed to discover the source of a student's difficulties. This includes professional clinicians, but most important, it includes those closest to each child, including the teacher and parent.

4. Of the two interdependent RTI spheres, the behavioral is far more complex than the academic, less studied and understood, more challenging, and, ultimately, more rewarding in terms of success for both the school and the individual student, such as Miguel.

While there are years of work and development ahead, the recognition of the inseparability of academics and behavior represents a genuine paradigm shift in learning and education—and this may be the greatest hope for children like Miguel.

 TECH BYTE

FLORIDA'S POSITIVE BEHAVIOR SUPPORT PROJECT

One of the most experienced states in the nation in the area of RTI and PBS is Florida. A good example of the depth and breadth of work being done in both the universities and schools can be seen in Florida's Positive Behavior Support Project website (http://flpbs.fmhi.usf.edu/), maintained by the State of Florida Department of Education since 2002. The home page is shown in Figure 7.2.

Figure 7.2   Screenshot of Home Page for Florida's Positive Behavior Support Project

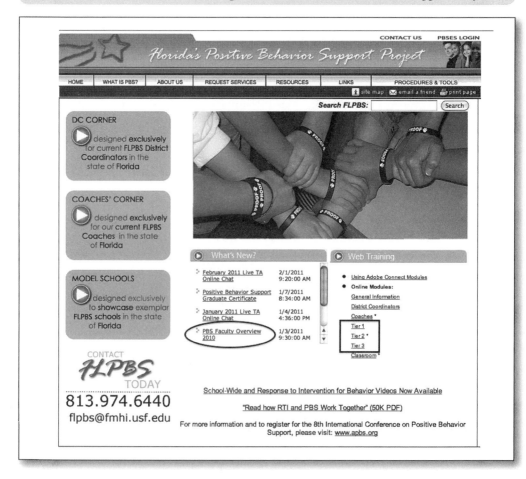

In the left-hand column are links to resources for the state's district PBS coordinators and PBS coaches, as well as to a showcase featuring schools the state has designated as outstanding in their PBS programs.

The center column, under the heading "What's New," includes four buttons linking to events that have occurred within the last 30 days. The bottom link, entitled "PBS Faculty Overview, 2010" (highlighted in an oval), leads to an animated slide show, which presents a 45-minute review of the state's PBS program. Slide 7 of the presentation, summarizing the core principles of PBS and RTI, is shown in Figure 7.3.

Figure 7.3 Screenshot of Slide on Florida's PBS Website

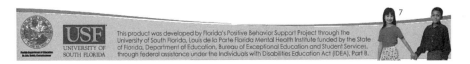

PBS and RtI:B

Core Principles of PBS

- Multi-tiered levels of support
- Team process
- Builds effective environments
- Evidence-based interventions
- Effective problem-solving
- Data-based decision-making
- Progress monitoring
- Fidelity of implementation

RtI:B Critical Components

- Multi-tiered levels of support
- Evidence-based instruction and interventions
- Effective problem-solving
- Data-based decision making
- Progress monitoring
- Fidelity of implementation

This product was developed by Florida's Positive Behavior Support Project through the University of South Florida, Louis de la Parte Florida Mental Health Institute funded by the State of Florida, Department of Education, Bureau of Exceptional Education and Student Services, through federal assistance under the Individuals with Disabilities Education Act (IDEA), Part B.

Returning to the home page (Figure 7.2), the right-hand column, entitled "Web Training," provides access to multiple hours of coordinated, systematic training, available to school districts, universities, and the general public, in a wide range of RTI and PBS topics. Links connect to animated instruction modules geared to district coordinators, PBS coaches, and classroom teachers. Of particular interest are the links (highlighted in a box) that connect to multiple hours of training in implementing PBS for each of the three RTI tiers.

Clicking on the Tier 1 button brings the viewer to a page containing a list of 13 training modules, shown in Figure 7.4, each providing approximately 20 to 30 minutes of instruction within an animated slide show. Topics include "Collaboration and Operation," "Data-based Decision-making System," "Developing Behavior Tracking Forms," "Teaching Appropriate Behavior," and "Implementing School-wide PBS."

Figure 7.4 Screenshot of Florida's Online PBS Training Menu

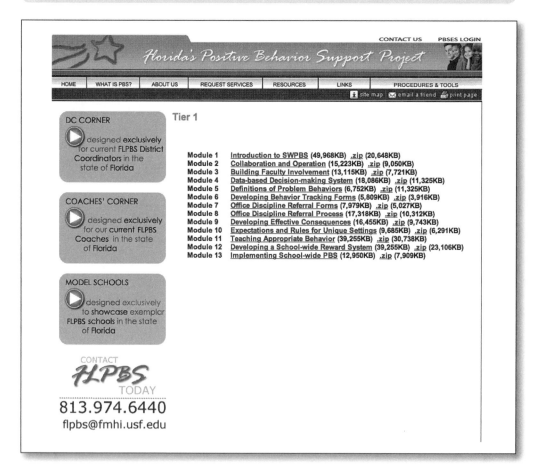

Clicking on "Tier 2" on the home page opens to a list of seven modules, shown in Figure 7.5, prepared specifically for Tier 2 team members, including guidance counselors, psychologists, PBS coaches, and mental health care providers.

The modules are each 60 minutes in length and cover topics such as "Establishing a Foundation for a Tier 2 System," "Targeted Classroom Support," "Measuring Fidelity," and "Making Decisions and Selecting Interventions."

Figure 7.5   Screenshot of Module Menu for Florida's Online PBS Training for Tier 2

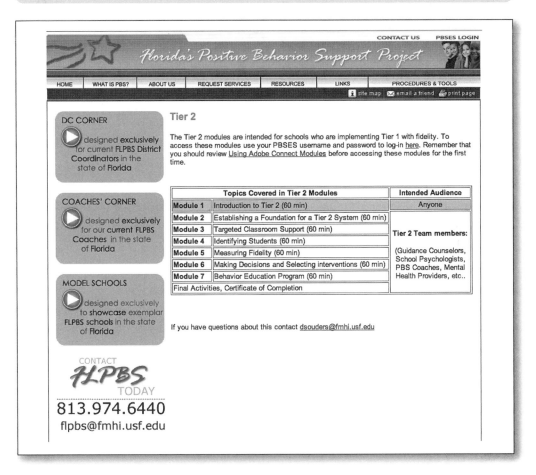

The website is massive, leading to dozens of hours of training. Although it is copyright protected as a state operated resource, it is available to the public without charge or restriction. With adaptation to local conditions, it is capable of sustaining a substantial staff development program in both RTI and PBS.

Emerging Agendas in Collaboration **8**

Working With Families in the RTI Process

John Kappenberg and Helene Fallon

Michelle Jackson is the mother of Andrew, a 12-year-old sixth grader. She is meeting with her son's reading teacher, Mary Hess. Andrew is a bright boy with inconsistent academic scores and frequent behavioral referrals. His parents are having him privately evaluated to determine if he has Asperger syndrome (AS), a form of high-functioning autism, which would qualify him for special education services. His WAIS-IV full-scale IQ measured in the above average to superior range, but social skills assessment places him in the fifth percentile of children his age. Along with all students in his class, Andrew has been evaluated as part of the Tier 1 universal screening process of his school's RTI program. The staff is puzzled by his erratic test results: high on certain days and low on others, with no apparent pattern.

Andrew's middle school program is based on a cohort design, which requires that as much classroom activity as possible be centered on student-peer interaction. This approach was approved by the board of education as a program that would meet state and federal standards for a scientifically based approach to instruction. The decision was widely applauded by the community and the district's professional staff.

The meeting is not going well: It is October, and Ms. Jackson has become increasingly upset over her son's response to the middle school program. She describes to Ms. Hess how Andrew resists going to school, is afraid of his classmates, frequently hides in the closet when it is time for school, and is afraid to be assigned to a new group of peers for an activity. "He wants to do his own work," Michelle tells Ms. Hess. "Isn't that enough to expect of a kid? Why do you insist that he work with other children just to learn how to solve math problems? Once the others start talking, Andrew gets completely confused and intimidated."

Ms. Jackson is a biology professor in the local community college and has used her research skills to become familiar with the presenting behaviors and learning needs of children with AS. She is trying to convince Ms. Hess that the cohort program is positively destructive to her son's educational and neuro-logical needs: Where Andrew needs structure and predictability, the program provides spontaneity and unpredictability; where Andrew needs quiet time, the program produces a high level of activity; where Andrew needs frequent breaks, the program encourages the students to develop mutual responsibility by staying with a project until it is completed.

Ms. Hess is trying to convince Andrew's mother that the cohort program has been through rigorous national testing, that it has been shown to be one of the most effective ways of reaching the largest group of children, that every other parent in the class is thrilled with the response so far, and that all that Andrew needs is a little more time to adjust to the change. "I am certain that Andrew is just showing his preadolescent independence," she tells Ms. Jackson. "In a few more weeks, he'll love being part of the group."

THE TEACHER AS PROFESSIONAL, THE PARENT AS CONSULTANT

It is hard to imagine a more complex aspect of RTI than the involvement of parents. Challenges come from an enormous collection of variables, including the wide array of opinions among professionals over the role that parents ought to play, and an even greater range of parental interest and preparation for participating in their child's formal education. In extreme situations, frustrated, anonymous critics of parent involvement have cited "massive parent disinterest, hostility, litigiousness, and misinformation." Parent advocates sometimes point to "dismissiveness, insensitivity, and aloofness" in the way school officials approach them. In most cases, the parent–teacher relationship is cordial, but it has an unspoken understanding that it involves a professional and a layperson, with the position of the professional normally accepted as authoritative and the role of the layperson as supportive.

The Parent–Professional Relationship

There is little doubt, in either perception or research, that parents play a critical role in the educational success of children (Lent, Brown, &

Hackett, 2000; Schulenberg, Goldstein, & Vondracek, 1991; Young & Friesen, 1992). A Phi Delta Kappa/Gallup Poll of the Public's Attitudes Toward Public Schools (Rose, Gallup, & Elam, 1997) reported that 86% of the public sees parental support as the most effective way to improve schools and, conversely, that lack of parent involvement is perceived as one of the greatest problems facing the schools.

With the passage of the No Child Left Behind Act in 2001, parent involvement—including participation in some of the decision-making processes, as well as support for school programs—became a federally mandated part of American education (Pub. L. 107–110, 20 U.S.C.A. 6301 *et seq.,* §§ 1112, 1114 (b) (2), 1116, and 1118 (a) (1) (2), (b) (2), (b) (2)-(4), (e)). While few parents or professionals have openly objected to this aspect of the law, a great many on both sides of the relationship would quietly prefer that parent–school partnerships remain as they had been for the past hundred years: Trained professionals provide the education, and parents provide support (Dodd & Konzal, 2000). We see examples of this wherever we search for general information on parent involvement. The masthead for a parent-centered website highlights the theme: "Successful parent involvement programs provide the link between the home and school that are essential to the growth and development of children, and enable principals, teachers and parents to work together towards a shared mission on behalf of learners" (Lewis, 1996). Variations on the statement, "The home is the first and most important school your child will ever have" ("Parents Involvement," n.d.), can be found on dozens of websites and publications and, in fact, represent a core belief of American life.

The Client Model of Parent–Professional Relationship

As with so many core values, the devil is in the details. When parents and school professionals try to develop a working partnership around a child's public school education, difficulties are more common than agreement. Applause for the *ideal* of parent involvement is easy to come by (Greenwood & Hickman, 1991); success in a long-term parent–professional relationship is often an exceptional achievement (Lopez, Scribner, & Mahitivanichcha, 2001). The majority of these relationships are traditional and perfunctory: "Although all schools routinely invite parents to attend informational meetings and conferences, few invite them to actively participate in extended and engaging activities" (Dodd & Konzal, 2000, p. 11, cited in Gonzalez-DeHass & Willems, 2003).

Like most contacts between professionals and the people they serve—whether they are called patients, clients, parents, or families—the traditional parent–educator relationship has been hierarchical. The professional status of the teacher or administrator becomes a platform that elevates his or her perspective above that of the parent, who usually lacks the professional's training and expertise. Both parties find themselves in a relationship that is inherently unequal (Tiegerman-Farber & Radziewicz, 1997).

The Client Model Within RTI

Inequality has restricted parent–professional interaction for generations, but within an RTI initiative, it becomes a serious impediment to the success of the program. RTI sets a major new agenda for a school's educational program, and any large change needs wholehearted commitment from all involved, including parents. This would apply to the introduction of any new learning initiative, but RTI presents a need beyond that of most other educational programs. A typical educational initiative may be compared to introducing a new model of jetliner to an airline. The entire team, from pilots to mechanics, needs training and testing until they learn how to operate the new plane. If the plane has been designed well, those who use it need only learn how to use it properly. It is a complete package, ready for application.

RTI: A Framework Without Content

Unlike other school programs, RTI is a *framework* for improving education, without the actual *content* of that education. It is the classical scientific method adapted to the field of student learning (Clark & Alvarez, 2010). According to Clark and Alvarez (2010), the "problem-solving methodology [of RTI] derives from the scientific method and includes four basic steps: (1) problem identification and definition, (2) problem analysis, (3) intervention plan development and implementation, and (4) evaluation of the plan's effectiveness" (p. 15).

For example, when cancer researchers test various drugs, they follow strict procedures based on scientific method, but the method itself doesn't offer any clue as to which particular sample might produce positive results in a particular trial. Success depends on following the correct research procedures, but following the procedures doesn't guarantee positive results. Success depends on the researchers having access, and being open, to the widest range of alternative ideas, and then testing those ideas within the framework of the scientific method. No matter how carefully they follow the prescribed research method, the scientists can't afford to miss out on any potentially effective idea that might lead to a cure. Without the material and the ideas, the method can do nothing; it is a blueprint without a contractor.

The Consultant Model of Parent–Professional Relationship

RTI requires educators to shift their thinking from that of an airline crew learning to use a new plane to that of a research scientist searching for a successful intervention. In RTI, fidelity of implementation is essential, but it is not enough.

The Need for Information, Resources, and Ideas Within RTI

RTI requires access to every possible idea and all relevant information in responding to the needs of an individual child. In most cases, the professional expertise and experience of the staff do not include the full range of insights needed to respond to a unique challenge that a student presents. Thus, the insight and input of the parent make up a source of expertise that the professionals cannot afford to miss.

Since it depends heavily on information, resources, and ideas, RTI requires professionals to widen the scope of their expertise. In particular, the traditional hierarchical relationship with parents may need to be reexamined. Parent involvement in RTI should not be limited to enlisting their support for programs that the schools have designed—we call this the *client model*. It needs to value parents as an essential resource in the RTI process, with unique knowledge of the capabilities and learning needs of their own child and an expertise that cannot be found anywhere else—we call this the *consultant model*.

The Client Model in the Business World: The Automobile Industry

We can better understand the client relationship by seeing the effect it can produce in the world of business. In the 1980s, the American automobile industry was being overtaken by higher quality Japanese cars, a management philosophy "coming apart at the seams" (Iacocca, 1984, p. 121), and in the case of Chrysler, a bottom line close to financial bankruptcy. One of the chief causes of the decline was a management approach that isolated top and middle management from employees and cut off the flow of critical information between the dealers, the shop floor, the designers, the engineers, and executive decision makers (Deming, 1994). It supported a "client" relationship with its workers, that is, management asked workers for "support" rather than input into decisions. Management set strategic goals; designers and engineers drafted designs; shop managers supervised the assembly lines; workers assembled the finished cars; information flowed in only one direction: from the top down. In the words of a contemporary observer, car makers had developed a "cultural isolation from non-automotive society" (Denison, 1984, p. 483). The results were catastrophic and, with hindsight, predictable.

Schools in the process of adopting RTI can avoid the mistake of isolating themselves from critical information on their students by reviewing their ideas about the role of parents. The research leaves no doubt that parent *support* can be a major advantage for a school when programs are in place and working as designed. But, as we have seen, RTI can function only with a continual flow of new ideas and information on individual students, and in many cases, the richest source of insight into individual students is the people who know them the best—their parents. To adopt a professional–client relationship with parents, to relegate the role of parents primarily to *support* of the school's programs, is to create a cultural isolation similar to that in the automobile industry in the 1980s.

The Parent as Consultant in an RTI Program

The alternative to the role of client is the professional–consultant relationship. Here, the experts in education view parents not simply as supporters for their professional expertise, but as a source of specialized expertise in their right, on their own child, that no one else can possibly provide, no matter how educated, experienced, gifted, or dedicated he or she may be. The parent's role in a family involves years of knowledge and experience with a child that can never be accessible to anyone outside the home.

Peggy Lou Morgan reminded parents of special needs children that "you have become the expert on your child. You know what his behavior means, and you automatically respond in the appropriate way. . . . that a lot of behavior issues are caused by what I call 'communication by behavior'" (Morgan, 2009, p. 3). For parents of general education children, this expertise is usually instinctive; for parents of special needs children, it often comes from living "a war with many battlefields" (p. 1). In either case, professionals who work with parents have in them a rich source of insight into their child's behaviors and capabilities that cannot be accessed through any other source. Inherently, parents have exclusive insight into major factors in a child's academic performance and social behavior. They are the only people who regularly interact with the child over long periods of time, across the many environments and transitions that a child faces. Their input in these areas is essential and irreplaceable.

Thus, RTI, with its focus on evaluating and improving the work of individual students, is heavily dependent on the knowledge and evaluations that only parents can provide. This is not a matter of support; it is a matter of specialized expertise. The most effective parent involvement is based on the parent as an invaluable consultant in the educational process. In this process, a parent–professional conversation might probe the parent's experience with the child, actions she has taken in the past, outcomes of those actions, the reasons for her interpretation the child's behavior in school and at home, and include similar questions, looking for insights aimed at discovering an effective intervention within RTI. (Recall that RTI is only a *process*; the *content* of that process has to be continually invented, discovered, and tested by the educational team, which includes professionals and parents.) Again, the parent is not just cooperating or supporting; he is contributing invaluable resources.

This means reversing the support relationship. Instead of asking parents, as clients, to support the school's RTI initiative, the school asks itself how it can support the parent as a consultant in the work of discovering the best interventions for the child. Table 8.1 illustrates the contrast between client and consultant relationships.

Table 8.1   Client and Consultant Relationships

	The Client Relationship	*The Consultant Relationship*
Expertise	The **professional** has specialized academic training in education.	The **professional** has specialized academic training in education.
	The **parent** is usually without academic training in education.	The **parent** has intensive knowledge gained from "field experience" working with the child.
Agenda	The **professional** sets the educational agenda for the child, based on professional judgment within the mandates of school and state educational standards.	The **professional** consults with the parent on how to discover and meet the child's needs within the framework of school and state standards.
	The **parent** is asked to support the agenda.	The **parent,** as consultant, contributes ideas on interventions that might address both considerations.
Assessment	The **professional** reports periodically to the parent on how the interventions are going in school.	The **professional** reports periodically to the parent on how the interventions are going in school.
	The **parent** is asked to adjust support for these interventions at home with the child.	The **parent** reports on how the interventions are going at home.
		Both parties discuss ways of adjusting the intervention and of coordinating these adjustments in both venues.

The case study of Michelle Jackson (the parent) and Ms. Hess (the teacher) that opened this chapter is an example of a conversation based on the professional–client model. The relationship is hierarchical: The teacher's role is to represent and enforce her school's cohort program, and to do this she needs to win the parent's support. The parent is struggling with conditions that she believes are harming her son and has to convince the person in authority to make an adjustment. The problems with this relationship become most evident when disagreements arise—just as the problems with management in the auto industry became evident only when heavy competition appeared. Table 8.2 presents a conversation that Michelle Jackson (parent) and Ms. Hess (teacher) might have had under a different, consultant model.

Table 8.2   Conversation Between Parent and Teacher Based on a Consulting Relationship

Parent. I'm really concerned—actually, I'm pretty upset—about the way Andrew is reacting to your cohort program. His father and I think he may be an Asperger child—it will be a few weeks before the testing is finished. But he just doesn't react at all to other children; when you force him to work with the others, he melts down.

Teacher. Tell me what you can about Asperger syndrome. I know it's an autism disorder and that it has some effect on social skills. Is that why you're having him tested?

Parent. That's right. We've done a lot of reading and met with some friends who have kids "on the spectrum," as they call it. A lot of his behavior fits the model. But regardless of the label, we know that he just doesn't work well in a program that forces him to socialize with other children in large groups. He gets completely disoriented; he runs for cover, it takes hours to get him back on track. . . .

Teacher. OK, I understand. I've seen it myself. I think first that we should see what the official diagnosis is, and then move on from there. If he is an Asperger child, we will need a lot of expertise, including your own. In the meantime, we have a schoolwide program in place that is working really well for almost all the kids in the class, even though it is a problem for Andrew.

Parent. I know that everyone else seems to love it. My problem is that Andrew is one of the 1% or 2% who don't fit the mold. I'm not going to let my child be a victim of something just because it works for everyone else's kid.

(Continued)

(Continued)

Teacher. Neither would I. My difficulty is that I need to find a way of working with Andrew at the same time that I need to make the cohort program work. It's my problem, not yours, but I'll need your help in making some adjustments that will work for him.

Parent. I'll tell you what I can, but I'm not the expert in teaching.

Teacher. But you're the expert on Andrew. I'll do anything I can to adjust his work in class until things improve, but I'm going to need to come up to speed on what works for a boy with his profile—and then what works for Andrew in particular. When we get the testing report, we'll have a lot clearer idea of what to do and who to turn to. In the meantime, would you be able to start by keeping a record of whatever he says and does that I would need to know?

The teacher has guided the conversation from one of hierarchy and authority (in the original scenario) to consultation and collaboration. Without surrendering control of her program, she recognizes the parent as an outside expert whose insights are essential to the child's success. The teacher needs and asks for the parent's perspective; she is also aware that more information will be coming when the outside testing results are known and is prepared to adjust her response at that time. In the meantime, the teacher is building a consultant relationship with the parent, in which each has an interdependent role to play. If the process continues successfully, several outcomes may be expected:

1. The parent's distress will be lowered and replaced with a sense of empowerment and involvement in her child's program;

2. the teacher will maintain control of her other responsibilities as a professional, that is, to teach the rest of the class and to support the school's investment in the cohort initiative;

3. and most important: The open-minded search for a program that works for this particular child is likely to produce a far better outcome for Andrew than if the parent and teacher engaged in a power struggle over which one was better prepared to decide what the child needed.

Part 2 will review several of the many resources that are available to parents, and to professionals who are working with parents, to build a consulting, rather than client–based, relationship.

RESOURCES FOR PARENT–PROFESSIONAL COLLABORATION

Family engagement, collaboration, and meaningful parent involvement have been the subjects of national and local advocacy for many years, and parent involvement has been a key component of RTI programs from their inception. Universities and educational institutions have done extensive research following the outcomes of students whose families are meaningfully involved. The results are consistent: Family engagement and parent involvement is crucial in long-term outcomes for children (Miedel & Reynolds, 1999). The resources available to professionals and parents are immense and, for the most part, fully accessible and available at no cost. National Technical Assistance Centers are funded by the U.S. Department of Education to provide information and resources to all stakeholders, including students and their families.

In recognizing the value of the parent-consultant model discussed in this chapter, working within the framework of a collaborative community of practice (CoP) can set the stage for building effective educational teams within the RTI process. Etienne Wenger defined CoPs as "groups of people who share a concern or a passion for something they do and learn how to do it better as they interact regularly" (Wenger, 2006, p. 1). A key component of a CoP is that all stakeholders are always invited and equally respected. There is an understanding that each participant brings an expertise to the conversation and the process. "A CoP is quite simply a group of people that agree to interact regularly to solve a persistent problem or improve practice in an area that is important to them" ("Communities of Practice," n.d.). The IDEA Partnership, on whose website this definition appears, is funded through the U.S. Department of Education's Office of Special Education Programs (OSEP) and hosted by the National Association of State Directors of Special Education (NASDSE). Their focus is collaboration, shared work, and CoPs.

The concept and framework of CoPs align closely with the parent–consultant model described earlier. Parents are seen as experts in regard to their child's educational needs; they need to be involved in planning and decision making from the very beginning of the RTI process. Bill East, the executive director of NASDSE and a former state director of special education, spoke to the importance of true collaboration in education. In a recent publication, he said,

> I worked hard with stakeholders but I didn't work smart. More times than not, I didn't involve them up front in the decision making process. Thinking deeply about community building has led

me to understand just how important it is to have stakeholder involvement from the very beginning. (Cashman, Linehan, & Rosser, 2007, p. viii)

CoPs have been supported and encouraged by OSEP initiatives and are mentioned in the most current federal Blueprint for Education Reform (U.S. Department of Education, 2010).

Projects of the IDEA Partnership and NASDSE contain a wealth of resources available to professionals and to parents, including materials, information, referrals to special education services, and technical assistance on the RTI process. These, and the resources included in the remainder of this chapter, have been developed by experts in the field of education and collaboration and can be invaluable as our schools move forward with current and future RTI mandates. Most of the websites listed are those of projects or organizations that have been financed through a national initiative. When a project is funded by federal, state, or local government, the materials are available to the public at no cost.

An overview of each organization is provided, along with a web address. Search tools on most organizations' home pages give easy access to specific information. Although it is evident that many of the organizations and resources have a focus on students at risk or with identified disabilities, it is critical to remember that RTI is a general education initiative and that the screening portion of the process includes all students.

IDEA Partnership. (www.ideapartnership.org)

Working within the context of CoPs, this organization has developed and made available collections of resources around educational topics, including a substantial, comprehensive collection on RTI. The IDEA Partnership is dedicated to improving outcomes for students and youth with disabilities by joining federal investments, state agencies, national organizations, and local stakeholders in shared work and learning. This dedication is evident in its collaborative work on RTI.

National Center for Learning Disabilities. (www.LD.org and www.ncldtalks.org)

Their mission is to ensure that the nation's 15 million children, adolescents, and adults with learning disabilities have every opportunity to succeed in school, work, and life. The site offers comprehensive resources regarding RTI collaboration, research, and implementation.

Consortium on Appropriate Dispute Resolution in Education, CADRE. (www.directionservice.org/cadre)

This is a federally funded technical assistance project that encourages collaboration in education. They offer an abundance of materials that give strategies to improve family engagement in educational programs. CADRE works with state and local education and early intervention systems, parent centers, families, and educators to improve programs and results for students.

Wrightslaw. (www.wrightslaw.org)

Parents, educators, advocates, and attorneys go to this site for authoritative, reliable information about special and general education law and advocacy for students. Wrightslaw has extensive information on RTI available for all stakeholders.

National Association of State Directors of Special Education, NASDSE. (www.nasdse.org)

NASDSE is dedicated to ensuring maximum achievement for all students and to engaging students, families, communities, professionals, and policymakers as full partners. Their website features information for all stakeholders who share the ideals in the NASDSE mission.

RTI Action Network. (www.rtinetwork.org)

This network is dedicated to the effective implementation of RTI in school districts nationwide. Their stated goal is to guide educators and families in the large-scale implementation of RTI so that each child has access to quality instruction, and so that struggling students—including those with learning disabilities—are identified early and receive the necessary supports to be successful.

The National Center on Response to Intervention. (www.rti4success.org)

This center offers information that reflects the latest research and expertise on RTI. It offers opportunities to participate in online learning events, discover practical resources, and participate in discussion boards, webinars, and more.

The Center for Applied Special Technology, CAST. (www.cast.org)

CAST works to improve learning opportunities and outcomes for all individuals through universal design for learning (UDL). Explore this website to find out more about UDL research and development, innovative learning tools, and professional services.

National Parent Training Information Center, PACER. (www.pacer.org)

PACER provides information, support, workshops, and referrals to both families and professionals. The website has a tremendous number of materials useful to all stakeholders.

U.S. Department of Education, ED. (www.ed.gov)

ED's mission is to promote student achievement and preparation for global competitiveness by fostering educational excellence and ensuring equal access. Visit this site to access an extensive and authoritative education collection of information, including information on RTI best practices.

Families and Advocates Partnership for Education, FAPE. (www.fape.org)

FAPE links families, advocates, and self-advocates to information about the Individuals with Disabilities Education Act. The project is designed to address the information needs of the 6 million families throughout the country whose children with disabilities receive special education services.

National Research Center on Learning Disabilities. (www.nrcld.org)

Their goal is to help educators, policymakers, and parents understand the complexity and importance of making sound decisions regarding whether a child has a specific learning disability. Research in this area—including studies of the role of and best practices associated with RTI—is the foundation underlying all of the materials available on this site.

Harvard Family Research Project. (www.hfrp.org)

Educators, policymakers, and families increasingly agree: Schools cannot do it alone. Children need multiple opportunities to learn and grow—at home, in school, and in the community. This project has worked for years doing research and developing materials to improve outcomes for students.

The National Center for School Engagement, NCSE. (www.schoolengagement.org)

NCSE provides training, resources, technical assistance, research, and evaluation to school districts, law enforcement agencies, and courts, as well as state and federal agencies.

National Association of School Psychologists, NASP. (www.nasponline.org)

NASP is a source of knowledge, resources, and information on RTI. It is the official organization for school psychologists, publishing materials relevant for and available to all stakeholders.

The National Joint Committee on Learning Disabilities. (www.ldonline.org)

This committee has the leading website on learning disabilities and learning disorders and differences. Parents and teachers of children with learning disabilities will find authoritative guidance on attention deficit disorder, attention deficit hyperactivity disorder, dyslexia, dysgraphia, dyscalculia, dysnomia, reading difficulties, and speech and related disorders.

Education Resources and Information Center, ERIC. (www.eric.ed.gov)

ERIC provides access to more than 1.3 million bibliographic records of journal articles and other education-related materials, with hundreds of new records added multiple times per week. Some of the works listed are available for download; others are presented as abstracts with references to the journals of their original publication.

The Iris Training Center. (www.iris.peabody.vanderbilt.edu)

The Iris Training Center offers free online interactive resources that translate research about the education of students with disabilities into practice. Their materials cover a wide variety of evidence-based topics, including behavior, RTI, learning strategies, and progress monitoring.

OSEP Parent Portal. (www.parentcenternetwork.org)

This federally funded project allows parents and professionals to easily link to a national network of parent centers and a wide range of resources.

OSEP Professional/Parent Library. (www.learningport.us)

This is a national online library of professional development resources compiled to help bridge research, policy, and practice.

The National Center for Culturally Responsive Education Systems. (www.nccrest.org)

This center supports state education agencies and local school systems to ensure a high-quality, culturally responsive education for all students, as well as resources to ensure cultural competence in the RTI process.

The National Parent Information Center, PIRC. (www.nationalpirc.org)

PIRC offers technical assistance to statewide PIRCs and their constituents by providing access to research-based materials and effective practices regarding parent training and parent involvement that contribute to improved student outcomes.

The National Parent Teacher Association. (www.pta.org)

The National Parent Teacher Association website provides links to resources relating to family and school partnerships and much more. It includes a policy brief on parental engagement in the Elementary and Secondary Education Act (No Child Left Behind).

The Family Center on Technology and Disability. (www.fctd.info)

This center offers a range of information and services on the subject of assistive and instructional technologies.

The National Network of Partnership Schools, NNPS. (www.partnershipschools.org)

NNPS aims to increase knowledge of new concepts and strategies; use research results to develop tools and materials that will improve policy and practice; provide professional development conferences and workshops; share best practices of parental involvement and community connections; and recognize excellent partnership programs at the school, district, organization, and state levels.

The National Dissemination Center for Children With Disabilities, NICHCY. (www.nichcy.org)

NICHCY is recognized as one of the central information hubs in the world of education. All of their materials are copyright free and available for wide distribution.

U.S. Department of Education Institute of Educational Services. (www.whatworksclearinghouse.org)

This U.S. Department of Education project is considered a trusted source of scientific evidence for what works in education.

U.S. Office of Special Education Programs (OSEP) Technical Assistance and Dissemination Network. (www.tadnet.org)

This network supports projects that provide information and technical assistance to states, local schools, educational professionals, and families.

These are a small sampling of the resources available to help families and professionals learn about the RTI process in education. In addition to the national websites included in this chapter, each state has its own materials, technical assistance centers, and guides on RTI practices. The technical assistance centers are available to help professionals and families navigate through necessary information and provide support to improve students' educational outcomes. A growing number are now focused specifically on parents' role in the RTI process. The quantity of information may seem overwhelming, but take your time and focus on one area to begin; the information is easily accessible. Remember, take advantage of the work and research that has already been done, and avoid reinventing the wheel.

 TECH BYTE

IDEA PARTNERSHIP INFORMATIONAL WEBSITE

In reviewing the case of Andrew, a student being evaluated for AS who is struggling in school, we will look at the IDEA Partnership informational website (www.ideapartnership.org) to see how the resources it provides might help to facilitate a positive outcome.

The IDEA Partnership is an example of an investment in stakeholder expertise that we have referred to as the consultant model of parent–professional relationship. Members of the partnership believe that those who are closest to the child have much to share about what works and can be valuable partners in finding new approaches to the challenges presented in educational programs. In this particular case, it would be beneficial for both the educator and the parent to access research-based, peer reviewed resources that have been shown to be successful with students who have profiles similar to Andrew's. The Autism Spectrum Disorder Collection has been developed by experts in the field of education and autism.

When entering the ideapartnership.org website, you will begin on the home page, shown in Figure 8.1.

Figure 8.1 Screenshot of IDEA Partnership Home Page

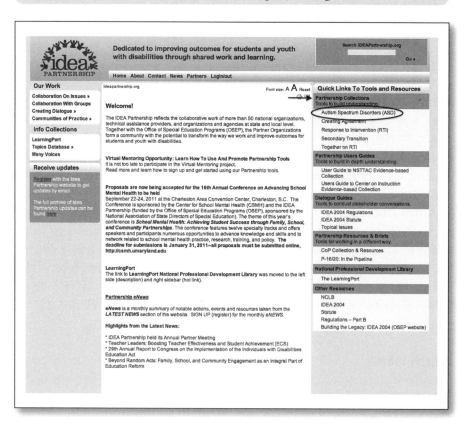

You will find resource links on both sides of the home page. For our search, we will be using the section of the site that is in the top right-hand corner underneath the heading, "Partnership Collections" (marked with an arrow ➝).

Below that heading, click on the link "Autism Spectrum Disorders (ASD)" (marked with an **oval**). Once you have clicked on the link, you will be sent to an Autism Spectrum Disorders (ASD) Collection home page, shown in Figure 8.2.

Figure 8.2   Screenshot of IDEA Partnership's Autism Spectrum Disorders Home Page

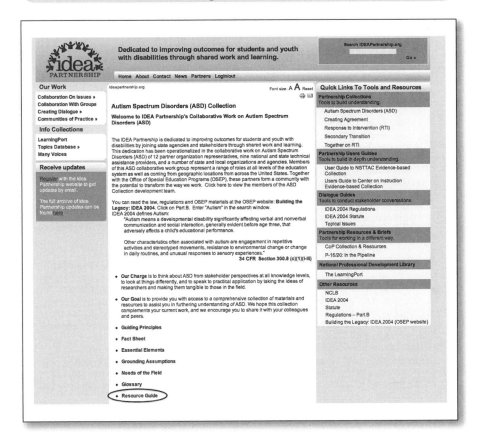

This page is full of resources. In this particular situation, it is suggested that you scroll down to "Resource Guide" (marked with an **oval**) and click on it. Again, you will be linked to a page full of information and resources, shown in Figure 8.3.

The second link (marked with an **oval**) is a comprehensive article on the subject of educating students with AS. If you scroll down a little further, you will see another link entitled "Autism: Interventions and Strategies for Success."

The resources are endless. You have hit gold and found a place that is a hub for a tremendous amount of research-based information on how to

Figure 8.3 Screenshot of IDEA Partnership's Autism Resources Page

AUTISM RESOURCES

This Resource Guide contains information that has been found to be helpful to individuals with autism spectrum disorders (ASD), their families and those who support them. It contains only websites that can be accessed at no cost.

Alaska Autism Resource Center
www.sesa.org
The AARC serves the needs of individuals with ASD, their families, caregivers, and service providers throughout the state of Alaska. They provide information, referral, training, and consultation via on-site and distance delivery. The Alaska Autism Resource Center (AARC) is a project of the Special Education Service Agency (SESA) located in Anchorage, Alaska.

Asperger Syndrome
http://www.education.com/special-edition/aspergers/
A free and rich resource of information on Asperger Syndrome for families and educators. Edited by Brenda Smith Myles, Ph.D., a consultant with the Ziggurat Group and Chief of Programs and Development for the Autism Society, the site includes multiple articles in such areas as the characteristics of Asperger Syndrome, social interventions, advocating for your child at school; academic Interventions, post-high school options, and developing and maintaining friendships. Over 20 articles written by nationally recognized experts appear on this site.

Aspy, R., & Grossman, B. G. (2007). *The Underlying Characteristics Checklist (UCC).* **Shawnee Mission, KS: AAPC.**
Developed as a component of the Ziggurat Model, the *Underlying Characteristics Checklist (UCC)* is an informal, nonstandardized assessment tool designed to identify characteristics across a number of domains associated with ASD. Three forms exist: UCC-CL for those with a classic presentation, UCC-HF for those with high-functioning autism/Asperger Syndrome, and UCC-EI for young children with ASD. The UCC is not designed or intended for diagnosis of ASD. The UCC is especially helpful for those working with school-aged individuals as the information gathered from the UCC provides a starting point for developing an IEP. The UCC and the Ziggurat Model in tandem lead to a program that is based on individual needs and uses the best practices in the field.

Autism Center for Diagnosis and Treatment
www.semo.edu/autismcenter
Located in Cape Girardeau, Missouri this center offers articles and a library as well as consultative and assessment services.

help children on the Autism spectrum succeed in their educational programs. This is one example of the IDEA Partnership's support system, which also includes collections around numerous other topics, including multiple aspects of RTI.

The other focus of our chapter is on collaboration. If you return to the IDEA Partnership's home page (Figure 8.1) and click on the "Creating Agreement" collection on the right-hand menu, you will be led to information and resources on how to work collaboratively and build effective educational teams.

Returning to the IDEA Partnership home page, you will see on the left more information collections and a section for "Our Work." This link brings you to pages that describe the comprehensive work of the partnership, in which all stakeholders are invited to participate.

The IDEA Partnership also sponsors and oversees a partner interactive site called "Shared Work" (www.sharedwork.org). Shared Work is both a communication tool and a collaborative workspace. It brings organizations, agencies, groups, and individuals together to exchange information on what is important to them, to learn together, to do work together, and to collaborate in addressing complex educational issues. Working as a community enables these groups to find new approaches to persistent issues and to gain support from each other in implementing these approaches ("Communities of Practice," n.d.). This shared work site gives professionals and families the opportunity to join national communities of practice around various issues. Both sites are worth investigating, since working collaboratively magnifies the talents and expertise of everyone involved in the well-being of children.

Leadership

9

The Role of District and School Administrators in Implementing RTI

Patricia Ann Marcellino and Dolores T. Burton

When Dr. Su Lee, an experienced elementary school principal, received the plan developed by a district team to meet her state's RTI requirements, she immediately began supplementing the district's existing academic intervention support (AIS) plan. She focused the RTI initiative first in the lower grades and then expanded it to the upper grades.

Dr. Lee meets weekly with her child study team (CST) to discuss children who are struggling with the curriculum and have been referred by their classroom teachers. As soon as the teacher completes a required form covering multiple information and assessments on a struggling child, a meeting is scheduled with the CST. Dr. Lee's team consists of the psychologist, social worker, nurse, resource room (i.e., special education) teacher, and an AIS teacher. They meet with the referring teachers every Tuesday for about 45 minutes, before the start of the school day. The CST recommends RTI strategies and materials on a child-by-child basis, examining each child's test scores and multiple assessments of the Tier 1 interventions that have already been implemented. The goal is to have the classroom teacher provide alternate strategies, since, based on the evidence of the student's difficulties, the current approaches have failed to meet his or her individual learning needs.

In this Tier 2 phase, frequent progress monitoring is implemented over a six-week period. After six weeks, the CST reconvenes with the classroom teacher, and a summative assessment is again conducted to evaluate the child's progress. The CST with the classroom teacher will recommend additional strategies and materials as needed. It is at this stage that various strategies and materials are changed and applied. For example, at this point in the Tier 2 process, the child may be placed in a small group with interventions recommended by CST that are consistent with research studies geared to the specialized needs of the group and each child in the group. The teacher continues to monitor the progress of each child in the small group. If the classroom teacher reports that the child is still struggling with the curriculum, then a more comprehensive battery of assessments is implemented. If the results of the progress monitoring and assessments indicate that the child needs more intensive and one-to-one interventions, then the CST will move the child into Tier 3, where instruction provided by an AIS teacher becomes individualized or continues within a small group. Progress monitoring is more frequent at Tier 3. If the child responds to this individualized or small-group instruction and performance improves, then the child will return to more traditional instruction in the classroom. But if the child is still not making satisfactory progress, then a special education referral is implemented.

At each stage of the process, Dr. Lee's team continually searches for research-based materials to support each child in the school. Dr. Lee reports that she was able to implement the district superintendent's RTI plan because she had the experience, people, resources, and instructional materials in place that are required for its implementation.

T he foundation of a successful RTI initiative is strong, professional, and action-oriented leadership from the district superintendent, secondary and elementary school principals, and their professional administrative staff members working at multiple levels of the school system (Barton & Stepanek, 2009; Canter, Klotz, & Cowan, 2008; Kelly, 2010; Pavri, 2010; Samuels, 2008; Sansosti, Noltemeyer, & Goss, 2010). This includes the following:

(a) *collaboration* among a school's internal stakeholders (teachers, staff, union members, parents, students) and a school district's external stakeholders (government officials, business executives, community representatives) working to build

(b) *consensus* among these internal and external stakeholders through

(c) ongoing *communication,* so all members within the school and district are kept informed about and engaged in the RTI process;

(d) *cross-training* and professional development working in partnerships, groups, and teams; and

(e) *celebration* of the achievements of students and teachers in regard to the learning objectives of the RTI program.

The good news is that when administrators lead a district or school toward continual approval and acceptance by community stakeholders under RTI, the process is no different than leading or reengineering any modern transformational change effort, regardless of whether it's the neighborhood school or district, the local family business, or a branch of a multimillion dollar company. Part of the process is demonstrated by leaders who are able to give direct answers to questions posed by stakeholders who ask *why, what, who, when, where* and *how* regarding RTI implementation. School districts are in the service of instruction and learning, and because of this, the superintendent, as the chief executive officer (CEO) of the district, and the school principal, as the chief instructional leader in the school, need to gain professional expertise in RTI and its multiple components. They should be knowledgeable and proactive leaders who directly raise and answer any questions that will be posed during the transformational change effort (Cambron-McCabe, Cunningham, Harvey, & Koff, 2005; Green, 2010; Houston, Blankstein, & Cole, 2007; Hoyle, Bjork, Collier, & Glass, 2005).

THE GROWTH OF RTI IN STATE EDUCATION PROGRAMS

Several national surveys reveal considerable variability in state regulations regarding the implementation of RTI (Kelly, 2010; Zirkel & Thomas, 2010). In New York State (NYS), for example, the Board of Regents and the Department of Education (NYSDOE) established guidelines for RTI, and in 2009 they recommended that

> effective July 1, 2012, all school districts in NYS must have an RTI program in place as part of its evaluation process to determine if a student in grades K–4 is a student with a learning disability in the area of reading. (DeLorenzo & Stevens, 2008)

NYS, with its diverse geographical areas, is sometimes anecdotally described as being three states in one because of its rural (e.g., Adirondack Mountain region), urban (e.g., New York City), and suburban (e.g., Long Island and Westchester) areas. Some school districts, especially in the suburban areas, are finding the implementation of RTI easily adaptable to their existing school structures, especially on the elementary level. In some districts, differentiated instruction and early intervention techniques have been common practices, especially in the lower grades.

Because high schools tend to be larger than elementary or middle schools, and other factors, administrators find it more difficult to implement RTI on the secondary level (see Chapter 10), but this has been implemented in some states, such as Iowa, Washington, and Minnesota, with varying degrees of success (Canter et al., 2008; Samuels, 2008; Sansosti et al., 2010). Overall, according to Zirkel and Thomas (2010), "The majority of the states have taken a permissive posture, presumably to allow for local choice" (p. 68) in regard to implementation of RTI at various school levels.

The Role of Leadership in RTI

Regardless of the size or grade levels of a school, one of the most critical factors in the success of an RTI implementation program is strong foundational leadership displayed by the superintendent and principal. Without wholehearted and personal support from the chief educational officers, no major initiative—including RTI—is likely to succeed. Strong leadership is based on getting the tasks done and supporting the people who perform those tasks by supplying the resources, the professional training, and—just as important—the ongoing determination needed to overcome obstacles.

A PROFESSIONAL PARTNERSHIP OF EDUCATIONAL LEADERS: THEIR FORMAL ROLES

One of the best models of educational leadership that administrators can use to sustain an RTI program is the philosophy known as *distributive leadership,* where expert teachers, acting as leaders and coaches for their peers, are distributed throughout the school system (Green, 2010; Spillane, 2006). These teacher leaders resemble middle managers: They become liaisons between the administration and classroom teachers, leading their teaching colleagues in the work of adopting research-based instructional practices and interventions. But even though teachers and teacher leaders are the ones who directly sustain the RTI process in the classroom, it is still the responsibility of the district superintendent, as CEO of the district (Hoyle et al., 2005), and the principal, as the instructional leader of the school, to carry out the special roles assigned in their formal leadership titles (Cambron-McCabe et al., 2005; Green, 2010; Hoy & Hoy, 2006; Knight, 2007; Smith & Piele, 2006).

To implement an RTI program effectively, the principal and superintendent must join forces as a leadership team. They must develop a united professional partnership committed to integrating the school's core curriculum with a new program for improvement of student skills based on the principles of RTI: universal screening, progress monitoring, and systematic introduction of new interventions until goals are achieved. The superintendent and principal, working in tandem, must understand that leading the introduction of RTI into a school is a *transformational* process, one that is impossible to achieve without the total commitment of both district and building leadership. They must display confidence and belief in the implementation of the RTI initiative so that others believe in it as well.

The distribution of leadership throughout the school is a key responsibility of these two educational administrators, working through and with their various teams, groups, and committees, who will make RTI succeed. The district superintendent is the *external change agent,* within and outside the district, and the school building principal is the *internal change advocate* working within the school.

The Superintendent

For the superintendent, the role of external change agent extends beyond the boundaries of the district and involves building a wide network of support with national, state, and local governmental officials, business executives, community-based stakeholders, and other district administrators who are implementing similar RTI models. These individuals play a major part in providing funding or informational updates regarding the successes (and any pitfalls encountered) in implementing an RTI program.

The Principal

For the principal, the role of an internal change advocate is rooted in two primary jobs within the school: those of instructional leader and building manager. The principal's key role as instructional leader is to coordinate, troubleshoot, defend, and—most of all—inspire the staff's efforts in RTI; the key role as building manager is to allocate the needed human, monetary, and technological resources. Table 9.1 lists the responsibilities of the chief instructional leader.

Table 9.1 Responsibilities of the Chief Instructional Leader

As the chief instructional leader, the principal needs to

- participate in designing a strong core curriculum.
- develop RTI interventions that are carefully aligned with it.
- introduce state-of-the-art research-based instructional strategies and learning techniques for teachers to execute.
- assist teachers to create assessments and data-gathering techniques.
- mentor new teachers.
- supervise the professional development of all the teachers and professional staff.
- facilitate multiple collaborative groups and teams.

The Staff

Classroom and lead teachers, coaches, and instructional team members have a responsibility to continue to evolve into high-performing quality educators who support their students' learning. The process should be generative and not punitive. Students and teachers should be assessed according to benchmarks that raise expectations and instruction and ensure the attainability of learning and e-learning objectives (Green, 2010; Hoy & Hoy, 2006; Knight, 2007; Picciano, 2011; Senge, 2006; Smith & Piele, 2006; Spinelli, 2011).

Moreover, to successfully fulfill their partnership, the superintendent and the principal must share several complementary roles, namely, those of political activist, team facilitator, system evaluator, and resource allocator.

The Role of Political Activist

Both the district superintendent and the principal need to become *political activists:* The superintendent must focus primarily on connecting, networking, interacting, and communicating with external stakeholders on a macro level; the principal focuses predominately on the internal stakeholders vested in the neighborhood school itself on a micro level. In keeping with their complementary roles, the superintendent and the principal need to maintain ongoing communication with other school principals and central district directors in student services (e.g., in guidance, psychology, special education, and technology). As political activists, they should communicate continually with vested individuals and groups outside and within the district and school, so that steadfast support for RTI is sustained. With the advances of technology, maintaining a network of communication is more manageable than ever before (Picciano, 2011). Information can be readily secured and disseminated through the various professional associations (local, state, and national), such as superintendents' and principals' associations, as well as through nonprofessional groups, such as chambers of commerce, Rotary, and parent–teacher organizations. The superintendent is the primary representative who communicates information about the RTI initiative to central administrators, school board members, school principals, local organizations, and citizens within the district who may or may not have children in the schools.

Team Facilitators

In their roles as *team facilitators*, the superintendent with the RTI district team, and the school principals with their CSTs, AIS teams, instructional support teams, peer support teams, and/or grade-level teams, have to make sure that team members collaborate effectively. Table 9.2 depicts the role that each team and team member needs to fulfill.

Table 9.2   Roles of Teams and Team Members

Each team and all team members should

- plan well and update their goals and implementation objectives.
- organize themselves so that they have the expertise and tools to do the job.
- share their successful and not-so-successful practices.
- continually evaluate their work in order to determine whether their goals and objectives are being achieved as planned.

As *team facilitators*, the superintendent and school principal have to make sure that each team member has a professional understanding of the role and duty to be performed, and that professional and respectful relationships are maintained among all members. (If not, the leaders will have to employ conflict-resolution practices or rotate members out of the team.) Because tensions can easily brew within teams, educational leaders have to be mindful of each group's interactions so that tensions do not surface and impact negatively upon the team (Katzenbach & Smith,

2003; Kling, 2000; Marcellino, 2006, 2010; Polzer, 2003). To relieve the tension, team and partnership contracts may become part of the process (Marcellino, 2008), with contracts outlining overall goals and team members' responsibilities.

System Evaluators

As *system evaluators*, the superintendent and principal need to assess and decide whether plans have to be updated, structures have to be reorganized, and resources have to be reallocated. Human, monetary, and technological resources have to be reassessed on a periodic basis so that optimum quality is sustained.

The principal evolves into the *central evaluator* within the school and assesses whether the RTI program has to be changed or refined. Investment in technology hardware, software programs, and a data management system is integral for assessment requirements (Creighton, 2007; Kowalski, Lasley, & Mahoney, 2008; Picciano, 2011). Teachers need professional training in the use of technology to chart each student's progress, as well as training in state-of-the-art instructional strategies and pedagogical techniques.

Resource Allocators

As *resource allocators*, the superintendent and the principal, working in tandem, need to secure resources for RTI (i.e., books, instructional materials, supplies, computers, software programs). Funds are also needed for the professional development of the teachers and staff members. Sometimes additional funds need to be secured through donations-in-kind, grants, and philanthropic pledges.

As resource allocators, they are required to oversee the distribution of the resources that are assigned by them (Lunenburg & Ornstein, 2008).

Table 9.3   Case Study, An Example of Professional Leadership at the Secondary Level

> *Dr. Natasha Patterson, currently a college instructor, has worked in a total of five suburban school districts in her 30-year career as a reading teacher, English teacher, assistant principal, department chairperson (on the high school level), and English language arts district coordinator. Throughout her career, she has*

(Continued)

(Continued)

consistently utilized early intervention and differentiated instructional techniques, similar to RTI, in her work on the middle and high school levels. In the state in which she works, decisions regarding the prioritizing of personnel and programs in individual school districts ultimately rest with the district superintendent and the school board members.

To illustrate the grassroots variability of administration in different districts, consider the two districts that Dr. Patterson worked in. One school district did not fully sustain its reading support classes. This district offered minimal reading services at the secondary level; only one reading teacher was employed at the high school. There were few push-in reading tutors or separate reading classes for below average students.

In contrast, Dr. Patterson also worked in another district that employed 50 reading tutors. In this district, reading was scheduled as a class in addition to English as a Tier 1 intervention. Pull-out programs were believed to be counterproductive, because students were taken out of their regularly scheduled classes, and these were usually the students who needed class time the most. Tier 2 group instruction at the secondary level was offered for groups of fewer than 10 students, with 5 to 7 being the ideal size. Small-group instruction and Tier 3 tutorials (one-on-one) were held daily.

The question guiding the latter district was, What will help our children the most? This district emphasized the integration of early intervention techniques when reading deficiencies were detected. The district administrators sought to partner with the teachers and have frequent conversations with them regarding student performance and learning.

The sharing of data regarding student performance and action plans was also part of grade level and departmental level meetings. Administrators provided and analyzed the assessment data with the teachers. Diagnosis was quick and ongoing. Assessment was conducted both before and after interventions were implemented and the results examined. Diagnosis was done immediately so that teachers and coaches could confer and share results. Once the assessment data arrived, the reading and math specialists conferred, shared results, and developed an action plan that was updated and ongoing. The plan was shared with the various CST, AIS, and other advisory teams. The plan was shared with the schools' various advisory teams (CST, AIS, and/or others that were in place). Student performance was continually reviewed. Assessment data from subject teachers were compared with standardized assessment data. Learning capability was compared with learning performance to determine whether a gap existed between the two.

At the secondary level, the advisory team (CST, AIS, or other designation) consisted of an administrator (usually the assistant principal), psychologist, social worker, head of guidance, reading specialist or reading remedial teacher, learning lab specialist, subject teacher, and tutor. When learning problems persisted, ultimately a decision was made regarding whether remediation or special education were services were needed.

Overall, the administration supported the teachers and provided professional training, especially in regard to analyzing assessment data. Teachers were treated with respect; they were considered the experts. If there were problems, administrators asked teachers to reflect on what they should be doing. Administrators understood that, as the professionals, the teachers knew the students best. Administrators believed that teachers were the ones who needed to devise the solutions.

Conversely, the teachers knew that the administration would support them with the resources that they needed. More important, creativity was emphasized; teachers did not teach solely to the test. For example, at times, administrators visited the classrooms and participated in reading to the students with the teachers.

Teachers were supportive of the administrators, the parents, and the students. A joint partnership ensued. As a result, students in this district benefited by consistently scoring at the highest levels in statewide reading and math tests. Ninety-eight percent of the high school students in this district were also accepted at our nation's colleges and universities.

BORROWING FROM BUSINESS TO IMPLEMENT AN INITIAL RTI PROGRAM

Although on the surface, the goals of business and education may seem to be different, many of the elements of management and leadership are appropriate for both.

Sharing a Knowledge Base and Improving the Model

Business management and educational administration share a common knowledge base, and as a result, various business and team models have been borrowed and adapted in education (Certo, 2008; Katzenbach & Smith, 2003; Lunenburg & Ornstein, 2008; Marcellino, 2010; Senge, 2006). Some of the most noteworthy models, such as Management by Objectives (MBO) developed by Peter Drucker (1999) and Total Quality Management (TQM) attributed to the followers of W. E. Deming (1994), were business endeavors that have been adapted to education. These comprehensive problem-solving models were research based and included extensive planning, organizing, leading, and evaluating efforts. However, the difference between these systems and RTI is that

MBO and TQM were essentially business-based models, whereas RTI is an education-based model with general education at its core.

Although business techniques are not absent from the RTI model, it is fundamentally an educational model. Moreover, as a program rooted in the disciplines of education, the impetus for RTI comes primarily from national changes in federal legislation (i.e., the No Child Left Behind Act of 2001 and the Individuals with Disabilities Education Act of 2004) coupled with differing state governmental edicts (Kelly, 2010; Zirkel & Thomas, 2010).

Applying the Classical Elements of Management and Leadership to RTI

Strong professional leadership includes developing a strategy that encompasses the classical components of management, namely, effective planning, organizing, leading, and evaluating (Certo, 2008; Lunenburg & Ornstein, 2008). This means that when a district or school introduces RTI, the initiative has to be included in each of four components, shown in Table 9.4.

Table 9.4 Components of an RTI School Initiative

> **An RTI school initiative needs to include**
>
> - *planning the core mission statement* and visionary goals (to answer the questions, "Why are we doing this?" and "What is going to happen each step of the way?").
> - *organizing personnel* into partnerships, groups, and teams who are supplied with the resources they need to do their jobs well (to answer the question, "Who is going to be involved?").
> - *leading a productive learning system* that emphasizes quality teaching (to answer the question, "When and where will it take place?").
> - *evaluating and* continually assessing the RTI through a systems analysis (to answer the question, "How are we doing?").

Several management processes may be implemented by the superintendent and school principal during the introductory phase of an RTI initiative, such as implementing aspects of POLE, conducting a SWOT analysis, and developing a three-year strategic plan focusing on RTI.

Implementing Aspects of POLE

POLE is this author's acronym for the classical business model that combines the four management functions of planning (P), organizing (O), leading (L), and evaluating (E), as shown in Table 9.5.

Table 9.5 Components of the POLE Business Model Applied to School Leadership

The superintendent and principals need to

- *plan* strategically with well-outlined and directed long-range and short-range goals.
- *organize* their human resources so that collaborative teams are formulated.
- *lead* by modeling fidelity to the goals of the school and district, so that quality teaching is maintained.
- *evaluate* student learning continuously to ensure that each child responds to the learning initiatives implemented.

While the principal and the superintendent are the lead players in initiating the development of an RTI program, the classroom teachers, instructional coaches, and subject and grade-level experts are the professionals who sustain the program. As middle managers, they provide the distributive leadership through which the goals and objectives of RTI are attained. Central and building administrators need to identify early on the professionals who have the skills to sustain an exemplary RTI program. If any of the program's components are unsuccessful, it is not the fault of the teachers; it is the responsibility of the educational administrators who are the formal leaders.

Conducting a SWOT Analysis

SWOT is a multilevel broad-based management technique (Certo, 2008; Ray, 1999) that examines a district's internal operations in regard to its strengths and weaknesses. The superintendent convenes a districtwide team, which analyzes the strengths (S), weaknesses (W), opportunities (O), and threats (T) to the district, using a four-cell matrix such as that shown in Table 9.6.

Table 9.6   Matrix for SWOT Analysis

Strengths	Weaknesses
Positive internal conditions that can be used for improvement.	Negative internal conditions that need to be addressed.
1. _____	1. _____
2. _____	2. _____
3. _____	3. _____
Opportunities	Threats
Positive external conditions that can be used for improvement.	Negative external conditions that need to be addressed.
1. _____	1. _____
2. _____	2. _____
3. _____	3. _____

The technique requires the district to focus on all aspects of its condition: internal and external, favorable and unfavorable. For example, in regard to its internal resources, analysis might lead to a focus on the allocation of human, monetary, and technological resources, as shown in Table 9.7.

Table 9.7   Review of Internal Resources Within a SWOT Analysis

Internal Resources

- *Human resources:* Is there an adequate number of teachers and staff experts allocated in the district across schools? Do they have the knowledge required to maintain fidelity in the operation of RTI?
- *Monetary resources:* Are the funds available in the budget sufficient for the purchase of instructional materials and professional training to maintain the RTI system? If not, what opportunities are available to increase those funds?
- *Technological resources:* Are there sufficient computers for faculty to chart student progress? Are software programs available for ongoing assessment of all learners in the district?

SWOT is a comprehensive analysis that evaluates not only the internal strengths and weaknesses of the resources available to the district, but also the external operation of the district in regard to its opportunities (Can the district avail itself of additional resources, including free use of technological programs? If so, through which channels, and how can this be accomplished?) and its threats (What other venues in the educational environment, such as private or charter schools, might take resources away from the district or school? What is the back-up plan if the district budget is voted down?). The school principal also performs a SWOT analysis, but the predominant focus of SWOT in this case is the school building and its resources (i.e., in regard to its strengths and weaknesses) as well as the availability of opportunities or the proximity of threats to the specific school. After applying a SWOT analysis, suggestions should be requested and discussed, and plans should be decided upon and implemented by the administrative and teacher teams.

Developing a Three-Year Strategic Plan Focusing on RTI

The last process that should be implemented by the superintendent and principal involves a tool that is specific in its application. A three-year strategic plan focusing on RTI should be generated. This plan should be revisited, evaluated, and updated on a periodic basis. Tasks need to be identified. As the building manager, the principal develops the plan along with any other administrators and key staff assigned to the building, such as assistant principals, directors, and department heads. Within the school, the plan links the school's goals for RTI directly to districtwide objectives. The plan focuses on the most effective utilization of human, monetary, and technological resources for instruction. A time line for Year 1, Year 2, and Year 3 needs to be compiled with the needed resources outlined. A sample implementation of a three-year strategic plan for the implementation of the RTI initiative is shown in Table 9.8

If RTI has been planned well, it will become a core part of the district's and school's culture and a visible symbol of their goals. It may become part of their mission statements or appear as an explicit goal in the district's and school's vision statements (perhaps even as Goal #1). More important, the RTI initiative and information should be prominently displayed in places like the district's and school's websites, and possibly illustrated in the school's logo and in district and school brochures, newsletters, flyers, and e-mail messages. The message of the RTI initiative, that "all children will learn," might become the mantra on school stationery and should be posted on signs throughout the school building. RTI achievements regarding learning objectives should be communicated

Table 9.8 A Sample Implementation of a Three-Year Strategic Plan for RTI

CRITERIA	Year 1	Year 2	Year 3
Schools: Learning goals of RTI are incorporated into the vision statements of the school. RTI state and local district standards for grade levels, various disciplines, and subject matter courses are revisited and implemented.	**Elementary School(s):** RTI is introduced in kindergarten, grades 1 and 2 **Middle or Intermediate School(s):** RTI is introduced in Grade 6 **High School(s):** RTI is introduced in Grade 9	**Elementary School(s):** RTI is introduced in kindergarten, grades 3 and 4 **Middle or Intermediate School(s):** RTI is introduced in Grade 7 **High School(s):** RTI is introduced in Grade 10	**Elementary School(s):** RTI is introduced in kindergarten, Grade 5 **Middle or Intermediate School(s):** RTI is introduced in Grade 8 **High School (s):** RTI is introduced in Grades 11 and 12
Professional Development and Training of Teachers: grade-level teachers and subject-level teachers	Teachers receive training regarding RTI through professional development in instructional methods, assessment, and technological integration.	Teachers receive continuing training regarding RTI through professional development in instructional methods, assessment, and technological integration.	Teachers receive continuing training regarding RTI through professional development in instructional methods, assessment, and technological integration.
Conversational meetings with administrators and teachers; teams are formed: CST, AIS, IST, PST, advisory & grade-level teams	Conversational meetings concerning RTI evolve between administrators and classroom teachers, special education teacher, Literacy/math coaches and teams	Continuing the conversations	Continuing the conversations

CRITERIA	Year 1	Year 2	Year 3
cross-training and coteaching	Cross-training is begun, and coteaching may be implemented.	Cross-training continues, and coteaching is implemented.	Cross-training continues, and coteaching is refined.
Technological Integration	Technology is incorporated into programmatic planning, curriculum, and assessment.	Technology is incorporated into programmatic planning, curriculum, and assessment.	Technology is incorporated into programmatic planning, curriculum, and assessment.
Assessments	Assessment is implemented on a periodic basis, and teachers begin to chart progress of individual students for RTI progress monitoring.	Assessment is ongoing, and teachers continue to chart progress of individual students.	Assessment is ongoing, and teachers continue to chart progress of individual students.
Assessment Reports	Midyear assessment report on RTI is generated.	First-year RTI assessment report is generated.	Comparison report of RTI in Year 1 and Year 2 is compiled.
Parents	Teachers continually inform parents of their child's progress.	Parents receive continuing updates about their child.	Parents receive continuing updates about their child.
Management and Allocation of Resources:	Managers secure resources for RTI and allocate these resources.	Managers secure resources for RTI and allocate those resources.	Managers continue to secure and allocate resources.
Instructional— human, monetary, and techological	Managers check for free programs and software. They contact philanthropic organizations for RTI donations in kind.	Managers continue to check for free programs and software. They contact philanthropic organizations for RTI donations in kind.	Managers continue to check for free programs and software. They contact philanthropic organizations for RTI donations in kind.

(Continued)

(Continued)

CRITERIA	Year 1	Year 2	Year 3
Adjustments to the master schedule	Elementary school: adjustments for group instruction and special education classes.	Additional adjustments to the master schedule when needed.	Additional adjustments to the master schedule when needed.
	Middle school and high school: Students are scheduled for additional instructional courses and programming in small groups.	Middle school and high school: Students are scheduled for additional instructional courses and programming in small groups.	Middle school and high school: Students are scheduled for additional instructional courses and programming in small groups.
	Meeting times are allotted for instructional group and team meetings.	Meeting times are allotted for instructional group and team meetings.	Meeting times are allotted for instructional group and team meetings.
Promotion and Outreach:	Internal and external stakeholders are updated.	Updates continue regarding RTI.	Updates regarding RTI are ongoing.
Website	Website posts general information about RTI.	Website posts general RTI progress reports.	Website posts general RTI progress reports.
Brochures and Flyers	Brochures and flyers are printed and circulated throughout the community announcing the RTI initiative to help all students succeed.	Brochures and flyers concerning RTI progress are circulated to the community.	Brochures and flyers concerning RTI progress are circulated to the community.
Local Newspapers	Local newspapers report RTI progress.	Local newspapers report RTI progress.	Local newspapers report RTI progress.
Building Support	Managers build support throughout the community, and hold conversations with community representatives and groups.	Managers continue the conversations and build community partnerships regarding the RTI process.	Managers have ongoing conversations and continue to build community partnerships.

Source: Adapted from Marcellino (2011).

throughout the district at community meetings and in local and regional newspapers. Some local newspapers will print verbatim the information that is submitted to them by school personnel describing student and teacher achievements. By cross-training teachers and staff members to collaborate productively in teams and groups, and celebrating the achievements of all the students, the partnership of the superintendent and principal is widened to include a community of learners continuously striving to improve and publicize the RTI program, their schools, and the district.

Continually Displaying Strong Professional Leadership

Throughout the RTI process, the superintendent and the principal should display professional leadership that is committed to collaboration, consensus building, communication, cross-training, and continual celebration regarding the achievements of the RTI program. An RTI program that is continually visited and revisited, as well as assessed and reassessed in order to evaluate whether its planned goals and objectives toward learning achievements at each grade level for each child in each school are being achieved, is one that will ultimately be successful. It will be built on a strong foundation of professional leadership and performance that is demonstrated by the superintendent and the school principals working in partnership with their teachers, parents, and community members.

 TECH BYTE

COMMUNICATING INTERNALLY
AMONG ADMINISTRATORS AND STAKEHOLDERS
WITHIN A SCHOOL DISTRICT USING **MOODLE**

Many school districts have instituted web-based communication sites so that administrators can easily communicate and interact with one another. This interchange allows administrators such as the super-intendent of schools and principals as well as other administrators to communicate privately over the Internet within a closed environment. But many of these "supportive" sites are costly to a school district, because there are usually fees that have to be paid up front to an outside vendor to set up the site, and then there are usually yearly required fees to maintain the system. In exchange for this service, the school district will receive support from the vendor when the system breaks down or needs to be expanded. But some school districts that are instituting cost-saving measures are choosing to set up *Moodle* as their private portal. According to the *Moodle* demonstration site, all content on the site is made available under a Creative Commons Attribution–Share Alike 3.0 License (http://demo.moodle.net).

Moodle is an open source community-based tool; it is in effect freeware. It does not cost anything to download *Moodle's* software to a school site. The only downside to *Moodle* is that rather than paying an outside vendor to facilitate and support communication, the school district must have its own task manager on hand to render support internally and maintain the system. If the necessary human resources are on hand, *Moodle* becomes the learning management system or portal that allows connection to other links, especially file-sharing systems, such as www.dropbox.com or www.google.com. By providing the links to various and multiple systems, the school system maintains the closed environment it seeks to protect its private integrity.

In addition, instead of installing multiple outside links, there is only one link that is necessary—*Moodle*. Within *Moodle*, additional links can be generated. The required interconnectivity and privacy that is necessary to share files among administrators and stakeholders within a school district can be maintained. Within *Moodle*, school district meetings and conferences can be held. *Moodle* can also be adapted for classroom use. For example, students can interact with one another in discussion forums that are set up by the teacher. In this way, teachers can check whether students understand a particular class lesson. Teachers have the ability to design, upgrade, and even change their *Moodle* classes on a daily, weekly, monthly, or semester basis. Furthermore, classroom photographs and images (which can be large entities to transport over the Internet) can be placed in a folder and easily shared.

RESOURCES

The following websites are national organizations and professional administrative associations that are useful to administrators who are considering implementing new initiatives in their districts and schools, including RTI initiatives.

American Association of School Administrators, AASA. (www.aasa.org)

This is a national networking organization for all school and district administrators.

Association of Supervisors and Curriculum Developers, ASCD. (www.ascd.org)

This is a national organization that provides research information to teachers and staff experts as well as administrators.

National Association of Elementary School Principals, AESP. (www.naesp.org)

This is a national networking organization for elementary school principals.

National Association of Secondary School Principals, NASSP. (www.nassp.org)

This is a national networking organization for secondary (middle, intermediate, and high school) principals.

GLOSSARY

Academic Intervention Service (AIS) Team, Child Study Team (CST), Instructional Support Team (IST), or Peer Support Team (PST): A school-based team that has been formed to apply its expertise and recommend various RTI strategies and materials for implementation in order to improve instruction and learning as it applies to students in the classroom, in a group, or on a one-to-one basis.

POLE: Dr. Patricia Ann Marcellino's acronym for the classical business management functions of planning (P), organizing (O), leading (L), and evaluating (E).

Strategic Development Plan: A results-oriented plan that has been devised to assess recommended actions over a specific time frame. In the context of Chapter 9, the strategic development plan has been spread over a three-year period, and the recommended actions focus on learning goals, professional development and training of teachers, management and allocation of resources, and promotion and outreach.

SWOT: An analysis of a district or school's strengths (S), weaknesses (W), opportunities (O), and threats (T). Strengths and weaknesses are internal; opportunities and threats are external.

Managing Time   **10**

RTI in the Middle and High School Master Schedule

Lydia Begley and Dolores T. Burton

Annie is a sixth-grade student who struggles academically and is currently receiving supportive services in math. As the first marking period of the school year progressed, her team of teachers noticed that she exhibited inconsistent academic performance in math, lacked motivation, and showed minimal effort in the completion of homework assignments in other curricula areas as well. Her grades (particularly in math) began to fall, and given these concerns, both of Annie's teachers wanted to implement a Tier 1 intervention.

Annie's teachers referred her to the building's instructional support team (IST) and completed an initial background form that gave the team some pertinent information about Annie's history (including strengths, reading level, math level, recent assessment scores in other academic areas, and other interventions recently attempted by the instructional team of teachers).

The IST in this building met every day during a regularly scheduled period. The team was led by the school psychologist, with other members consisting of a guidance counselor (who acted as the students' case manager), two special education teachers, one general education teacher, and the assistant principal. In addition to representing the administration, the assistant principal is highly trained in the RTI process and is a full participant in all aspects of the IST. The team convened and Annie's case was presented.

Annie's two academic teachers presented their concerns to the full team along with her present level of performance (known as PLOP). In math, Annie had achieved an overall average of 61.9%, and her most recent assessment had yielded a 57% correct on one performance-based test and a score of 26 correct out of 50 (52%) on another. In addition, her homework performance was poor, and her math teacher felt that it did not indicate an acceptable level of understanding of the material presented.

Annie's humanities teacher also reported inconsistencies with completion of homework assignments and had set a minimum goal for Annie of 70% on-time submission.

The team decided on two Tier 1 interventions:

Implementation of a long-term daily study log to monitor Annie's progress in studying for two subjects per night (DiPipi-Hoy, Jitendra, & Kern, 2009). This log would require Annie to study for 10 minutes in math and one other subject (depending on the need) each evening. It would be signed by Annie's parent and checked each morning by Annie's humanities teacher.

In addition to the study log, a homework log for math would be implemented and checked. This study would be separate from and in addition to assigned written homework. Also, Annie's math teacher would conduct frequent check-ins during class to ensure that Annie was on task during the instructional period (Buffum, Mattos, & Weber, 2008).

The team completed a progress monitoring report and recorded the goals for improvement. They also decided that the interventions would last two weeks, and at the conclusion of the two-week period, the IST would convene again to determine if these two interventions were successful or whether to introduce any new RTI strategies and extend the timeline for further monitoring.

During the two-week period of intervention, Annie's teachers incorporated several formative assessments to determine Annie's progress. Two math quizzes (assessing newly learned information) were administered, and one math unit exam containing information learned over a series of weeks was also given. Annie's grades improved on these assessments, and the team decided to continue using the homework log and the long-term study log to assist Annie in time management. Annie was also urged to attend extra help sessions at least one time per week to continue to improve her skills in math.

Annie is only one of a number of students who can benefit from discussion at a secondary IST meeting. Throughout the year, Annie's teachers will continue to monitor her performance, both academically and behaviorally, to determine if further interventions or measures are needed to ensure her success as a middle school student. These conversations are not atypical and are beginning to be held in many secondary schools around the nation.

T hroughout this book, it has been shown that RTI is a multitiered approach to teaching that includes identifying and supporting students with specific learning and behavior needs. Furthermore, the primary goal of RTI intervention is to provide high-quality, scientifically based instruction in the general education classroom. The RTI process includes ongoing student assessment and monitoring of individual student progress that tracks results of a variety of targeted or "tiered" interventions to improve learning over a period of time. As these interventions are introduced to all learners (beginning at the elementary school level), a multitiered approach is used to provide differentiated instruction for all students based on their needs and learning styles. Although there is no single RTI model that is universally practiced at all grade levels, generally, the three (sometimes four or five) separate tiers of specific learning strategies offer increasing levels of intensity of instruction to accelerate students' rates of learning, based specifically on individual needs. General education teachers, special education teachers, and specialists (including support staff) closely monitor progress, adjust instruction depending on the learning rate and level of performance, and form ISTs to routinely discuss individual students' progress. Data are collected and analyzed, and this analysis forms the basis of decision making. Ultimately, members of the IST share these data with the student's parents in an effort to collaboratively make educational decisions on behalf of the student.

At the secondary level (middle and high school), a comprehensive approach to implementing RTI and the dialogue associated with it can be especially challenging. Some schools view it as a means to special education classification and feel that most secondary students should already have been identified at much earlier levels (i.e., elementary grades). As a result, schools often feel that RTI principles do not apply to middle and high school learners. Others implement RTI from a compliance point of view, doing just enough to meet minimum mandates to stay within the legal requirements. For some schools, the shift in thinking to what RTI requires of teachers in terms of their essential practices is so difficult that they are reluctant to see the overall instructional benefits from interventions and view the implementation of RTI as overwhelming (Buffum, Mattos, & Weber, 2010).

In addition, since RTI has been implemented primarily in the elementary grades, secondary schools struggle to find a clear model of what it would look like for students in middle and high school. Teachers may become frustrated with the time it takes to try tiered interventions and grow impatient with the time it takes to meet, collaborate, collect data, and assess students' performance. This is a major obstacle, because only when teachers personally believe that RTI is an effective model for identifying students with learning disabilities do they actively work toward implementing the interventions that improve performance (Duffy, 2007).

The particular demands of secondary schools—high student caseload per teacher, high-stakes testing, rigorous high school curriculum (e.g.,

Advanced Placement, college-level curriculums, or International Baccalaureate programs)—may also limit on the amount of time that teachers perceive they have to provide tiered interventions for students. Some teachers may also resist the level of involvement that RTI requires them to have in the building's IST, preferring instead to be considered the "content driven specialist" who knows how best to deliver a challenging curriculum (Gusky, 2010).

We sometimes find ourselves needing to debunk the myth that nothing can be done for students at the secondary level who have been unsuccessful in the elementary grades and are now unmotivated to learn and succeed as adolescents. Middle and high school teachers may be less optimistic that RTI strategies can be successful with adolescents, because they think it is essentially too late for them to make any significant difference with students who are truly struggling. This can be particularly true with students who experience difficulty in the area of literacy, an area that many secondary teachers feel ill prepared to teach (see Chapter 5).

At the secondary level, as content becomes more challenging, a student's difficulty with literacy and prior content mastery is exacerbated. Students are introduced to textbooks that may be far above their ability, and, on any given day, they are expected to evaluate, synthesize, and navigate their way through complex assignments that require them to read materials beyond their grade level. Often, teachers of secondary students believe that reading problems should have been corrected at the elementary level, and as a result, they do not see any aspect of the teaching of reading as their responsibility (Ehren, 2008). In light of this, no conversation about RTI strategies in secondary schools would be complete without addressing literacy.

Finally, and perhaps most important, whether RTI strategies focus on content area skills or specific reading skills, we need to examine the broader base of knowledge and skills that our students need to learn in the 21st century. We need to prepare secondary students for jobs and careers that are emerging faster than curriculum is being written. Students who graduate today need to know how to learn, unlearn, and learn again, and the ability to analyze, synthesize, evaluate, and apply information is critical in a "flat world" where technology is changing the economic landscape. These are the skills that are crucial to success in careers that may not yet exist.

In spite of the individual preferences or perceptions on the part of secondary teachers, RTI strategies and interventions have the potential to provide educators with a coordinated schoolwide effort toward improvement that benefits all students (Ehren, 2008). Our ultimate challenge as instructional leaders is how to assist our staff in embedding RTI strategies into their everyday practices by providing them with professional development in fidelity of implementation and research-based practices.

SETTING THE STAGE FOR RTI AT THE SECONDARY LEVEL

Most RTI models are based on a three-tier, or three-step, process of support for students that includes high-quality classroom instruction and screening interventions (Tier 1), targeted interventions (Tier 2), and intensive interventions in addition to core instruction and comprehensive evaluations (Tier 3) (Buffum et al., 2010). Much has been written about response to intervention since its official federal endorsement in 2004, and there is a wide range of "models" for its process. The great majority of these are well documented and studied at the elementary level, but there is little research to guide secondary schools as they try to embed RTI interventions in the upper grades. Furthermore, although many secondary schools have resources to assist struggling students, most of these are isolated and lack a unified effort that would pull them together in a cohesive way (Duffy, 2007).

In addition, at the elementary level, it is not uncommon for students to be pulled out of class for tutoring, either on a one-to-one basis or in small groups. However, at the middle and high school levels, these techniques need to be crafted into the master schedule as part of a teacher's daily class load. Adolescent students are also more sensitive to being "pulled" or isolated from their peers, and many may be forced to make difficult choices in terms of giving up more favorable electives (i.e., band, chorus, art, etc.). As a result, interventions need to be crafted within tiers that suit an adolescent's lifestyle (e.g., a half-semester targeted small-group intervention class geared for students who need reading strategies for content area material). Flexible building-level and district administrators might also consider adjusting the teaching workday to create an "X" period so that students could receive support before or after the school day in order to take advantage of the full range of courses and electives without begrudging the intervention help offered.

CREATING THE INSTRUCTIONAL SUPPORT TEAM AT THE SECONDARY LEVEL

Since RTI strategies and structures are more established at elementary schools than at the secondary levels, when we consider models for secondary students, it is more difficult to determine what those structures will look like and, more important, how to create a master blueprint for how they will operate.

However, one consistent element of RTI across all K–12 areas is the need to support the process with intensive staff training and involvement through the program known as ISTs (Fontana, Doerries, & Stickney, n.d.). These evolved from the instructional consultation model introduced by Sylvia Rosenfield and Todd Gravois (1996) and include a flexible group of multidisciplinary teachers, usually six to nine members, which typically involve general and special education teachers, a school counselor, and/or a school psychologist. Some teams even include a school nurse who can offer valuable alternative perspectives (Sprick & Borgmeier, 2010). Their expertise and commitment strengthen the process and provide valuable insights to help teachers diagnose and support struggling students.

Since ISTs often meet fairly regularly on behalf of numerous students, the level of involvement of any one particular staff member can be high. As a result, it is often a good idea for school teams to try to recruit and enlist a large number of teachers to serve on the team. Schools that are able to do so reduce the commitment required of any single member and can therefore increase the willingness of teachers to serve on the team.

The inclusion of administrators on the IST, although not necessary, is an advantage, because their presence publicly demonstrates their support for the work done by the team. In addition, the administrator can offer the building leadership's perspective on discussions that may have an organizational impact and alert the team to issues that might impede its progress. Also, the building leader needs to be kept informed of all high-profile cases and report their outcomes to district-level administrators. On the other hand, the administrator's presence may cause certain members to be more reluctant to speak honestly about their ability to meet a struggling student's needs. In the best of circumstances, the IST will strike a balance that allows team members to feel professionally competent and simultaneously keeps the building-level leader informed of its concerns and decisions about individual students.

Role of the Secondary IST

At the elementary level, ISTs often have an established protocol coordinated by school psychologists, support personnel, regular education teachers, and special education teachers. Depending on the school district, ISTs in individual buildings may be configured differently (e.g., kindergarten centers, primary buildings, intermediate buildings, etc.), and different grade levels may be housed in varied settings depending on each configuration.

At some point, however (depending on the size of the school district), students from the district's elementary schools will merge into the secondary complex. In these cases, the RTI procedures and processes in place at the elementary schools will need to be reexamined. This can become a challenging task for the secondary IST, since individual elementary schools (even within the same district) often do not operate in the same way in terms of interventions. It becomes critical, therefore, for the secondary IST to establish specific roles for individual team members (such as the role of data coach), focus on clear-cut criteria for Tier 1 resources, discuss mastery skills, and provide opportunities for teachers to collaborate among themselves regarding students' performance and achievement. As teachers begin to identify students in need of more assistance, a universal screening device, appropriate to the secondary level, needs to be in place to identify students who lack specific skills, and teachers must understand what these skills are in order to provide the required targeted intervention that is appropriate to the middle school or high school student. The decision to introduce these screening procedures, particularly in the early stages of setting up an effective IST, is crucial to the success of the team and needs to involve the expertise of all members.

The Precious Commodity of Time

Once the secondary IST is established, and before it can begin its work to identify students at risk, it needs to establish a set meeting time. Each school and district needs to examine its own organizational structure to determine the best time for its IST to confer. The secondary school culture is somewhat different from that of the elementary school in terms of its organizational structure and use of time within the school day. The nature of the elementary school day permits administrators the flexibility to create time for an IST to meet on a fairly regular basis. Usually (although not always), many of its members are based within the one school, and the administrator can pull the team together fairly easily to discuss students at risk. This is not as easily accomplished at the secondary level due to factors, such as staff shared among several buildings and rigid blocks of instructional of time, that prohibit mobility. This presents a challenge for scheduling professional staff.

It is recommended that the IST reserve a specific block of time each week to discuss the student caseload, with the frequency depending upon the number of students typically referred to the team in a week. In some organizations, specific contractual obligations and restrictions may interfere with an administrator's ability to convene the full team; however, here is where a positive and constructive relationship with the teachers' union will assist in creating a climate of collaboration. In some districts, teachers who serve on the IST are relieved of a "duty" period, or time served on the committee may count as a professional period or obligation. For some school districts and administrators, success with RTI implementation at the secondary level may depend heavily upon the creative use of contractual and bargaining language and a constructive relationship with professional organizations.

Once the building team has established a set time period to meet, it is often possible to discuss two students at one IST meeting, since an initial student RTI case should typically not exceed 30 minutes, and follow-up meetings often do not exceed 20 minutes. An efficient IST that provides all members with appropriate paperwork and information in advance of meetings can therefore manage between 25 and 40 Tier 3 cases in the course of a typical school year. The website Intervention Central (www.interventioncentral.org) contains a wealth of free resources that can assist teachers and administrators with additional articles and ideas about potential configurations for building support teams.

Table 10.1 illustrates the differences between two typical IST models.

Table 10.1   Models of Instructional Support Teams

Elementary Instructional Support Team	*Secondary Instructional Support Team*
Meeting Day/Time: Mondays—8:30–9:00 A.M.	Meeting Day/Time: Fridays—Period 3
Members:	**Members:**
(Chair) Psychologist	(Chair) Psychologist
Reading Teacher	Assistant Principal
Speech Teacher	Seventh-Grade English Teacher
O/T	Eighth-Grade Math Teacher
P/T	Reading Teacher
School Nurse	Guidance Counselor
Child's Classroom Teacher	Child's Classroom or Team Teachers

In the first model, the elementary support team consists of a wide variety of professionals in the building, and they meet together as a group before school to discuss the various students who have been referred to the IST. In the second model, the IST is a bit smaller, and their designated time to meet is one 40-minute period once per six-day cycle (a common scheduling module). The assistant principal is a participating member, and the team also consists of teachers who are free during the designated period because it is their duty period. As the master schedule is developed during the summer, the building principal tries to select certain teachers who would be positive, contributing members of the team and arranges for their duty period to coincide with the IST period.

Decisions of the Secondary IST

One of the first decisions made by the IST is to clarify its mission and understand its roles and responsibilities as a team. The team's primary function is to assess the need for professional development, provide technical assistance and support to staff for implementing academic interventions with students introduced within the RTI framework, and monitor the progress of these interventions (Batsche, 2008).

The IST is normally convened by an administrator as part of the RTI introduction process at the school or district level. Usually, at one of the initial IST meetings, an individual emerges as a team leader; this person acts as facilitator for the group and coordinates each case discussion. He or she may also serve as the data coach, facilitating meetings for all staff in the building or for grade-level groups, gathering and organizing the Tier 1 or Tier 2 data, providing coaching for data interpretation, and supporting the staff in collecting performance data on individual students and small groups of students. In some schools and districts, an RTI specialist may be employed as a consultant to train each building's IST and provide professional development as they work collaboratively to build their infrastructure and begin to implement RTI support measures. This consultant/trainer model provides the district with an onsite expert who can easily answer staff questions and provide important information and resources needed by the members of each IST.

With or without a specialist, the team needs to develop a problem-solving approach to assist teachers with research-based strategies to use as they approach each individual case. In some schools, teams create a bank of these strategies, make them available on a common teacher website, and utilize them routinely as a means of data collection. A "teacher share" of ideas, perhaps established on a building's or district's collective computer database, is instrumental in creating a forum for those teachers whose time is more restricted to access computer resources. Teachers and administrators with expertise in computer skills might want to explore this option with their IT department, since such a collective database can promote online collaboration among colleagues. Moreover, the use of district e-mail, while not necessarily a preferred model of communication, can also lead to a productive exchange of collegial ideas, particularly with teachers who are shared personnel between buildings and who may not be available to attend IST meetings due to additional time constraints.

RTI STRATEGIES

Secondary schools that are trying to implement RTI can easily begin the conversation with their staff about data by engaging teachers in a professional dialogue about the kinds of Tier 1 strategies they use on a daily basis in their classrooms. This conversation is fundamental, because these strategies produce the preliminary "data" that will be utilized at the IST meetings. In some schools, this can first be accomplished at a faculty meeting led by the building principal, the school psychologist, or the resident RTI specialist in the building.

Numerous websites list RTI interventions for students at all levels, and while these sites are easily accessible, and many are free, it is often more effective for teachers to create and share a list of research-based strategies that work well for them. One initial nonthreatening and low-key activity that can get faculties to work together and initiate these discussions is to ask teachers to post their strategies on charts. At a faculty meeting, provide poster-sized charts, each labeled with a headline, such as "Strategies for Reading Comprehension," "Strategies for Improving Study Skills," and "Strategies for Fluency." These charts can be posted around the room. Make markers available, and using a "carousel" method, ask small groups of teachers to visit each poster and jot down specific strategies that they have utilized in their classrooms that fit that particular category. At the completion of this exercise, the faculty can see how many interventions are already in place in each other's classrooms. The activity builds the faculty's sense of self-efficacy and enhances their confidence that Tier 1 RTI strategies are not too overwhelming.

This list of intervention strategies generated by the staff can easily be reproduced as a handout or placed on the building's RTI internal website as a permanent reference. A more comprehensive list of interventions can be found at www.interventioncentral.org.

Decisions About Data

For many secondary teachers, the collection of student data has traditionally consisted of tests, quizzes, and project-based assessment grades.

By the time students enter middle school, those who are struggling have already been classified, and those who are still experiencing problems in academic areas are often failing classes and suffering from issues with self-esteem. At this point, the IST becomes critical in assisting regular education teachers with both academic and behavioral interventions to determine if a particular student's performance can benefit from an alternative form of intervention. Although RTI strategies and procedures may have been in place at the elementary grades, students who arrive in middle and high schools performing below grade level in reading, writing, or mathematics are often in even greater need of the benefits from RTI instructional strategies than they were in the earlier grades (Duffy, 2007).

Table 10.2 illustrates one possible model of the academic and behavioral structures that a district may utilize in its RTI strategy.

Table 10.2 A Model for Academic and Behavioral Tiered Interventions at the Secondary Level

Tier 1—80% to 90% of All Students	Tier 2—5% to 10% of All Students (Targeted)	Tier 3—1% to 5% of All Students (Targeted)
Academic		
High-Quality Scientifically Based Instruction	Curriculum Support for Struggling Students	Individual or Small-Group Instruction
• Vocabulary review • Word mapping • Split page note taking • Graphic organizers • Summarizing information • Text look back • Question generating • Mnemonic devices • Partnered reading • Cover/copy/compare • Choral reading • Reciprocal reading • Partner retell • Summarizing reading • Linking pronouns to referents • Interactive reading	• Math and/or reading labs • Extended writing opportunities • Scholastic's Read About or Read 180	• Scholastic's System 44 • Wilson Orton-Gillingham

Tier 1—80% to 90% of All Students	Tier 2—5% to 10% of All Students (Targeted)	Tier 3—1% to 5% of All Students (Targeted)
• Story maps • Reteaching • "Chunking" information • Centers • Exit slips • Six traits		
Behavioral		
Positive reinforcement for all students	Antibullying programs	Individual counseling
Schoolwide programs/incentives	Small-group counseling	Behavioral intervention plans (BIP)
Schoolwide surveys	At-risk groups	Intense assistance
Schoolwide social skills (i.e., social-emotional learning)	Parent training	
Classroom management techniques	Behavioral intervention plans (BIP)	
Guidance programs	Weekly counseling plans	
Parental input/involvement seminars		

Let's return to our sixth-grade student Annie, who is experiencing some academic difficulty in the first quarter of middle school.

Although her team of teachers has tried a Tier 1 intervention by involving her parents in reviewing and signing her homework log, there are other Tier 1 interventions that they could try to improve the chances of Annie's success in the classroom. Annie, in addition to the rest of the students in the class, might benefit from the addition of these two Tier 1 "best practice" strategies:

(1) Summarizing—At the conclusion of key lessons or units, teachers might ask the students to construct three to five sentences summarizing what they learned. This can be done as an oral exercise, or it can be written. This strategy gives students a chance to formulate their thoughts about a particular topic

and articulate those thoughts in a cohesive way before moving on to other new information. This also provides the teacher with an informal assessment about knowledge learned.

(2) Cover/copy/compare—This intervention involves some preparation by the teacher. The teacher constructs a worksheet (in this example, for a math problem) that shows a problem alone on the front side, and the problem with its answer on the back. Students work independently to solve the problem on the front, and then they turn the sheet over to find the correct solution to self-check their answers. This offers students a chance to learn independently as their skills improve. In this model, students' work can be monitored by working with a partner, a tutor, or even a parent.

As the IST begins to evaluate students, one of the critical decisions it needs to make is the type of data that will be utilized in its RTI strategy. Members of the IST play a key role in supporting teachers as they collect and interpret data. To be effective, the team needs to decide on universal student-driven data sources that will provide baseline information upon which to make informed decisions about students. These may include the following:

- Universal screening measures
- Progress monitoring measures
- Classroom assessments
- Diagnostic assessments
- Districtwide assessments
- High-stakes testing (accountability) assessments

A more complete listing of assessments is included in Table 10.3.

Table 10.3   Assessments and Their Uses

Assessment	Appropriate for
Individual state assessments	Screening for Tier 1
Northwest Education Association's Measures of Academic Performance (MAP)	Screening for Tier 1
CTB/McGraw Hill's Acuity Assessment	Screening for Tier 1
AIMSweb (up to eighth grade)	Benchmark and universal screening

Assessment	Appropriate for
Bader Reading and Language Inventory	Informal reading inventories (IRIs)
Iowa Test of Basic Skills (up to eighth grade)	Decoding and math computation
Peabody Individual Achievement Test	Reading comprehension
Gray Oral Reading Test	Fluency and reading comprehension
Woodcock Reading Mastery Test	Decoding and comprehension

As the members of Annie's IST begin to consider Annie's case, several assessments can provide the team with valuable information.

> (1) Having reached the sixth grade, Annie has taken state assessments in Grades 3, 4, and 5 in English language arts and math. The results of these assessments can be examined by the team to determine Annie's progress and mastery of content area skills.
>
> (2) As a supportive math student who is already receiving math services, Annie was given the math portion of the Iowa Test of Basic Skills. This exam measured beginning math concepts, problem solving, and math operations, and it will provide Annie's teachers with her grade equivalent score and percentile rank on each portion of the test. Since the Iowa Test of Basic Skills provides percentile ranks on each subtest, Annie's teachers can compare her progress to that of her classmates and of other students in the same grade nationwide.

Data obtained from these different sources yield a range of information about instruction. In addition, classroom and districtwide assessments may be used to assess the effectiveness of local classroom instruction. Diagnostic or progress monitoring interventions should be used to assess a student's response to supplemental instruction.

Once they have identified what type of data they will use, the secondary-level IST needs to identify what the criteria will be for assigning students to Tier 1, Tier 2, and Tier 3 and what the screening and monitoring procedure will be for each of the tiers. In addition, specific standardized tools need to be agreed upon to obtain baseline data. Will teachers use standardized assessments that are norm referenced (e.g., California Achievement Tests or Iowa Tests of Basic Skills)? These two tests are frequently utilized to provide a screening of reading and math achievement and can establish a baseline of achievement information to monitor year-to-year development. Or, depending on the specific issues presented by an individual case, a team may choose to implement a reading assessment, such as the Group Reading Assessment and Diagnostic Evaluation or GRADE (American Guidance Service, 2001) and the Woodcock Reading Mastery Tests–Revised or WRMT-R (Woodcock, 1998). The GRADE test is a diagnostic exam and is administered to students in prekindergarten through 12th grade primarily to determine what developmental skills they have mastered and where they need instruction or intervention. This exam is group administered, norm referenced, and based on scientific research. GRADE provides teachers with the components they need to accurately and effectively assess students' competency in reading. The WRMT-R is a norm-based, diagnostic exam that measures precise ability in reading achievement for students in kindergarten through 12th grade. This individually administered exam consists of a variety of subtests that examine a student's ability in such areas as vocabulary, decoding, and comprehension.

These two assessments are often administered to secondary students who experience reading difficulties to monitor their progress as interventions and supportive services are implemented. Some schools who have certified reading specialists on staff may prefer to administer the WRMT-R to secondary students, because the teachers believe that the individual testing environment of this test is more conducive to getting a "true read" on a student's performance in reading than the group environment of the GRADE. As a result, when data are brought to the IST regarding the student's progress, results may indicate a truer measure of progress made.

In addition to selecting the types of instruments utilized, the team will also need to make decisions regarding the frequency of data collection during a student's progress monitoring. This may depend on what targeted intervention is being monitored (e.g., fluency of reading, homework completion, etc.). A time span for an intervention is agreed upon (sometimes six to eight instructional weeks), an intervention goal is established, and the facilitator of the meeting summarizes what was discussed and agreed upon for the minutes. An RTI progress monitoring worksheet (see Table 10.4) can be designed by the RTI team to assist the teacher with data collection and recording until the next meeting. Other monitoring worksheets, charts, and graphs are available free to teachers and can be found at www.interventioncentral.org.

Table 10.4 Sample Progress Monitoring Report

| Student: _____ |
| Teacher: _____ |

| Define ONE problem/concern: |

| Present Level of Performance (PLOP): |

| Goal: |

| Intervention(s) to be implemented: |

| Assessment tool(s) being used to measure progress: |

| Monitor/Assess For Improvement: |

Time Elapsed	Date	PLOP: *Present Level of Performance*	*Continue/Adjust/ Discontinue Intervention*
2 weeks			
4 weeks			
6 weeks			
8 weeks			
10 weeks			

Keeping Track of Data

At the elementary level, examples of data collection often involve measuring and monitoring a student's progress in reading. As a result, data regarding oral reading fluency, word attack, and sight word vocabulary might be charted by the general education classroom teacher. As elementary students move into the secondary schools, however, teachers might choose to target different skills (such as homework completion). Regardless of what is being monitored by the teacher, two essential strategies remain the same: (1) A specific goal for improvement must be established, and (2) a specific method needs to be selected to monitor the student's progress toward meeting that goal during that intervention period (formative assessment), and then to determine if the intervention was successful in helping the student attain the goal (summative assessment). Perhaps one of the greatest stumbling blocks to the implementation of RTI in secondary schools is the daunting task of collecting data on students and the time required to effectively do it. Most teachers wonder how they will fit this additional task into their already busy instructional day.

For RTI to be effective, the teacher must choose a method for collecting data that will provide useful information about an individual student, but, just as important, that can be managed within the classroom setting. In addition, the information must be related to the curriculum and be measurable over time (e.g., structured note taking, study organizers, and math worksheet generators). These classroom-generated assessments can be combined with more structured assessments that are monitored by building- and/or district-level administrators to provide a more comprehensive picture of the student's overall performance in terms of strengths and weaknesses.

Table 10.5 provides a sampling of websites that are available to teachers to assist with data collection.

Table 10.5   Websites for RTI Data Collection

Type	Description	Website
Math Worksheet Generator	This site has a free math worksheet generator to create computation worksheets with easy problems interspersed among more challenging ones.	www .interventioncentral .org/htmdocs/tools/ mathprobe/allmult .php

Type	Description	Website
Behavior Report Card	This site allows teachers or parents to create daily behavior report cards as a way to collect ongoing ratings of students' behavior, work habits, and work completion. Customized forms are available in either daily or weekly formats, and there are ready-to-use progress monitoring charts.	www .jimwrightonline. com/php/tbrc/tbrc .php
Online Testing	This site has storage space for tests and quizzes that can be used and reused. Questions are saved in a variety of formats and can be saved in a teacher's personal account for future storage and use.	www.quizinator.com
ChartDog	ChartDog is a web-based program that constructs customized progress monitoring graphs from data created by teachers. It provides users with a concrete way to monitor a student's progress for a specific period of time and visually graph results.	www .jimwrightonline .com/php/ chartdog_2_0/ chartdog.php

The IST can be helpful in assisting teachers with templates for documents, charts, and even technologies that can store, calculate, and keep track of student data. This type of support may be critical to the overall infrastructure of an RTI program (Batsche, 2008), and many of these templates are available to teachers for free. Several computerized programs, available by subscription and shown in Table 10.6, can also assist with collection of data that require subscriptions.

Table 10.6 Computer Assisted Progress Monitoring Sites—Fee Based

Type	Description	Purpose
AIMSweb (www .aimsweb .com)	This is a benchmark and monitoring system that screens and assesses student progress, monitors at-risk students, and evaluates effectiveness of interventions in reading, math, spelling, and writing.	Web-based management and reporting system that efficiently captures RTI data.

(Continued)

Type	Description	Purpose
EasyCBM (www .easycbm .com) free to individual teachers (up to Grade 8)	This site has two components (teacher and district) that offer benchmark/screener tests and progress monitoring measures that give different users different levels of access to data relative to reading and math within the system. The math assessments for grades K–8 are based on the Focal Point Standards in Mathematics from the National Council of Teachers of Mathematics.	An assessment tool for individual teachers or school districts that samples from a year's worth of curriculum to assess the degree to which students have mastered the skills and knowledge deemed critical at each grade level.
EdCheckup (www .edcheckup .com)	This progress monitoring system tracks literacy skills (oral reading, silent reading, beginning reading, and four aspects of writing, including sentence copying, sentence dictation, paragraph dictation, and written expression). The site also assesses math computation using a cloze math format.	A K–8 progress monitoring system that evaluates student performance and measures student progress toward goals in reading, writing, and math.
STEEP (www .isteep .com)	This website offers commercial products that include both reading and math assessments that span grades 1–12. Schools and districts can purchases assessments separately or can pay a fee based on student enrollment for more comprehensive services, including web-based data management.	Computer administered screenings for reading and math that span grades 1–12. Offers benchmark screening and use of web-based data system for management of paper-based assessments, progress monitoring, and so forth.

Source: Compiled from information at www.interventioncentral.org.

CONCLUSION

Although RTI is becoming increasingly well known and accepted at the elementary levels, its implementation at the secondary level is less widespread. Teachers at this level need to be assured that RTI strategies are, in essence, best practice teaching methodologies that benefit all students, and that, with support from administration and peers, RTI implementation can be embedded into the tapestry of secondary schools.

 TECH BYTE

PODCASTS

Podcast #1: "RTI at the Secondary Level"

Teachers and administrators who are contemplating the implementation of RTI in the secondary schools often do not know where to begin. The use of the brief podcast below is one way for administrators to begin the conversation among colleagues at the secondary level. Jay Engeln (a high school principal) shares his (and his colleagues') perspectives on some of the critical issues facing teachers and administrators in making RTI work in the high school setting. In the podcast, Jay discusses typical hurdles faced by staff in implementing RTI and stresses the importance of data-driven decision making. He suggests that many schools often have interventions in place and stresses the value of collaboration.

How to Use This Podcast: This podcast is a good starting point to begin the conversation about RTI at the secondary level. Teachers and building leaders might use this video as a kickoff to staff development about RTI. Jay Engeln provides us with some of the key ideas and concerns of RTI implementation in secondary schools (i.e., time, data analysis) and urges us to consider how our own school's current configuration has the structures in place to implement RTI. The questions he poses can become good building blocks for faculty discussions on how to create a model that is collaborative and successful for all students.

Watch and listen to the podcast at www.rtinetwork.org/professional/podcasts/jay-engeln-rti-at-the-secondary-level.

Podcast #2: "Supporting Struggling Adolescent Readers"

Many students who struggle academically exhibit difficulties with reading. This podcast offers teachers and administrators information on how to support struggling adolescent readers. Concrete suggestions for teachers and tutors are provided to help reluctant readers improve comprehension, motivation, and sight word vocabulary, and to enhance prior knowledge of content area. The podcast also provides teachers with further references to expand upon their knowledge of adolescent literacy. This is an excellent resource for further study into the area of literacy and its relationship to RTI.

How to Use This Podcast: This podcast offers several specific teaching tools to help struggling learners. After listening to this podcast, teachers might want to work collaboratively in groups; each group might want to select one of the strategies mentioned in the podcast and brainstorm how the strategy might work in their particular subject area or grade. One group might consist of several content area teachers and a reading teacher, and their focus might be to select trade books on a variety of topics that are related to the content taught in one particular grade. Reluctant readers or struggling learners could build their background knowledge about a particular topic by learning about it through a high-interest nonfiction trade book that sustains their interest and is at a reading level that is commensurate with their ability. Another way to utilize ideas presented in this podcast is to have a group of special education and regular education teachers create a list of semantic maps or graphic organizers that have been successfully utilized to expand students' learning. These lists can be shared with grade-level and building-level teams to create a common core of RTI best practices.

Listen to the podcast at www.reading.org/Resources/Resources ByTopic/ResponseToIntervention/Overview.aspx. To locate this podcast on this website, scroll down on this link until you see the word "Podcasts." Click on the title "Supporting Struggling Adolescent Readers," and the podcast will begin.

RESOURCES

In addition to the references found at the end of this book, teachers and principals who wish to learn more about RTI can get more information from a variety of sources. Below is an annotated list of Internet sites and resources for future study:

National Center on Response to Intervention. (www.rti4success.org)

To meet the challenges of RTI, the American Institutes for Research and researchers from Vanderbilt University and the University of Kansas (with funding from the U.S. Department of Education's Office of Special Education Programs) have established this organization. Its website contains a wealth of information on RTI implementation in each of the 50 states and offers visitors free resources and access to tools utilized throughout the nation.

Intervention Central. (www.interventioncentral.org)

This comprehensive website provides teachers, schools, and districts with free articles and tools to implement RTI. The site's author, Jim Wright, is an RTI consultant and trainer from central New York who has worked for 17 years as a school psychologist and administrator. This site contains a multitude of free resources, including academic and behavioral publications and assessment materials. Many resources are available for download.

The RTI Action Network. (www.rtinetwork.org)

This is an organization that is dedicated to effectively implementing RTI in school districts across the country. The website offers teachers free resources to obtain information about RTI on all levels (pre-K to higher education) as well as the ability to connect with others through the use of discussion boards, blogs, and discussion threads.

What Works Clearinghouse. (http://ies.ed.gov/ncee/wwc/)

This website is an initiative of the U.S. Department of Education; it contains user-friendly guides for educators that address instructional challenges with research-based recommendations for schools and classrooms. The site also provides tiered interventions that will assist educators in making informed decisions about students.

The Technical Assistance Center on Positive Behavioral Interventions and Supports, PBIS. (www.pbis.org/)

This center has been established by the Office of Special Education Programs and the U.S. Department of Education to give schools capacity-building information and technical assistance for identifying, adapting, and sustaining effective schoolwide disciplinary practices. The center's goal is to promote and improve the social behavior of students in U.S. schools as a means to enhance academic performance and to demonstrate that positive behavioral interventions can be effective when implemented in schools as part of an overall schoolwide behavior support system. The website contains resources, links, videos, and information regarding PBIS and its implementation.

The Florida Center for Reading Research. (www.fcrr.org/)

The mission of the Florida Center for Reading Research is to conduct basic research on reading (growth, assessment, and instruction) that will contribute to the scientific knowledge of reading and benefit students in Florida and throughout the nation. Pursuant to its research, the center disseminates information about research-based practices related to literacy instruction and assessment for children in preschool through 12th grade and provides technical assistance to Florida's schools and to the state's department of education for the improvement of literacy outcomes in students from pre-K through 12th grade. The center's website also focuses on RTI and provides teachers with information on training, information on the state's plan for intervention, and potential models for RTI.

The Center on Teaching and Learning, University of Oregon. (http://reading.uoregon.edu/curricula/or_rfc_review.php)

The center offers teachers a variety of resources on the teaching of reading. Specifically, curriculum resources are available, and supplemental and intervention programs are reviewed, explained, and offered as models.

Epilogue

Why Implement RTI?

Dolores T. Burton and John Kappenberg

RTI is based on a very simple premise: All children can learn. The goal of RTI is to improve instruction and educational outcomes for *all* students. Its foundation is three fold: providing high-quality instruction to students, using reliable and valid data to make decisions, and preventing rather than fixing student failure. Attendees at the National Summit on Learning Disabilities, a learning disabilities summit conference convened by the Office of Special Education Programs (OSEP) in August 2001 (Bradley, Danielson, & Hallahan, 2002) endorsed RTI as "the most promising method of alternative identification" and stated that RTI promotes the implementation of effective practices in schools.

Data from the National Assessment of Educational Progress (NAEP) have shown that large percentages of students in the United States are not proficient in reading or mathematics. For example, only 31% of fourth-grade students and 29% of eighth-grade students in the United States were classified as proficient or better on the NAEP reading assessment in 2007. Reid Lyon, Jack Fletcher, and their colleagues (2001) suggested that through early identification and intervention for reading difficulties, the number of children in special education can be reduced by 70%.

Every child who can benefit from special education should, after careful diagnosis and proper assessment, be given the support necessary for him or her to succeed. However, this must be done in a thoughtful way, as only 57% of the students placed in special education graduate from high school, and often they are labeled and segregated from other students, and few ever return to general education (Hosp & Madyun, 2007).

An additional concern is that children from minority groups are overrepresented in special education (Stuebing, et al., 2002). Black-White achievement gaps in Grade 4 mathematics existed in 2007 in the 46 states for which results were available, and gaps in Grade 4 reading existed in

197

2007 in the 44 states for which results were available. As educators we have the responsibility to provide educational opportunities to all students regardless of race, gender, or socioeconomic status so they may reach their potential.

The focus of RTI is on improved student outcomes for all students through the provision of high-quality science- or research-based instruction and interventions that are matched to student academic or behavioral needs. Through a multitiered framework, the RTI process enables districts to provide early support and assistance to students who are struggling to attain or maintain grade-level performance. No longer do teachers, parents, and students have to wait for students to fail before interventions can begin. According to the National Association of State Directors of Special Education (NASDSE), RTI "is a practice of providing high quality instruction and interventions matched to student need, monitoring progress frequently to make decisions about changes in instruction or goals and applying child response data to important educational decisions" (NASDSE, 2006, p. 3).

This book was written to help educators and parents to develop a background in multiple aspects of RTI, from its structure to the content of individual interventions. It was designed with case studies to demonstrate how theory is turned into practice, and it includes resources for continued study on best practices in instruction, assessment, and all components of RTI. It was written in the hope that with informed parents and educators, all students will have the opportunity to reach their potential and succeed in our ever changing global interconnected world. Our children deserve no less.

References and Resources

Abramson, L. (2009). *U.S. unveils education stimulus rules.* Retrieved from http://www.npr.org/templates/story/story.php?storyId=120340616&ft=1&f=3

Adams, J. J., Foorman, B. R., Lundberg, I., & Beeler, T. (1998). *Phonemic awareness in young children.* Baltimore, MD: Paul Brookes.

Adams, M. J. (1990). *Beginning to read: Thinking and learning about print.* Cambridge: MIT Press.

Adams, T. L. (2000). Overlapping of Gardner's multiple intelligences and NCTM process standards. *Childhood Education, 77*(2), 86–94.

Ambach, G. M. (1884). State and local action for education in New York. *Phi Delta Kappan,* (66), 202–204.

Ambrose, S. E. (1990). *Eisenhower: Soldier and president.* New York, NY: Simon & Schuster.

American Federation of Teachers. (1999). *Teaching reading is rocket science: What expert teachers of reading should know and be able to do.* Washington, DC: Author.

American Guidance Service. (2001). *Teacher's administration manual: Group Reading Assessment and Diagnostic Evaluation (GRADE).* Circle Pines, MN: Author.

Baer, J., Kutner, M., & Sabatini, J. (2009). *Basic reading skills and the literacy of America's least literate adults: Results from the 2003 assessment of adult literacy (NAAL) supplemental studies* (NCES 2009-48l). Washington, DC: National Center for Education Statistics, Institute of Education Sciences, U.S. Department of Education.

Baker, S., & Good, R. H. (1995). Curriculum-based measurement of English reading with bilingual Hispanic students: A validation study with second-grade students. *School Psychology Review, 24,* 561–578.

Barton, R., & Stepanek, J. (2009). Three tiers to success. *Principal Leadership, 9*(8), 16–20.

Batsche, G. (2008). *Developing a plan.* Retrieved from http://www.rtinetwork.org/component/labels/create-your-rti-plan

Batsche, G., Elliott, J., Graden, J. L., Grimes, J., Kovaleski, J. F., Prasse, D., Reschly, D., et al. (2006). *Response to intervention: Policy considerations and implementation.* Alexandria, VA: National Association of State Directors of Special Education.

Bender, W., & Shores, C. (2007). *Response to intervention: A practical guide for every teacher.* Thousand Oaks, CA: Corwin.

Bens, I. (2005). *Facilitating with ease! Core skills for facilitators, team leaders and members, managers, consultants and trainers.* San Francisco, CA: Jossey-Bass.

Bergan, J. R. (1995). Evolution of a problem-solving model of consultation. *Journal of Educational and Psychological Consultation, 6*(2), 111–123.

Bradley, R., Danielson, L., & Hallahan, D. (Eds.) (2002). *Identification of learning disabilities: Research to practice.* Mahwah, NJ: Erlbaum.

Buckley, S. (2003). Literacy and language. In J. A. Rondal & S. Buckley (Eds.), *Speech and language intervention in Down syndrome* (pp. 132–153). London, UK: Whurr.

Buffum, A., Mattos, M., & Weber, C. (2008). *Pyramid response to intervention: RtI, professional learning communities, and how to respond when kids don't learn.* Bloomington, IN: Solution Tree.

Buffum, A., Mattos, M., & Weber, C. (2010). The why behind RTI. *Educational Leadership, 68*(2), 10–16.

Burns, M. K., & Gibbons, K. A. (2008). *Implementing response to intervention in elementary and secondary schools.* New York, NY: Routledge.

Burns, M. K., Hall-Lande, J., Lyman, W., Rogers, C., & Tan, C. S. (2006). Tier II interventions within response-to-intervention: Components of an effective approach. *Communiqué, 35*(4), 38–40.

Cambron-McCabe, N., Cunningham, L. L., Harvey, J., & Koff, R. H. (2005). *The superintendent's fieldbook.* Thousand Oaks, CA: AASA & Corwin.

Canter, A., Klotz, M. B., & Cowan, K. (2008). Response to intervention: The future of secondary schools. *Principal Leadership, 8*(6), 12–15.

Carr, E. G., Horner, R. H., Turnbull, A. P., Marquis, J. G., Magito McLaughlin, D., McAtee, M. L., Smith, C. E., et al. (1999). *Positive behavior support for people with developmental disabilities: A research synthesis.* Washington, DC: American Association for Mental Retardation.

Carr, E. G., Levin, L., McConnachie, G., Carlson, J. I., Kemp, D. C., & Smith, C. (1994). *Communication based intervention for problem behavior: A user's guide for producing positive change.* Baltimore, MD: Paul H. Brookes.

Cashman, J., Linehan, P., & Rosser, M. (2007). *Communities of practice: A new approach to solving complex educational problems.* Alexandria, VA: National Association of State Directors of Special Education.

Center on Teaching and Learning, University of Oregon. (n.d.). *What are Dynamic Indicators of Basic Early Literacy Skills (DIBELS)?* Retrieved from https://dibels.uoregon.edu/dibels_what.php

Certo, S. C. (2008). *Modern management.* Upper Saddle River, NJ: Prentice Hall.

Chen, Y. (2002). *Assessment of reading and writing samples of deaf and hard of hearing students by curriculum-based measurements.* Unpublished doctoral dissertation. Minneapolis: University of Minnesota.

Child Development Institute. (n.d.). *Language development in children.* Retrieved from http://www.childdevelopmentinfo.com/development/language_develop ment.shtml

Christ, T. (2008). Best practices in problem analysis. In A. Thomas & J. Grimes (Eds.), *Best practices in school psychology V* (pp. 159–176). Bethesda, MD: National Association of School Psychologists.

Clark, J. P. (1998). Functional behavioral assessment and behavioral intervention plans: Implementing the student discipline provisions of IDEA '97. *Section Connection, 4*(2), 6–7.

Clark, J. P., & Alvarez, M. E. (Eds.). (2010). *Response to intervention: A guide for school social workers.* New York, NY: Oxford University Press.

Clark, T. (2004). *Ask not: The inauguration of John F. Kennedy and the speech that changed America.* New York, NY: Henry Holt.

Clonin, S. M., McDougal, J. L., Clark, K., & Davison, S. (2007). Use of office discipline referrals in school-wide decision making: A practical example. *Psychology in the Schools, 44*(1), 19–27.

Communities of Practice. (n.d.). Retrieved from http://ideapartnership.org/index .php?option=com_content&view=section&id=11&Itemid=45

Council for Exceptional Children. (2007). *Position on response to intervention: The unique role of special education and special educators.* Retrieved from http:// www.cec.sped.org/AM/Template.cfm?Section=Home&CONTENTID=9237& TEMPLATE=/CM/ContentDisplay.cfm

Council for Exceptional Children. (n.d.). *Exceptionality: Learning disability.* Retrieved from http://www.cec.sped.org/AM/Template.cfm?Section=Learning_ Disabilities&Template=/TaggedPage/TaggedPageDisplay.cfm&TPLID=37& ContentID=5629

Covey, S. R. (1989). *The seven habits of highly effective people.* New York, NY: Free Press.

Covey, S. R. (2004). *The seven habits of highly effective people.* New York, NY: Free Press.

Creighton, T. B. (2007). *Schools and data: The educator's guide for using data to improve decision-making.* Thousand Oaks, CA: Corwin.

DeLorenzo, J. P., & Stevens, J. (2008, April). *Memo re implementation of response to intervention programs.* Retrieved from http://www.p12.nysed.gov/specialed/ publications/policy/RTI.htm

Deming, W. E. (1994). *The new economics for industry, government, education.* Cambridge: Massachusetts Institute of Technology, Center for Advanced Engineering Study.

Denison, D. R. (1984). Book review: The decline and fall of the American automobile industry, by Brock Yates (New York, NY: Empire Books, 1983). *Human Resource Management, 22*(4), 483–486.

Deno, S. L. (1985). Curriculum-based measurement: The emerging alternative. *Exceptional Children, 52,* 219–232.

Deno, S. L. (2003). Curriculum-based measures: Development and perspectives. *Assessment for Effective Intervention, 28*, 3–12.

Deno, S. L., & Mirkin, P. K. (1977). *Data-based program modification: A manual.* Reston, VA: Council for Exceptional Children.

Devenow, P. (2002). *A study of the CBM maze procedure as a measure of reading with deaf and hard of hearing students.* Unpublished doctoral dissertation. Minneapolis: University of Minnesota.

Dillon, S. (2009, November 12). After criticism, the administration is praised for final rules on education grants. *The New York Times*, p. A20.

DiPipi-Hoy, C., Jitendra, A. K., & Kern, L. (2009). Effects of time management instruction on adolescents' ability to self-manage time in a vocational setting. *Journal of Special Education, 43*(3), 145–159.

Dodd, A. W., & Konzal, J. L. (2000). Parents and educators as partners: Conducting students learning. *The High School Magazine, 7*(5), 8–13.

Donovan, S., & Cross, C. T. (Eds.). (2002). *Minority students in special and gifted education.* Washington, DC: National Academies Press.

Doran, G. (1981). There's a SMART way to write management's goals and objectives. *Management Review, 70*, 35–36.

Doyle, M., & Straus, D. (1993). *How to make meetings work!* New York, NY: Berkley.

Drucker, P. F. (1999). *Management challenges for the 21ˢᵗ century.* New York, NY: HarperCollins.

Duffy, H. (2007). *Meeting the needs of significantly struggling learners in high school: A look at approaches to tiered intervention.* Retrieved from http://www .betterhighschools.org/pubs/usergd_stlr.asp

Duncan, A. (2009). *Teacher preparation: Reforming the uncertain profession: Remarks of Secretary Arne Duncan at Teachers College, Columbia University.* Press release. Washington, DC: U.S. Department of Education. Retrieved from http://www .ed.gov/news/speeches/2009/10/10222009.html

Education for All Handicapped Children Act. (1975, 1977). *Pub. L. 94-142*, 20 U.S.C. §1400–1485, 34 CFR-300

Ehren, B. (2008). *Response to intervention in secondary schools: Is it on your radar screen?* Retrieved from http://www.rtinetwork.org/component/labels/create-your-rti-plan.

Espin, C. A., & Deno, S. L. (1993). Curriculum-based measures for secondary students: Utility and task specificity of text-based reading and vocabulary measures for predicting performance on content-area tasks. *Diagnostique, 20*, 121–142.

Feldman, K. (n.d.). *Response to intervention and reading: Intervening effectively in literacy.* Retrieved from http://www.calstat.org/podcasts/pdfs/rti_literacy.pdf

Fernald, A., Taeschner, T., Dunn, J., Papousek, M., de Boysson-Bardies, B., & Fukui, I. (1989). A cross-language study of prosodic modifications in mothers' and fathers' speech to preverbal infants. *Journal of Child Language, 16*, 477–501.

Fisher, S. E., & DeFries J. C. (2002). Genetic dissection of a complex cognitive trait. *Nature Reviews Neuroscience, 2*, 767–782.

Flesch, R. (1955). *Why Johnny can't read—and what you can do about it.* New York, NY: Harper.

Fontana, J. L., Doerries, D., & Stickney, D. (n.d.). *Instructional support teams help sustain responsive instruction frameworks.* Retrieved from http://www.cec.sped .org/AM/Template.cfm?Section=Home&TEMPLATE=/CM/ContentDisplay .cfm&CONTENTID=10372

Friederici, A. D., & Thierry, G. (2008). *Early language development: Bridging brain and behavior.* Bangor, ME: Max Planck Institute for Human Cognitive and Brain Sciences.

Fuchs, D., & Fuchs, L. (1997). Use of curriculum-based measurements in identifying students with disabilities. *Focus on Exceptional Children, 50,* 1–16.

Fuchs, D., & Fuchs, L. (2005). Responsiveness-to-intervention: A blueprint for practitioners, policymakers, and parents. *Teaching Exceptional Children, 38*(1), 57–61.

Fuchs, D., & Fuchs, L. (2006, January/February/March). Introduction to response to intervention: What, why and how valid is it? *Reading Research Quarterly, 41*(1), 92–99.

Fuchs, D., Fuchs, L., & Bahr, M. (1990). Mainstream assistance teams: A scientific basis for the art of consultation. *Exceptional Children, 57,* 128–139.

Fuchs, L., Deno, S. L., & Mirkin, P. (1984). Effects of frequent curriculum-based measurement and evaluation on pedagogy, student achievement, and student awareness of learning. *American Educational Research Journal, 21,* 449–460.

Gardner, H. (1983). *Frames of mind: The theory of multiple intelligences.* New York, NY: Basic Books.

Gersten, R. (2009). *RTI and mathematics.* Webinar retrieved from http://www .rti4success.org/webinars/video/890

Gersten, R., Compton, D., Connor, C. M., Dimino, J., Santoro, L., Linan-Thompson, S., & Tilly, W. D. (2008). *Assisting students struggling with reading: Response to intervention and multi-tier intervention for reading in the primary grades. A practice guide* (NCEE 2009-4045). Washington, DC: National Center for Education Evaluation and Regional Assistance, Institute of Education Sciences, U.S. Department of Education. Retrieved from http://ies.ed.gov/ ncee/wwc/pdf/practiceguides/rti_math_pg_042109.pdf

Gonzales, P., Williams, T., Jocelyn, L., Roey, S., Kastberg, D., & Brenwald, S. (2008). *Highlights from TIMSS 2007: Mathematics and Science Achievement of U.S. Fourth- and Eighth-Grade Students in an International Context* (NCES 2009–001). Washington, DC: U.S. Department of Education, National Center for Education Statistics. Retrieved from http://nces.ed.gov/timss/

Gonzalez-DeHass, A. R., & Willems, P. P. (2003). Examining the underutilization of parent involvement in the schools. *School Community Journal, 13*(1), 85–99.

Graden, J., Casey, A., & Bonstrom, O. (1985). Implementing a prereferral intervention system: Part II, the data. *Exceptional Children, 51,* 487–496.

Graden, J., Casey, A., & Christenson, S. L. (1985). Implementing a prereferral intervention system: Part I, the model. *Exceptional Children, 51,* 377–384.

Graden, J., Zins, J. E., & Curtis, M. (1989). *Alternative educational delivery systems: Enhancing instructional options for all students.* Washington, DC: National Association of School Psychologists.

Green, R. L. (2010). *The four dimensions of principal leadership: A framework for leading 21ˢᵗ century schools.* Boston, MA: Allyn & Bacon.

Greenwood, G. E., & Hickman, C. W. (1991). Research and practice in parent involvement: Implications for teacher education. *Elementary School Journal, 91*(3), 279–288.

Gresham, F. M., MacMillan, D. L., Beebe-Frankenberger, M. E., & Bocian, K. M. (2000). Treatment integrity in learning disabilities intervention research: Do we really know how treatments are implemented? *Learning Disabilities Research & Practice, 15*(4), 198–205.

Gresham, F. M., VanDerHeyden. A., & Witt, J. C. (2005). *Response to intervention in the identification of learning disabilities: Empirical support and future challenges.* Riverside: Graduate School of Education, University of California–Riverside.

Grigorenko, E. L. (2001). Developmental dyslexia: An update on genes, brains, and environments. *Journal of Child Psychology and Psychiatry, 42,* 91–125.

Guskey, T. (2010). Lessons of mastery learning. *Educational Leadership, 68*(2), 53–57.

Harvey, R. (1995). *The return of the strong: The drift to global disorder.* London, UK: Macmillan.

Hawken, L. S., Pettersson, H., Mootz, J., & Anderson, C. (2006). *The behavior education program: A check-in, check-out intervention for students at risk.* New York, NY: Guilford Press.

Help! Teacher can't teach!: The multlifaceted crisis of American schools. (1980). *Time.* Cover story published June 16, 1980. Retrieved from http://time.com/time/magazine/article0,9171,924217,00.html

Hiebert, E. H., Pearson, P. D., Taylor, B., Richardson, V., & Paris, S. G. (1998). *Every child a reader.* Ann Arbor, MI: Center for the Improvement of Early Reading Achievement.

Hoffer, T., B., Venkataraman, L., Hedberg, E. C., & Shagle, S. (2008). *Final report on the National Survey of Algebra Teachers for the National Mathematics Advisory Panel Subcommittee.* Retrieved from http://www2.ed.gov/about/bdscomm/list/mathpanel/report/nsat.pdf

Horowitz, S. (2009). *Learning disabilities: What they are and what they are not.* Retrieved from http://www.ncld.org/ld-basics/ld-explained/basic-facts/learning-disabilities-what-they-are-and-what-they-are-not

Hosp, J., & Madyun, N. (2007). Addressing disproportionality through response to intervention. In S. Jimerson, M. Burns, & A. VanDerHeyden (Eds.), *The handbook of response to intervention: The science and practice of assessment and intervention* (pp. 172–181). New York: Springer.

Houston, P. D., Blankstein, A. M., & Cole, R. W. (2007). *The soul of educational leadership: Out-of-the-box leadership.* Thousand Oaks, CA: Corwin.

Hoy, A. W., & Hoy, W. H. (2006). *Instructional leadership: A research-based guide to learning in schools.* Boston, MA: Allyn & Bacon.

Hoyle, J. R., Bjork, L. G., Collier, V., & Glass, T. (2005). *The superintendent as CEO: Standards-based performance.* Thousand Oaks, CA: AASA & Corwin.

Hudson, R. F., High, L., & Al Otaiba, S. (2007). Dyslexia and the brain: What does current research tell us? *The Reading Teacher, 60*(6), 506–515.

Hughes, S., Kolsyad, R. K., &. Briggs, L. D. (1994). Dyscalculia and mathematics achievement. *Journal of Instructional Psychology, 21*(1), 64–68.

Iacocca, L. (with William Novak). (1984). *Iacocca: An autobiography.* New York, NY: Bantam Books.

International Reading Association. (2009). *Response to intervention: Guiding principles for educators from the International Reading Association.* Newark, DE: Author.

Iowa Department of Education. (2006). *Progress monitoring for teachers of students who have visual disabilities.* Des Moines, IA: Bureau of Children, Families, & Community Services. Retrieved from http://www.iowa.gov/educate/index .php?option=com_docman&task=doc_download&gid=3313

Jackson, F. B. (2002). Crossing content: A strategy for students with learning disabilities. *Intervention in School and Clinic, 37*(5), 279–282.

James, F. (2004). *Response to intervention and the Individuals with Disabilities Education Act (IDEA), 2004.* Retrieved from http://www.reading.org/ downloads/resources/IDEA_RTI_report.pdf

Jennings, M. (2009). *Before the special education referral: Leading intervention teams.* Thousand Oaks, CA: Corwin.

Jimerson, S., Burns, M., & VanDerHeyden, A. (Eds.). (2007). *Handbook of response to intervention: The science and practice of assessment and intervention.* New York, NY: Springer.

Jitendra, A. (2002). Teaching students math problem-solving through graphic representations. *Council for Exceptional Children, 34*(4), 34–38.

Johnson, E., Pool, J., & Carter, D. (2008). *Screening for reading problems in grades 4 through 12.* Retrieved from http://www.rtinetwork.org/essential/assessment/ screening/screening-for-reading-problems-in-an-rti-framework

Jordan, N. C., Kaplan, D., Nabors Ola´h, L., & Locuniak, M. N. (2006). Number sense growth in kindergarten: A longitudinal investigation of children at risk for mathematics difficulties. *Child Development, 77*(1), 153–175.

Kaminski, R. A., & Good, R. H. (1996). Toward a technology for assessing basic early literacy skills. *School Psychology Review, 25,* 215–227.

Katzenbach, J. R., & Smith, D. K. (2003). *The wisdom of teams.* Boston, MA: Harper Business.

Kavale, K. A., & Forness, S. R. (2000). What definitions of learning disability say and don't say: A critical analysis. *Journal of Learning Disabilities, 33,* 239–256.

Kelly, T. (2010, August). *Supporting diverse learners through response to intervention: Theory, research, and implications for educational leaders.* Paper presented at the National Council of Professors of Educational Administration Annual Conference, Washington, DC.

Kimmel, H., Deek, F. P., Farrell, M. L., & O'Shea, M. (1999). Meeting the needs of diverse student populations: Comprehensive professional development in science, math, and technology for teachers of students with disabilities. *School Science and Mathematics, 99,* 241–249.

King, N. (2009, November 12). Stimulus to reward states that overhaul school systems. *The Wall Street Journal,* p. A7.

Kling, J. (2000). Tension in teams. *Harvard Management Communication Letter, 3*(7), 1–3. Article reprint #C0007A. Boston, MA: Harvard Business School Publishing.

Knight, J. (2007). *Instructional coaching: A partnership approach to improving instruction.* Thousand Oaks, CA: Corwin.

Kornhaber, M., & Krechevsky, M. (1995). Expanding definitions of teaching and learning: Notes from the MI underground. In P. Cookson & B. Schneider (Eds.), *Transforming schools* (pp. 120–149). New York, NY: Garland.

Kowalski, T. J., Lasley, T. J. II., & Mahoney, J. W. (2008). *Data-driven decisions and school leadership: Best practices for school improvement.* Boston, MA: Pearson Allyn & Bacon.

Lent, R. W., Brown, S. D., & Hackett G. (2000). Contextual supports and barriers to career choice: A social cognitive analysis. *Journal of Counseling Psychology, 47,* 36–49.

Lerner, J. W. (2003). *Learning disabilities: Theories, diagnosis, and teaching strategies.* Boston, MA: Houghton Mifflin.

Levine, A. (2006). *Educating school teachers.* Washington, DC: The Education Schools Project.

Lewis, J. (1996). *Perspective of parent involvement in public education cited in Parent Involvement Exchange.* Retrieved from http://parentalie.com

Lopez, G. R., Scribner, J. D., & Mahitivanichcha, K. (2001). Redefining parental involvement: Lesson's from high-performing migrant-impacted schools. *American Educational Research Journal, 38*(2), 253–288.

Lunenburg, F. C., & Ornstein, A. C. (2008). *Educational administration: Concepts & practices.* Belmont, CA: Thomson Wadsworth.

Lyon, G. R. (1998, March). What is basic? *Educational Leadership, 5*(6), 14–18.

Lyon, G. R., Fletcher, J. M., Shaywitz, S. E., Shaywitz, B. A., Torgesen, J. K., Wood, F. B., Schulte, A., et al. (2001). Rethinking learning disabilities. In C. E. Finn, Jr., A. J. Rotherham, & C. R. Hokanson, Jr. (Eds.), *Rethinking special education for a new century* (pp. 259–287). Washington, DC: Progressive Policy Institute, Thomas B. Fordham Foundation.

Lyon, G. R. (2002). Reading development, reading difficulties, and reading instruction: Educational and public health issues. *Journal of School Psychology, 40,* 3–6.

Marcellino, P. A. (2006). A teambuilding model for the educational leadership classroom. In F. Dembowski & L. Lemasters (Eds.), *NCPEA 2006 yearbook— unbridled spirit: Best practices in educational administration* (pp. 216–225). Lancaster, PA: Pro>Active.

Marcellino, P. A. (2008). Action-research: Adopting team contracts to initiate team learning. *American Association of School Administrators Journal of Scholarship and Practice, 5*(1), 15–20.

Marcellino, P. A. (2010). Revisiting and redesigning a faculty-developed team instructional model. In B. Irby, B. Alford, G. Perreault, & L. Zellner (Eds.), *Promoting critical ideas of leadership, culture and diversity: The 2010 yearbook of the national council of professors of educational administration* (pp. 39–56). Lancaster, PA: Pro>Active.

Marcellino, P. A. (2011). *A sample implementation of a three year strategic plan.* Syosset, NY: C&P Consulting.

Marston, D. (2006). *Problem-solving model and response to intervention.* Paper presented at Response to Intervention Symposium, Austin, TX. Retrieved from http://www .rti4success.org/index.php?option=com_content&task=view&id=853

Marzano, R. (2010). Reviving reteaching. *Educational Leadership, 68*(2), 82–83.

Maslow, A. H. (1943). A theory of human motivation. *Psychological Review, 50*(4), 370–396.

Mayer, M. (1993). *Robert Maynard Hutchins: A memoir.* Berkeley: University of California Press.

McGrath, A. (2005). A new read on teen literacy. *U.S. News & World Report,* posted February 20, 2005. Retrieved February 8, 2011, from http://www .usnews.com/usnews/culture/articles/050228/28literacy.htm

Mellard, D. (2004). *Understanding responsiveness to intervention in learning disabilities determination.* Retrieved from http://www.nrcld.org/about/ publications/papers/mellard.pdf

Melnyk, B. M., & Fineout-Overholt, E. (2005). *Making the case for evidence-based practice.* Philadelphia, PA: Lippincott Williams & Wilkins.

Mercer, C. D. & Mercer, A. R. (1997). *Teaching students with learning disabilities* (5th ed.). Upper Saddle River, NJ: Prentice-Hall, Inc.

Miedel, W. T., & Reynolds, A. J. (1999). Parent involvement in early intervention for disadvantaged children: Does it matter? *Journal of School Psychology, 37*(4), 379–402.

Miller, G. A. (1956). The magical number seven, plus or minus two: Some limits on our capacity for processing information. *The Psychological Review, 63,* 81–97.

Moats, L. C. (1995). The missing foundation in teacher preparation. *American Educator, 19*(9), 43–51.

Moats, L. C. (1999). *Teaching reading is rocket science.* Washington, DC: American Federation of Teachers.

Montague, M., Warger, C., & Morgan, H. (2000). Solve it! Strategy instruction to improve mathematical problem solving. *Learning Disabilities Research and Practice, 15,* 110–116.

Morgan, P. L. (2009). *Parenting an adult with disabilities or special needs.* New York, NY: AMACOM Books.

Mueller, T., & Brewer, R. (2008). *Strategies at hand: Quick positive behavior support strategies.* Arlington, VA: Council for Exceptional Children.

Murray, C., & Cox, C. (1989). *Apollo: The race to the moon.* New York, NY: Simon & Schuster.

National Association of State Directors of Special Education (NASDSE) and the Council of Administrators of Special Education (CASE) at the Council for

Exceptional Children. (2006). *Response to intervention: NASDSE and CASE white paper on RtI.* Retrieved from http://www.nasdse.org/Portals/0/Documents/Download%20Publications/RtIAnAdministratorsPerspective1-06.pdf

National Center for Education Statistics. (2006). *A first look at the literacy of America's adults in the 21st century.* Washington, DC: U.S. Department of Education.

National Center on Response to Intervention. (2010). *Essential components of RTI – A closer look at response to intervention.* Washington, DC: U.S. Department of Education, Office of Special Education Programs, National Center on Response to Intervention.

National Commission on Excellence in Education. (1983). *A nation at risk: The imperative for educational reform.* Washington, DC: Author. Retrieved from http://www2.ed.gov/pubs/NatAtRisk/index.html

National Council of Teachers of Mathematics. (2000). *Principles and standards for school mathematics.* Reston, VA: Author.

National Council on Teacher Quality. (2006). *What education schools aren't teaching about reading and what elementary teachers aren't learning.* Retrieved from http://www.nctq.org/p/publications/reports.jsp

National Governors Association Center for Best Practices (NGA Center) and the Council of Chief State School Officers (CCSSO). (2010). *Common core state standards for English language arts & literacy in history/social studies, science, and technical subjects.* Retrieved from http://www.corestandards.org/about-the-standards

National Reading Panel. (2000). *Report of the National Reading Panel. Teaching children to read: An evidence-based assessment of the scientific research literature on reading and its implications for reading instruction.* Retrieved from http://www.nichd.nih.gov/publications/nrp/smallbook.htm

Nelson, J. R., Benner, G. J., Reid, R. C., Epstein, M. H., & Currin, D. (2002). Convergent validity of office discipline referrals with the CBCL-TRF. *Journal of Emotional & Behavioral Disorders, 10*(3), 181–188.

Neuman, S. B. (2002). *The use of scientifically based research in education.* Transcript of working group conference. Washington, DC: U.S. Department of Education.

New York State Education Department, Office of Vocational and Educational Services for Individuals With Disabilities. (2007). *Quality indicator review and resource guides for literacy.* Albany, NY: Author.

Office of Special Education Programs, Center on Positive Behavioral Interventions and Supports. (2004). *School-wide positive behavior support: Implementers' blueprint and self-assessment.* Eugene: University of Oregon.

Office of Special Education Programs, National Center on Student Progress Monitoring. (2008). *What is progress monitoring?* Retrieved from http://www.studentprogress.org

Parents involvement helps in child's education. (n.d.). Retrieved from http://www.essortment.com/all/parentsinvolvem_rhuj.htm

Parks-Recore, L. (2008, March). *Response to intervention and literacy.* Presentation at Clinton-Essex-Warren-Washington Board of Cooperative Education Services (CEWW BOCES), Plattsburg, NY.

Pavri, S. (2010). Response to intervention in the social-emotional-behavioral domain: Perspectives from urban schools. *TEACHING Exceptional Children Plus, 6*(3), 1–15.

Picciano, A. G. (2011). *Educational leadership and planning for technology.* Upper Saddle River, NJ: Pearson Merrill Prentice Hall.

Piersel, W. C., & Gutkin, T. B. (1983). Resistance to school-based consultation: A behavioral analysis of the problem. *Psychology in the Schools, 20,* 311–320.

Pinker, S. (1997). *The language instinct: The new science of language and mind.* London, UK: Penguin.

Planck, M. (1949). *Scientific autobiography and other papers* (F. Gaynor, Trans.). New York, NY: Philosophical Library.

Polzer, J. T. (2003, February). *Leading teams.* Harvard business review industry and background note, prod. #403094-PDF-ENG. Boston, MA: Harvard Business School.

Preschool Curriculum Evaluation Research Consortium. (2008). *Effects of preschool curriculum programs on school readiness.* Washington, DC: National Center for Education Research, Institute of Education Sciences, U.S. Department of Education.

President's Commission on Excellence in Special Education. (2002). *A new era: Revitalizing special education for children and their families.* Washington, DC: U.S. Department of Education, Office of Special Education and Rehabilitative Services.

Puma, M., Bell, S., Cook, R., Heid, C., Shapiro, G., Broene, P., Jenkins, F., et al. (2010). *Executive Summary, Head Start Impact Study: Final Report,* ERIC document ED507847. Retrieved from http://www.eric.ed.gov/PDFS/ED507847.pdf

Ray, R. G. (1999). *The facilitative leader: Behaviors that enable success.* Upper Saddle River, NJ: Prentice Hall.

Remillard, J. T. (2000). Can curriculum materials support teachers' learning? Two fourth-grade teachers' use of a new mathematics textbook. *Elementary School Journal, 100,* 331–351.

Riccomini, P. J., & Witzel, B. S. (2010). *Response to intervention in math.* Thousand Oaks, CA: Corwin.

Ritchie, K. D., & Speece, D. L. (2004). Early identification of reading disabilities: Current status and new directions. *Assessment for Effective Intervention, 29*(4), 13–24.

Rivera, D. M., & Bryant, B. R. (1992). Mathematics instruction for students with special needs. *Intervention in School and Clinic, 28,* 71–86.

Rose, D. H., & Meyer, A. (2002). *Teaching every student in the digital age: Universal design for learning.* Alexandria, VA: ASCD.

Rose, L. C., Gallup, A. M., & Elam, S. M. (1997). The 29th Annual Phi Delta Kappa/Gallup Poll of the public's attitudes toward the public schools. *Phi Delta Kappan, 79*(1), 41–56.

Rosenfield, S. A. (1989). *Instructional consultation.* Hillsdale, NJ: Lawrence Erlbaum.

Rosenfield, S., & Gravois, T. (1996). *Instructional consultation teams.* New York, NY: Guilford Press.

Rourke, B. P., & Conway, J. A. (1997). Disabilities of arithmetic and mathematical reasoning: Perspectives from neurology and neuropsychology. *Journal of Learning Disabilities, 30*, 34–46.

Samuels, C. A. (2008). High schools try out RTI. *Education Week, 28*(19), 20–22.

Sandomierski, T., Kincaid, D., & Algozzine, B. (2007). Response to intervention and positive behavior support: Brothers from different mothers or sisters with different misters? *Positive Behavioral Interventions and Supports Newsletter, 4*(2), 1–4.

Sansosti, F. J., & Noltemeyer, A. (2008). Viewing response-to-intervention through an educational change paradigm: What can we learn? *The California School Psychologist.* Retrieved from http://findarticles.com/p/articles/mi_7479/is_200801/ai_n32281793/

Sansosti, F. J., Noltemeyer, A., & Goss, S. (2010). Principals' perceptions of the importance and availability of response to intervention practices within high school settings. *School Psychology Review, 39*(2), 286–295.

Saranson, S. B., & Doris, J. (1979). *Educational handicap, public policy, and social history.* New York, NY: Macmillan.

Schulenberg, J., Goldstein, A. E., & Vondracek, F. W. (1991). Gender differences in adolescents' career interests: Beyond main effects. *Journal of Research on Adolescence, 1*, 37–61.

Senge, P. M. (2006). *The fifth discipline: The art and practice of the learning organization.* New York, NY: Currency Doubleday.

Shavelson, R. J., & Towne, L. (2002). *Scientific research in education.* Washington, DC: National Academy Press.

Shaywitz, S. E. (2003). *Overcoming dyslexia.* New York, NY: Knopf.

Shinn, M. R. (1995). Best practices in curriculum-based measurement and its use in a problem-solving model. In J. Grimes & A. Thomas (Eds.), *Best practice in school psychology III* (pp. 547–568). Washington, DC: National Association of School Psychologists.

Shinn, M., & Walker, H. M. (2010). *Interventions for achievement and behavior problems in a three-tier model including RTI.* Bethesda, MD: National Association of School Psychologists.

Smith, S. C., & Piele, P. K. (2006). *School leadership: Handbook for excellence in student learning.* Thousand Oaks, CA: Corwin.

Snow, C. E., Burns, M. S., & Griffin, P. (Eds.). (1998). *Preventing reading difficulties in young children.* Washington, DC: Commission on Behavioral and Social Sciences and Education.

Spellings, M. (2007, July 30). *Statement by Secretary of Education Margaret Spellings in response to Chairman Miller's remarks to the National Press Club.* Press release. Washington, DC: U.S. Department of Education. Retrieved from http://www.ed.gov/news/pressreleases/2007/07/07302007.html

Spillane, J. P. (2006). *Distributed leadership.* San Francisco, CA: Jossey-Bass.

Spinelli, C. G. (2011). *Linking assessment to instructional strategies: A guide for teachers.* Boston, MA: Pearson.

Sprick, R. (2009). CHAMPs: *A proactive and positive approach to classroom management.* Eugene, OR: Pacific Northwest.

Sprick, R., & Borgmeier, C. (2010). Behavior prevention and management in three tiers in secondary schools. In M. Shinn & M. H. Walker (Eds.), *Interventions for achievement and behavior problems in a three-tier model including RTI* (pp. 1–34). Bethesda, MD: National Association of School Psychologists.

Stanovich, K. E. (1994). Romance and reality. *The Reading Teacher, 47,* 280–291.

Stiggins, R. (2004). New assessment beliefs for a new school mission. *Phi Delta Kappan, 86*(1), 22–27.

Stuebing, K. K., Fletcher, J. M., LeDoux, J. M., Lyon, G. R., Shaywitz, S. E., & Shaywitz, B. A. (2002). Validity of IQ discrepancy classifications of reading disabilities: A meta-analysis. *American Educational Research Journal, 39,* 469–518.

Sugai, G., Horner, R. H., Dunlap, G., Hieneman, M., Lewis, T. J., Nelson, C. M., Scott, T., et al. (2000). Applying positive behavior support and functional behavioral assessment in schools. *Journal of Positive Behavior Interventions, 2*(3), 131–143.

Tiegerman-Farber, E., & Radziewicz, C. (1997). *Collaborative decision making: The pathway to inclusion.* New York, NY: Prentice Hall.

Tilly, W. D., III. (2002). School psychology as a problem solving enterprise. In A. Thomas & J. Grimes (Eds.), *Best practices in school psychology IV* (pp. 25–36). Bethesda, MD: National Association of School Psychologists.

Torgesen, J. K. (2004). Avoiding the devastating downward spiral: The evidence that early intervention prevents reading failure. *AFT News.* Retrieved from http://www.aft.org/newspubs/periodicals/ae/fall2004/torgesen.cfm

Torgesen, J. (2005, November). *Designing and using assessment systems to prevent reading difficulties in young children.* Paper presented at the Western North Carolina LD/ADD Symposium. Retrieved from http://www.fcrr.org/science/powerpoint/torgesen/NC-assessment-r.ppt

U.S. Department of Education. (2002, April 1). *Guidance for the Reading First Program.* Washington, DC: Author. Retrieved from http://www.ed.gov/programs/readingfirst/guidance.doc

U.S. Department of Education. (2010). *A blueprint for reform: Reauthorization of the Elementary and Secondary Education Act.* Washington, DC: U.S. Department of Education, Office of Planning, Evaluation and Policy Development. Retrieved from http://www2.ed.gov/policy/elsec/leg/blueprint/blueprint.pdf

U.S. Department of Education, Office of Special Education Programs. (2004). *Topic: Identification of specific learning disabilities.* Retrieved from http://idea.ed.gov/explore/view/p/%2Croot%2Cdynamic%2CTopicalBrief%2C23%2C

Vail, P. (1993). *Emotion: The on/off switch for learning.* Rosemont, NJ: Modern Learning Press.

Van Garderen, D., & Montague, M. (2003). Visual-spatial representation, mathematical problem solving, and students of varying abilities. *Learning Disabilities Research & Practice, 18*(4), 246–254. doi: 10.1111/1540-5826.00079

Vanneman, A., Hamilton, L., Baldwin Anderson, J., & Rahman, T. (2009). *Achievement gaps: How Black and White students in public schools perform in mathematics and reading on the National Assessment of Educational Progress*

(NCES 2009-455). Washington, DC: National Center for Education Statistics, Institute of Education Sciences, U.S. Department of Education.

Vinovskis, M. (2009). *From a nation at risk to no child left behind: National educational goals and the creation of federal education policy.* New York, NY: Teachers College Press.

Wegielnik, S. (2011). *PBS at Westbrook.* Westbury, NY: Westbrook Preparatory School.

Wenger, E. (2006). *Communities of practice: A brief introduction.* Retrieved from http://www.ewenger.com/theory/index.htm

Wilson, J. W. (2011). *Cracking the learning code.* Advanced Learning Institute. Retrieved from http://crackingthelearningcode.com/bonus2.html

Witt, J. C., VanDerHeyden, A. M., & Gilbertson, D. (2004). Troubleshooting behavioral interventions. A systematic process for finding and eliminating problems. *School Psychology Review, 33,* 363–383.

Woodcock, R. W. (1998). *Woodcock reading mastery tests—revised.* Circle Pines, MN: American Guidance Service.

Young, R. A., & Friesen, J. D. (1992). The intentions of parents in influencing the career development of their children. *Career Development Quarterly, 40,* 198–207.

Zabala, J. S. (1998). *The SETT framework: Critical areas to consider when making informed assistive technology decisions.* Retrieved from http://www2.edc.org/NCIP/Workshops/sett/SETT_Framework_article.html

Zirkel, P. A., & Thomas, L. B. (2010). State laws and guidelines for implementing RTI. *Teaching Exceptional Children, 43*(1), 60–73.

Index

CORWIN

A SAGE Company

The Corwin logo—a raven striding across an open book—represents the union of courage and learning. Corwin is committed to improving education for all learners by publishing books and other professional development resources for those serving the field of PreK–12 education. By providing practical, hands-on materials, Corwin continues to carry out the promise of its motto: **"Helping Educators Do Their Work Better."**